BETWEEN GODS

Alison Pick is the author of the novel *Far To Go*, longlisted for the 2011 Man Booker Prize, and winner of the Canadian Jewish Book Award for fiction. She is also the author of two collections of poetry, and a novel, *The Sweet Edge*, all of which were published to wide acclaim.

Also by Alison Pick

Far to Go

BETWEEN GODS

Alison Pick

TINDER
PRESS

First published in 2014 by Doubleday Canada

First published in Great Britain in 2015 by Tinder Press
an imprint of HEADLINE PUBLISHING GROUP

1

Cataloguing in Publication Data is available from the British Library

ISBN 978 1 4722 2509 2

Headline's policy is to use papers that are natural, renewable and recyclable
products and made from wood grown in well-managed forests and other
responsible sources. The logging and manufacturing processes are expected
to conform to the environmental regulations of the country of origin.

HEADLINE PUBLISHING GROUP
An Hachette UK Company
Carmelite House
50 Victoria Embankment
London EC4Y 0DZ

www.tinderpress.co.uk
www.headline.co.uk
www.hachette.co.uk

For Ayla and for Lynn

When I looked for light, then came darkness.
– Job 30:26

Stand by the roads and consider; inquire about ancient paths:
which way is good? Travel it and find rest for your soul.
– Jeremiah 6:16

PAIN DISAPPEARS. THESE YEARS LATER – not even so many of them – summoning the details is hard: what exactly it was that made me feel so alone, so outside myself and my life, so lifeless I no longer wanted to be alive. To say I wanted to *kill* myself implies a will, a volition I certainly didn't have. But to be mercifully dead?

Oh yes.

It was dark that year. All year. I cried when Degan left for work in the mornings, terrified of the solitude I have relished my whole life. In my memory, I see myself standing on our back porch in a perpetual dusk, filling my lungs with smoke as though at the base of some terrible chimney. In fact I know I kept rules for myself, smoking only one cigarette a day, or maybe one a week. Maybe I never smoked at all. But looking back, I remember one long smoking binge and an accompanying desire to be obliterated.

Good things did happen during that time. I landed a big publishing deal; I got married. But what I remember is the way my heart raced when I found myself awake again each awful morning. The panic when Degan ran to catch the streetcar. Jim Bryson on my stereo singing, 'I got tired of sleeping in Toronto' while all around me the temperature plunged, the air so clear and brittle it seemed it might actually shatter. It hurt to move. Was this just a bad case of the blues, as common as a cold in a country where one in four people are diagnosed with depression? Or maybe it was my 'artistic temperament' that did me in. The part of the brain that pumps out art appears predisposed to annihilation through tailpipes and slipknots.

These are just two hypotheses about the roots of depression. There are, of course, many others. For example, there's the idea that it can originate before birth, the unresolved trauma of an ancestor passed down one generation, then down another, like a baton in a relay race. Perhaps my hand was open, ready to receive it – the suffering that had been coming my way for so long.

This wasn't the first time I'd found myself in a dark place. Far from it. But something was different now; something more was at stake. Now there were others involved, people I loved; there might even be people ahead of me in time, waiting to be born. But before that could happen, I needed to look deeper, to finally address the ghosts buried beneath me.

As I started tunnelling, I made a desperate attempt to halt the despair, blindly grabbing for therapy, sun lamps, vitamin D. But all the while I was sucked into a vortex that no amount of leafy greens or exercise could touch. There was, I would soon learn, nothing to do but submit. Whoever lived below me, in my shadows, had me. A hand on my ankle, her nails digging in.

PART ONE

*For the things we have to learn before we
can do them, we learn by doing them.*
– Aristotle

ONE

THE PLANE DEPOSITS ME, LIKE A wadded-up tissue, at the airport in Toronto. I've barely slept all week, my eyes puffed up and bleary from crying. I catch a cab downtown and hurry to my appointment with the woman who is sewing my wedding dress. She gets down on one knee to measure me, as though she is the one proposing. 'Who are you marrying?' she asks, speaking around a mouthful of pins.

I can barely remember Degan's name.

It is 2008. On my finger is my grandmother's wedding ring, engraved with my grandfather's name and the year they were married, 1936, seventy-two years ago.

After the fitting, I lug my suitcase to my hotel. I fall into a heavy slumber and dream of train stations, missed connections. When I wake, the sun is just starting to set. I'm supposed to be at the Griffin Poetry Prize gala, the literary event of the season, by 7:00. It's 6:45.

I throw on my little black dress, lipstick and concealer – a futile attempt to hide the evidence of my tears.

My taxi whisks me south to an enormous warehouse in the heart of the Distillery District. Inside, the building is gussied up to evoke a romantic Tuscan street fair, bright baubles and streamers hanging from the ceiling, crepe paper butterflies hovering over the tables. I'm handed a glass of wine at the door, which I down in one swallow. The room is wall-to-wall bodies, a who's who of the literary scene.

I head for the bar.

Mark Blume is ahead of me in line, a writer I know casually among a sea of writers. Curly brown hair, a blue silk necktie. We say our hellos. 'You're in town now?' he asks.

'We're moving back to Toronto.'

'You're leaving Newfoundland?'

'Yes.'

'Where's Degan?'

'He's coming next week.'

And then, for some reason, I tell him, 'I'm wondering about the Jewish . . .' I pause, searching for the right word. 'The *community*. Here in Toronto.'

He looks at me as if I'm drunk – and it's true: I haven't eaten and the single glass of wine has gone straight to my head. It's too late to take the question back, though. I relieve the barmaid of a tall frosted glass and lean my elbows on the bar.

He hesitates. 'I wish I could help you. But I don't really . . .' He hesitates again. 'I don't really do anything *Jewish*.'

Mark is a funny man who likes to hold forth with a stiff drink in his hand. He wants to holler while cleavage bumps against the limbo pole, not to discuss theology. I hiccup softly into the back of my hand. He looks at me more closely. 'But I know who you should talk to,' he says.

We elbow our way through the tangle of guests to an enormous chocolate fountain. Among the writers dunking their strawberries is a poet Mark introduces as Sol Jalon. I know next to nothing about him: not that he's Jewish, certainly not what his wife does as a living. Later in the year, when I learn about *bashert*, the Hebrew word for fate, this moment is what I will think back to. Being just broken enough to spill my question to a near stranger, who takes me by the arm, heavy and reeling, and introduces me to Sol. Who in turn introduces me to his wife.

A rabbi? *Her?*

Rachel Klein has dimples and lovely dark curls. She's in her early thirties, like me, or maybe a few years older. She looks like the popular girl in my cabin at summer camp, like a kid I might have gone to ski school with or invited over for slumber parties on the weekend.

The revelry has escalated into a din over which conversation can't be heard, so we push our way outside to the booze-soaked pavement, where the glamorous faction is smoking. Don McKay, one of the prize-nominated poets, is being interviewed by the press. There are flashbulbs, smoke rings, lots of little black dresses. But the rabbi's attention is on me.

She says, 'Tell me everything.'

I want to die, I think. I'm tired of being alive.

But I know this is not what Rabbi Klein is asking.

'I grew up not knowing I'm Jewish.' I hesitate. 'Half Jewish.'

I fiddle with Granny's wedding ring, spinning it on my finger.

Rachel beams at me, her focus undivided, and I force myself to keep talking. 'My grandparents escaped Czechoslovakia in 1939. They bribed a Nazi for visas, came to Canada and renounced their Judaism. They spent their lives posing as Christians – going to church instead of synagogue, eating plum pudding at Christmas instead of matzah at Passover.'

Rachel sighs. Quietly, but I hear it. 'And you grew up knowing nothing about it?'

'As a kid I was forbidden from discussing it. But now I'm going back and asking questions.'

'Why now?'

'I'm writing a novel.'

She squints at me. 'And?'

Already she can read me. Already she sees there's something else.

'I get . . . depressed,' I tell her. I don't know how else to say what has recently made itself clear to me: that the ancestors lined up behind me, the ones my family pretended had never existed, the ones who died in the gas chambers, are also the ones pulling me into my darkness.

Rachel peers at me. 'What are you thinking now?'

I take a deep breath and exhale slowly.

'Secrets cause such pain,' I say finally.

'Yes.' Rachel smiles. 'But here you are, telling me about it. So it's not a secret anymore.'

'That's true,' I concede.

'You're feeling a pull? Toward Judaism?'

I nod.

She beams at me. 'What a happy story.'

TWO

MY GRANDMOTHER NEVER LIKED babies. At least, this is how the story goes. We have a picture of Dad as a small boy sitting on her knee. She is wearing a blue silk blouse and large pearl-drop earrings, holding a thin cigarette loosely between her manicured fingers. She has just learned that her parents have been murdered. She stares off into the distance. It is as though the child in her lap – my father – has been placed there by a stranger, or belongs to someone else entirely.

Granny covered her depression with words. Armed with a cocktail and a cigarette, she made herself the centre of any group. She knew history, politics, opera, literature. If anyone else tried to speak, Granny talked right over them.

At the end of our summers with her when I was a child, she would stand in the doorway in her pale blue and white checked Hermès dressing gown, crying as my father pulled our family station wagon down the long driveway. She was terrified of being left alone.

During the first crippling depression I suffered in my early twenties, I called her at the condominium in Florida where she wintered. 'I'm starting to think life is inherently painful,' I told her.

I remember the uncharacteristic silence. I could hear the ice cubes clinking in her rye and then the sharp inhale on her cigarette. From farther behind her came the muffled sound of waves crashing on Longboat Key. Her silence lengthened. For once, she was searching for words.

When she finally spoke, I was relieved to hear her glamorous European accent; relieved she was still there at the other end of the line at all.

'Yes,' she said simply. 'You're right.'

Granny was twenty-two when the Nazis entered Czechoslovakia. She was newly married, with a baby. Her husband – my grandfather – was out of the country that day; from his position of relative safety, he was able to secure the visas they needed to leave.

My grandparents used those visas: I'm alive today as proof.

There were visas for Granny's parents, too; she had agreed to flee the country only because her parents would follow. The plan was for the family to meet in Canada when all the 'Jewish business' had blown over. But Granny's parents delayed. They couldn't believe they were in danger.

They would leave next week, they said.

Then the week after.

Finally, of course, it was too late.

I think of those visas sometimes, sitting on a dusty oak desk in a vacated flat, bathed in momentary sunlight from a thin space below the drapes and then falling into darkness again.

Granny passed her depression on to my father, who refers to it as 'the bad blood'. I think of his description when I wake in the early-morning hours, swamped with existential dread. The bad blood arrives as though a tap has been turned on. My body is flooded with the toxic liquid. My heart, against my will, pumps it into every part of my being. The bad blood makes it hard to do simple things: wash a cereal bowl, lift sunglasses to my face. Later – months or years – it leaves with the same squeak of finality, the heavy, rusted tap being wrested closed.

The idea of blood as the source of disease is, of course, ancient. The Greek and Roman philosophers and physicians believed blood was one of four humours that, when out of balance, had dire consequences. Before Sigmund Freud's popularization of the unconscious mind, 'tainted blood' was often seen as the source of insanity. It's a notion that persists – blood has a way of asserting itself. During the Spanish Inquisition, great numbers of Jews were forced to convert to Catholicism. Generations later, their ancestors found their way back to the truth of who they were. They had a phrase for history's siren song: *la sangre llama.*

The blood is calling.

I met Degan just after Granny died. We attended a writers' conference together in Saskatchewan. We were the only two participants from Ontario and we decided to carpool. Our first date wasn't a coffee or a glass of wine before a movie but three straight days in my parents' old station wagon, driving three thousand kilometres across the country. We spent our first night together in a ratty motel room outside of Wawa. We were young writers; we needed to save money. And I knew right away I could trust him.

I went into the bathroom to put on my pyjamas and came out to find Degan propped up against the pillow of his single bed, surrounded by newspapers. Not just the *Globe and Mail* and the *Toronto Star*, but the *Guardian*, the *New York Times*. What, I wondered, could a person want with so much news?

I climbed into the twin bed on the opposite side of the room. We looked – it did not escape me – like an old married couple who had drifted, over the years, into a companionable friendship.

We read in our separate silences, said good night and turned out the light.

Degan arrives in Toronto the week after the Griffin Prize. He brings with him the last boxes and bags from our old home at the far edge of the country. He kisses me hello in the front hall of our new apartment. His hair is messy and there are circles under his blue eyes. 'How did your meeting with the wedding dress lady go?' he asks.

He passes me a box. My legs buckle under its weight.

'It went fine,' I lie. I stagger across the hall and place the box on a pile of others. The new apartment has mirrors on all of the doors fronting the hall; from where I'm standing, facing the stairs, I can see the back of my own head.

'We should nail down the date for the wedding,' Degan says.

I pause with a hand on my low back, like a pregnant woman.

'Right?' he says. 'Get on top of it and all that?'

'I guess.'

'I was thinking May.' He rolls his shoulders back, absently digging at the muscles. 'But May might be buggy. If we do it outside.'

I'm quiet.

'Well?'

'Can we talk about this later?' I ask.

He nods his assent, turns away from me in a silence I can't read. We spend the rest of the evening making house, unpacking late into the hot June night. Putting away colanders and cutting knives and knee socks and boxes and boxes of books. There's a near-constant wail of sirens from up on St. Clair, and several eruptions of drunken yelling. '*Who* called it? *Who* called it?' we hear a man holler, followed by the shattering of glass. The sky darkens but never to black, tempered always by the neon glow of the street lamps and signs. In the morning,

Degan will start his new job as a counsellor at a college downtown. This is the reason we have moved back to Toronto; this and to be closer to our families. We're engaged, after all. Who knows what else might be in our future.

It's after midnight when we finally fall into bed – which is to say, onto an old futon over which we've draped an ill-fitting sheet. Degan rolls toward me, puts an arm across my chest. 'I'm happy we're here,' he says.

I should feel something. I don't know what. But something.

'What are you going to do tomorrow?' he asks, nuzzling my neck.

I pull away from his stubble. 'Can't you stay home with me?'

I know he's looking forward to the first day of his new job, but I can't help myself. I'm overcome with a sudden anxiety at the thought of being alone in the apartment.

Degan's eyes soften. 'I wish I could.' He pushes my hair off my forehead. 'Organize your books,' he says. 'And make sure you get out of the house. Go for a walk. Or a run. That'll make you feel better.'

He knows me so well. Still, I roll away from him and curl my body around a pillow. I feel wooden, like an actor on a set.

THREE

I WAS IN MY EARLY TWENTIES WHEN I had my first stint of psychotherapy. It took place on the top floor of a private home on a leafy suburban street in Guelph, my university town. To get to the office, I had to climb a staircase. There was nothing special about the staircase – it wasn't hidden behind a false wall, say, or carpeted with psychedelic paisleys – but climbing it gave me a shiver, part dread, part anticipation, as if I were progressing up and into another world entirely.

I had originally called to book an appointment with a woman named Karen. Karen had star power. She had written a bestseller about hugging.

Because of this, or perhaps because of her genuinely remarkable therapeutic skills, she was in demand. She got back to me, saying she was booked solid. But her husband, Ben, had some openings.

I agreed reluctantly.

Mere months ago I had been a girl with many friends, a high achiever. Now I found myself dressed in chunky Guatemalan sweaters, twenty pounds heavier than when I'd started university the previous year, my body mimicking the weight I felt inside. I would wake in the night with my heart pounding. In the morning, I'd rally my resources to face the cereal bowl. I'd tried, without luck, to will myself back into wellness, to *apply* myself, but nothing had worked. Therapy was my last resort.

The day of my first session I climbed those stairs slowly and Ben was there to greet me at the top. His wife may have been a rock star, but Ben was a soft-spoken septuagenarian in corduroys. He reached out and took my hand. 'Welcome,' he said.

I detected, I thought, a slight Californian accent.

He led me into his office, where there was a chair and a small couch. I watched to see which place he would take; he indicated that I should sit first.

I took the chair. It seemed safer.

I don't remember our introductions that day, who told whom a little bit about themselves first. I remember only that at a certain point in the meeting he held up two fingers in the form of a peace sign. The diverging fingers were to illustrate two parts of the self: the conscious and the unconscious. These, of course, were not the words he used. Instead, he explained the concepts slowly, as though to a small child: that there are parts of ourselves we know and parts of ourselves we don't know.

'The parts of ourselves we have repressed,' he said, 'exert a great power over our lives.'

I held on tightly to the wooden arms of the chair. I had a sudden and overwhelming desire to go to sleep. My eyes blinked rapidly, involuntarily, as though trying to clear themselves of the form Ben's fingers had taken. I voiced several feeble protests, but I knew he was right; had, I realized, known all along.

He held up his two fingers again in a vee to demonstrate the split, and with that peace sign, the world as I knew it fell apart. Or, more accurately, doubled. There was no longer one world, one truth, I could count on, but two.

The known and the unknown.

The acknowledged and the unacknowledged.

The next week when I arrived at Ben's office, the chair was gone. There was only the small couch, on which, I saw immediately, we would both have to sit. I accepted this with a childlike resignation. It was clear to me how the rest of the therapy would go: the enforced collapsing of boundaries, the gentle but relentless nudging toward that which I had always – wisely, I realized now – denied. That we would be sitting so close together, on the same couch – which was actually more like a loveseat – was a physical manifestation of the emotional openness I was expected to bring. After this, anything could happen.

For example: Several sessions later, in the middle of our conversation, Ben took off his sweater, to reveal a shirt buttoned at the neck but nowhere else. His hairy chest and belly protruded above his corduroys. I accepted this as though it was part of the process, drawing my knees in closer to my chest but continuing dutifully with whatever childhood memory I had been dredging up. Toward the end of the meeting, Ben happened to look down and find his shirt undone. The colour drained from his face. 'Why didn't you *tell* me?' he asked. It was the first time I could discern the individual person behind the generalized listener.

I couldn't rightly answer him; couldn't find a polite way to say that the whole exercise of revealing one's feelings seemed so bizarre to me, so freakish and uncomfortable, that the exposure of skin, the baring of the private body, seemed a logical consequence, in keeping with the proceedings.

Ben did his shirt up, being careful not to miss a button. We went on talking. Several minutes later, though, he stopped and said again, 'I'm so embarrassed. Why didn't you say anything?'

And again I was at a loss, shrugging, and answering with some timid platitude that must have given him more

information about me than the entire rest of the session –
perhaps all our sessions combined.

Here was a girl used to silence. Here was a girl who knew
how to hide.

FOUR

ON THE MORNING OF MY THIRTY-SECOND birthday, my phone rings early. I feel around for it on the nightstand. 'Hello?'

I hear muffled breathing, a grunt that sounds like something heavy is being lifted. For a moment I think it's some kind of crank call. Then my parents' voices: 'Happy Birthday to you – *dun-da-da-dun*! Happy Birthday to you – *dun-da-da-dun*! Happy Biiiiirthday, dear Alison – *dun-da-da-dun*! Happy Birthday to you!'

My father punctuates the end of the song with tuba noises in the style of an Eastern European oompahpah band, true to his heritage, so the whole performance takes several minutes. I sit up in bed, lean my back against the headboard. Beside me, Degan pulls a pillow over his eyes.

'So?' Dad asks brightly. 'How are you liking Toronto?'

'We just got here,' I say.

'Wait until you get a taste of the cost of it!'

'Thanks for the welcome,' I tease.

'The economy is crashing! Are you following the real estate news?'

'Dad,' I say. 'Take some deep breaths.'

He mocks a heavy exhale.

There's more muffled kerfuffle in the background, more grunting. Then he says abruptly, 'I'd better go. I have to walk the dog,' and hangs up.

By the time I'm done on the phone, I hear the shower

running. Degan comes out with a blue towel wrapped around his waist. 'Happy Birthday, babe,' he says.

'Am I getting old?'

'Kind of.'

'I'm an old lady.'

'You're five years younger than me.'

'Always,' I say.

He towels off his hair, buttons his shirt. Grabs a pair of pants from the back of the chair.

'Any big plans today?' he asks.

Good question.

'I might do some reading about Judaism,' I say.

'Don't go crazy or anything.'

'Ha ha.'

His face goes serious and he nods. I've told him about meeting Rabbi Klein at the Griffin, about her comment 'What a happy story'.

'I've always thought,' he starts to say, but he is distracted, checking his phone, pulling a comb through his hair.

'You've always thought what?'

'I don't know. You and your family history. The secrecy. But you've always seemed kind of . . . Jewish.'

'Really? What do you mean?'

'I'm not sure,' he says. 'It's just a feeling.'

There's a crash from down on the street, a garbage can being knocked over.

'I'm late,' he says. 'We'll talk tonight. And celebrate your birthday.'

'Okay, good luck today. Hope it goes well.'

He kisses me and runs to catch the streetcar.

When he's gone, I wander through our rooms in my pyjamas, picking things up and putting them back down. I check Facebook, where I click on a raft of birthday messages. I notice my Jewish friends are also wishing each other a Happy New Year. It must be Rosh Hashanah. Even if I wanted to, I wouldn't know where to mark it, or how, or who with. Instead, I spend the day on the rumpled futon sheet reading *Help Me* by Eli Bloomberg, a young Jewish writer struggling with his Hasidic upbringing. I enjoy the read. There is comfort in the knowledge that Judaism is confusing for someone else, too, even for someone born and raised as a Jew. I Google him and see he'll be interviewing another writer at the International Festival of Authors here in Toronto on the coming weekend. I decide to go hear him.

The event takes place on Sunday afternoon. I leave the house without telling Degan where I'm going. The bus down to the waterfront is packed full of old Italian men in undershirts, women with strollers, teenagers in flip-flops snapping their gum. By the time I change buses and find my way to the theatre, the interview has already started. Eli Bloomberg sits onstage in an armchair opposite his subject. He seems immediately familiar. Not that I actually *recognize* him, but I have a strange sense of understanding what he's about. He's wearing a green blazer and his hair looks purposefully dishevelled.

Something about him reminds me of Kramer from *Seinfeld*. A smarter, more attractive Kramer.

I listen intently, take some notes. His questions are perceptive. When the interview wraps up, though, I collect my things and hurry toward the exit. Judaism draws me, repels me, draws me back. I'm exhausted just from sitting in the audience, a supposedly passive observer. All I can think about is getting home and crashing. And Degan will be wondering where I am.

Just as I've reached the door, I glance back and see Eli looking at me. He's been talking to a petite brunette, but he walks away from her, leaving her with her mouth open, literally mid-sentence.

'I know you from somewhere,' he says to me.

I shrug and step back into the building; the door sighs heavily on its hinges.

'Really?'

He nods.

'I thought you seemed familiar, too.'

Up close, his eyes are a deep shade of green, his skin almost olive.

We run through our hometowns, our childhood friends, our schools, but find no common ground. 'I just read *Help Me*,' I say. 'So maybe that's why. You're pretty much the way I imagined you on the page.'

He brings a hand to his face, and I recognize the look other writers get when they're wondering what you thought of their book.

'I liked it,' I assure him. 'Would you sign it for me?'

'They're not selling it here.' He shrugs, gesturing behind him to the festival's bookstore.

'I brought my own copy.' I pull it from my purse.

'Oh,' he says, his face brightening. 'Sure.'

He bends over my book to sign it, his shirt pulling up to show the smooth, hairless skin on his lower back. I see the brand name on the back pocket of his jeans. I try, but cannot picture him in the black Orthodox garb he must have grown up wearing. The woman he was talking with earlier has been waiting patiently to finish her sentence, but she now realizes

Eli is done with her. 'Anyway,' she says to him, 'I'll catch you later?'

He doesn't look at her. 'Yeah,' he mumbles. 'So long.'

He passes me the signed book, holds my eye for half a second too long.

Next morning there's an email: 'Dear Alison, Nice to meet you briefly yesterday. I can't believe how familiar you seemed. Maybe I've heard you read? Are you working on anything? Publishing? Reading anything good lately? E.'

I write back right away: 'Good to meet you, too! My new book of poems is coming out in the spring. I'm working on a novel around the Holocaust, so I've been focusing my reading in that direction. What do you think I'd like?'

'I don't know you well enough to say,' he answers. 'Yet. How about dinner?'

FIVE

I'M DIGGING THROUGH MY WALLET for an elusive twenty-dollar bill when I come across Rabbi Klein's business card. On the back she has written a single word: Kolel.

I check out the website: The Adult Centre for Liberal Jewish Learning. Something about the extensive list of programs and classes, this untapped store of knowledge about my family's lost faith, makes me giddy with possibility. Their 'signature course' is called Doing Jewish:

> *Begin with basics and explore Jewish life from a liberal perspective: holidays, life cycle, basic Jewish philosophy, and creating a Jewish home.*

When Degan gets home from work, I tell him about the class.

'Why don't you sign up?' he asks, tossing his bag onto the floor in the corner of the hall.

'I don't know. I feel kind of nervous about it.'

'Nervous why?'

'I don't know,' I say again. 'I'm not Jewish, right?'

'You sort of are.'

'And I'm pretty tired.' *Tired*, we both know, means depressed.

'Maybe it will cheer you up,' Degan says. He goes to the fridge and cracks a beer, then starts digging around for something to eat. The top shelf holds two tubs of plain organic yogourt, the bottom a limp head of broccoli. The crispers are empty. 'I'll call for takeout,' he says. Since arriving in Toronto, we've had takeout almost every night.

'I'm going to get groceries tomorrow,' I say.

He reaches for the phone and the pizza coupons.

'Do you really think I should take it?' I ask.

'Take what?'

'The class.'

'Why not?' He lifts his beer and has three long swallows.

I nod. 'Oh,' I say, 'and there's something else. I met a guy.'

He raises his eyebrows.

I laugh. 'Not a *guy* guy. A writer.'

'What kind of writer?'

'A Jewish one.'

Degan runs a thumb lightly around the lip of the bottle. 'Okay,' he says.

'I'm going to have dinner with him,' I say.

'Okay,' he says again.

He starts dialling the pizza number.

'Do you mind?' I ask.

'Mind what?' Then: 'Hello?'

'If I have dinner with him?'

'I'd like to order a large pizza for delivery,' he says into his phone. And then, to me: 'I trust you.'

◈

The Doing Jewish course starts on a Wednesday night in early October. I don't know what I'm expecting: a large lecture hall, maybe, and a stuffy professor with horn-rimmed glasses and a PowerPoint presentation. Instead, I am shown into a small, brightly lit room decorated with young children's crayoned attempts at the Hebrew alphabet. The teacher bustles in after me with her papers flying.

'I'm Rabbi Glickman,' she says, and nods curtly, challenging anyone to contradict her. She is small and thin, with her hair cropped close to her head. Her features have a tightness in contrast to the openness of Rachel Klein's.

There is a dry-erase board at the front of the class. With a bold black marker she writes: WHAT IS JUDAISM?

The class is silent. Eight or ten strangers trying not to meet each other's eyes.

'Is it a race?' Rabbi Glickman asks.

A blond woman in her forties with a wide gap between her front teeth puts up her hand. 'It's a religion.'

'Like any other?'

'It's harder to join.'

Titters from our classmates.

'Your name is?' the rabbi asks.

'Debra.'

'Okay, Debra. Why do you think it is harder to join?'

'The Jews are the chosen people. You can't *choose* to be chosen.'

Debra glances at an Asian woman sitting across the room. 'At least,' she says quickly, 'that's how the thinking goes.'

'But what about conversion?' another woman asks. 'I really want to convert. Or at least, my boyfriend really wants me to.'

Around the circle, several of the women nod in recognition.

The conversation quickly progresses to conversion, which is, I learn, the reason everyone else is here. To officially become Jewish in Toronto is a complex process. You have to take a yearlong, intensive class called the Jewish Information Course, or the JIC. To take *that* course, you have to be sponsored by a rabbi. Our class, it seems, is full of engaged couples – one partner Jewish, the other hoping to sign up before they get married – whose sponsoring rabbis have suggested they take this course first, as a kind of trial run.

The whole process is news to me. I have always assumed that I could reclaim my family's Judaism when I wanted, like a lost suitcase at an airport security desk.

We go around the table and introduce ourselves properly. A man with dreadlocks and an Israeli accent says he is totally secular, but that he and his wife – the Asian woman – want to raise their children in a one-religion home. The next four women say they are dating Jewish men who encouraged them to sign up for the class. Debra tells us that she's the daughter of a minister but wants to explore other faiths. She feels inexplicably drawn to Judaism, though a friend told her she could never be Jewish. Conversion or not. To forget it.

And what about me? I wonder. Will *I* ever be Jewish? Am I already?

A few years back, at a writing residency at the Banff Centre for the Arts, an older writer I admire told me that I had no choice in the matter. I *was* Jewish. Because my family died in Auschwitz. Because it's in my blood.

La sangre llama.

But when it's my turn to introduce myself, and when I explain my background to the rabbi, her reaction is more staid.

'You're Jewish,' she says. '*Sort of.* But to really be accepted, you would need to go through a process.' She clears her throat. 'Because your mother is Christian.'

SIX

IRONICALLY, I FIRST STUMBLED on our family secret at Christmas. I was maybe eleven years old. We were at my aunt and uncle's house; a huge Christmas tree shone with a hundred white lights in the corner. Over my head, in the crowd of adults, my auntie Sheila was speaking to my mother, saying something about a couple they both knew, the husband Jewish, the wife a Gentile.

I was cruising a plate of Black Magic chocolates, trying to guess which one would have a pink centre.

Above me, I heard Auntie Sheila: 'So their daughter isn't Jewish. Because Judaism always comes from the mother.'

I bit into a chocolate and screwed up my face: marzipan.

My mum: 'So our girls . . . ?'

'Our girls aren't technically Jewish, either,' Auntie Sheila said. 'Secret or no secret.'

'Even though their fathers . . .'

'Right,' Auntie Sheila said.

I remember this moment as if it were in a cartoon: a little light bulb appearing in the air above my head, and the sound effect, the clear *ting* of a bell. My brain was working fast, trying to process this information. Who did they mean by 'our girls'? They meant my cousins. They meant my sister. They meant *me*.

I put my half-eaten marzipan back on the plate.

I was not Jewish because my *mother* was not Jewish. But my *father*, the implication seemed to be . . .

Then, when I was twelve, my friend Jordan stopped me on the playground. 'Your dad is Jewish,' he said.

I remembered the conversation between my mother and my aunt but still wasn't sure what it meant. I had a crush on Jordan, and I weighed my possible responses and their various consequences. Jordan was Jewish. Would he be offended if I denied it? Would I get in trouble if I agreed?

'No, he's not,' I said at last.

'Yes, he is. My mum says.'

'No, he isn't.'

'He is, too.'

'No, he's *not*,' I repeated, my desire to protect my father finally outweighing my desire to find common ground.

'What you need –' Jordan said, slinging an arm around my shoulder; he was more confident than the other twelve-year-old boys were '– what you need is a good Jewish name. We should call you Rosie.'

He had stumbled, I knew, on the English translation of my Czech great-grandmother's name, Ruzenka. I giggled.

I denied the truth several more times and then managed to divert Jordan with a game of kissing tag. It was easily done. But I felt a growing unease. The clues were beginning to add up. Something wasn't right in our family. Something was lurking, biding its time. It seemed to be pulling at me, a persistent tugging I wasn't sure I could resist much longer.

I was born in the middle of the 1970s, but my home life was straight out of the fifties. My mother cooked and took care of the children. My father worked and made money. In our house the values that are archetypically masculine – assertiveness, agency, success – were prioritized at the expense of the feminine traits of nurture and interdependence.

Feelings were tolerated as one tolerates a needy aunt who comes to visit yearly: we put up with her, we were polite, but behind her back we were all rolling our eyes.

Predictably, the feminism I cleaved to as a young woman was the variety in which a woman gained purchase by behaving like a man. I'd spent my childhood as Daddy's girl, prized for my chutzpah (although this, of course, is the last word he would have used). He loved to see me ham it up in front of the video camera, bossily instructing the unseen viewer on the correct way for a queen to mount her throne. If I felt sad about something, he did not shame or berate me, but he also didn't draw me out.

'What's all *that* about?' Dad would ask if I ever fussed or cried.

So by the time depression came for me in my early twenties, I already had two decades of unexpressed grief accumulated inside me, the grief of small pains and slights. Yes, in the big picture I was a content child with a very happy childhood. None of the classic traumas had ever darkened my door. But it turns out Granny was right. Life is inherently painful. And several generations of unshed tears eventually become a flood.

◡◠

Luckily, my psychotherapist Ben was an exceptional listener. He barely spoke. He nodded. He sighed empathetically. Every now and then he suggested a connection between the present and the past, his suggestion so subtle I was sure I'd come up with it myself.

'How are you feeling?' he would ask, and then he would

wait, his hands folded quietly in his lap, while I fished around inside myself for something.

'I've been thinking,' I'd start to say, and he'd let me continue.

When I was done, he'd repeat the question: 'And how are you *feeling*?'

Our meetings exhausted me. I arrived home wrung out like a dirty old rag. Once, I thought to record a session – an attempt to hang on to the insights that erupted so fast and furious, breaking briefly into the air, only to be swallowed back up by the great ocean of unconsciousness. There was nowhere for them to go but back to where they came from. Several years later I listened to the tape, anticipating a deluge of psychological insight. Instead, there was silence. The odd muffled sniff. Heavy sighing. A statement by Ben or me, followed by such a long period of quiet that I thought the recorder had broken. Such intense, tiring inner labour and nothing to show for it on the outside.

Ben was Jewish. I knew this at the same level that I knew he had grey hair and sported comfortable corduroys. I told him about my 'interesting background' – I must have – but it didn't form the basis for any of our work. The Holocaust is unfathomably deep material. I was still toiling away at the upper reaches of my blindness, admitting that my childhood had not been as perfect as I'd always assumed. It took twelve, or perhaps twenty, sessions to distinguish between what I *thought* I'd had – parents who were perfect – and the reality – parents who were human. Hundreds of dollars. Hours of mental anguish untangling the threads of acceptance and blame. There is no perfect parent. To exist is to get hurt. And the extra confusion of a case like mine: more money than we knew what to do with, everybody smiling and apple-cheeked. Not a whiff of anything remotely like abuse.

And yet. Turns out my father was not at all consistent.

Turns out he was absent, then present, then absent, like the sun moving in and out of the clouds. Turns out he could sit through a half-hour of dinner-table conversation with a blank look in his eye, not registering a single word that was said. To admit this meant admitting that the parent I had idealized was other than how I had needed him to be. Another five sessions on that alone. Long, pregnant pauses, tears, my psyche struggling and thrashing as though being drowned.

But if my father's dissociation was related to the family history with the Holocaust, it wasn't something Ben and I discussed.

Dad had done some psychotherapy himself as a young man. He had been part of one of the T-groups that were popular in the seventies, a group led by a man named Dr Martin Fischer. 'He was good,' Dad would often say. 'It's so hard to find someone *good*.'

When I was a newborn, Dad sometimes took me to group. I picture myself as a baby asleep in my car seat, my little hands curled up at the sides of my head, and try to imagine what it meant that Dad, who could easily have left me with my mother, chose to bring me along.

It was, I think, a kind of pledge. He would work through his past. He would not pass it down to me.

Does every parent dream this impossible dream?

When depression first came for me, Dad was the one who encouraged me to find someone to talk to. He never asked for details about my sessions with Ben, but he asked if I was still going, and whether it was helpful.

And one day, a few months in, he called me on the phone. 'If you want me to come, I will.'

I put down the bowl of grapes I was painstakingly washing. 'Where?'

'To a therapy session. If there's anything you want to talk about with me there.'

In the background the dog barked. 'Go beddie!' Dad reprimanded her.

'Oh,' I said, mortified. 'I don't think so.'

'Are you sure?'

'Yep,' I said. And then something occurred to me. 'Why don't you go alone?'

'What do you mean?'

'You're always saying you'd like to find someone good. I think Ben might qualify.'

I was thinking, of course, of Dad's own 'bad blood', and of the futile pledge he had made to me as a baby. I was thinking of the long gaps between sentences when we talked, gaps that Dad seemed to fall headlong into, disappearing from both himself and from me.

Eventually he agreed. But he saw Ben only once. He was interested in the puzzle of the psyche, he told me, in figuring out how the pieces of a family story fit together. Ben was too focused on feelings. And Dad was done with feelings. There wasn't anything soft and subterranean left inside him that he needed to express.

&

Dad found out by accident that he is Jewish. In his early twenties he toured Europe with some college friends. At the Jewish cemetery in Prague, the tour guide pulled him aside. 'Don't you know that Pick is a Jewish name?'

I can see it so clearly. Dad pauses, his eyes on one of the tombstones, its stylized menorah. It's a fall day and he pulls his sweater tight around his chest. His heart is suddenly pounding. He feels both that he is being told something ridiculously, impossibly implausible, and something that makes his whole life make sense. He looks around for his friends, and finally spots them over by the iron gates, rolling cigarettes.

'I'm not Jewish,' he says.

The tour guide shrugs. 'Your name is.'

'Well, *I'm* not.'

The guide shrugs again. 'Suit yourself.'

Back home in Canada, Dad needed not weeks, not months, but *years* to work up the nerve to ask whether what the guide said was true. When he finally approached his mother in the kitchen, she got a look in her eye – part fear, part relief – and called upstairs to her husband, 'He knows!'

Dad asked and his parents confirmed what the guide had said. They told him about their relatives who were killed in the concentration camps. Dad's grandparents, the aunts he'd never known.

I try to imagine what this must have been like for Dad. To spend your whole life thinking you were one thing, only to find out you are something completely different. That everything you thought you knew – your church, your school, the food your family ate – was a carefully constructed fabrication, designed to mislead even the most casual observer. Implicit in this charade, unspoken and therefore all the more terrible, was the knowledge that the truth had killed your family.

SEVEN

FAMILY LIFE IS DEFINED BY TRADITION. Degan and I are slapdash: We fall into bed at different times. We eat our dinner on the run. Come Friday, though, we slow things down. A few years after we met, we agreed to a day each weekend when we would turn off the phone, turn off the Internet and relax into each other's company. It's a ritual we call, our tongues firmly in our cheeks, '24 Hours Unplugged'.

There's always a moment of panic after pulling the plug, a huge chasm yawning in front of us. But we have learned how important it is to do it anyways.

This Friday it feels especially needed. The week has been crazy, Degan adjusting to his new job, me ticking my way through the tasks of adjusting to a new city: finding the closest gym, the closest post office; figuring out where to buy dish soap. As dusk falls, we put our cells away. We turn off our computers, the frenzied screens falling peaceful like the faces of sleeping children. We cook slowly, and eat together in the strange and fertile silence. After dinner we retreat to the couch, where we sit on opposite ends, our feet touching lightly in the middle.

I've been waiting all week for the chance to get to the reading that has been assigned for Doing Jewish, from Anita Diamant's *Living a Jewish Life*. Now I pull out the book. I turn it over in my hands like a talisman, savouring its unbroken spine. I read the blurbs on the back and the dedication on the opening page. I flip to the Contents page: the first chapter

I've been assigned is about Shabbat, the Jewish day of rest.

A Jewish day of rest?

I read, for the first time, about the day of study and prayer that is the cornerstone of all Jewish life. Every Friday evening, Jews around the world light candles, recite blessings and rejoice in a taste of the world to come. In the modern world, a crucial part of the ritual is turning off technology.

I look over at my phone, as inert as a stone; at the clean kitchen, dishes gleaming, and the actual fire Degan has kindled in the hearth.

'Hey, babe,' I say.

He glances up from his own book.

'*Listen* to this.' I read him the description, and a slow smile spreads across his face. 'Yup – "24 Hours Unplugged",' he says. 'The Jews have been spying on us.'

'I know.'

'For centuries.'

'Copycats.'

He laughs.

'Isn't it bizarre?' I say. 'It's like we invented something out of my ancestors' tradition. I mean, how does that happen? What are the chances?'

'Do you think you'd heard about Shabbat and forgotten? That you suggested "24 Hours Unplugged" based on something someone told you?'

I shake my head. 'I've never heard of Shabbat before right now.'

'Maybe Jordan?' Degan knows the story of my outing on the playground.

'Nope. Really.'

'Weird,' he says.

He lowers his face to his reading, but I'm too excited to stop. 'It's almost like a genetic memory,' I say. 'Like my *cells* were remembering something my consciousness had been told to forget.'

Degan is silent.

'Right?'

'Yeah,' he says. 'Sure.'

From behind him comes the steady tick of the clock on the stove.

'I mean, the ritual we have "invented" (I make quotes in the air with my fingers) constitutes, point for point, a secular version of Shabbat. We rest, we eat, we make love.' I clear my throat. 'We watch videos, which is like our version of praying.'

He laughs again.

'In a way, we're living as Jews,' I say.

'I know,' Degan says. 'I get it. It's cool.'

I can see he wants to get back to his book and I let the subject drop, but I feel an overpowering urge to tell someone who would fully understand the implications. Someone Jewish. But who? Jordan lives on the other side of the country. My father hardly counts. What about Eli, his dinner invitation? I think back to a scene in his book where he goes away to reflect on his Hasidic upbringing. His girlfriend telephones him again and again. Again and again he ignores her calls.

He sounds like an asshole, I think. But he is also undeniably compelling.

 ~

Eli and I agree to meet up at a restaurant called Utopia on College Street. It's a Tuesday evening in the full blush of autumn, the maple trees showing off their prettiest dresses. I lock my bike and see him right away on the busy sidewalk, a head taller than anyone else, moving toward the intersection.

His bright orange sweater matches the fall leaves. He hasn't spotted me, and I walk for a minute beside him in the crowd, bump my shoulder lightly against his. He pulls away instinctively, and then sees it's me who has nudged him. 'Oh!' He laughs, 'You scared me!'

We go inside, joking, already comfortable.

The restaurant is almost as noisy as the street, and packed with young hipsters sporting plaid shirts and tattoos. I go downstairs to the bathroom; on my way back to the table, I see Eli surreptitiously mussing his hair.

I order a lamb burger, sweet potato fries and a beer.

'I'll have the same,' Eli tells the waitress. 'But no beer.'

I raise my eyebrows.

'Allergic.'

I realize I know nothing whatsoever about this person.

Soon, though, we find we have many things in common. We skip the small talk and launch into a heated conversation about the writing life, about the loneliness at the heart of the true creative enterprise. We talk about the relentless desire to write something good, something *perfect*, and the inevitable accompanying disappointment. There are so many books in the world. Why add another unless it's special?

I gesture at the spine of a novel poking out of his bag. 'For example,' I say, 'that one.'

'You didn't like it?'

'Not really.'

'Why not?'

I squint. 'Well, for one thing, the women weren't complex enough.'

His eyes travel down, taking in the ring on my hand. 'Are you married?' he asks finally.

He's the kind of man, I see, who isn't afraid to take what he wants. Our emails have flirted around this subject, but now that he's got me in person he can address it head-on.

'No, not married.' I stop with a french fry halfway to my mouth. I haven't told Degan where I am tonight, who I'm meeting. I wait to hear myself say, 'Engaged,' but no sound comes out of my mouth. I find myself twisting my ring around my finger so the diamond doesn't show.

Eli wears a ring, too. I don't inquire.

'So,' I say, instead. 'I really did like your book. I wasn't just being nice.'

'Thanks,' he says. 'Are you Jewish?'

'Why?'

He shrugs. 'Jews react to it differently.'

'Half,' I say. 'But I grew up thinking I was Christian.' I explain, and tell him about my recent discovery, that I've been making Shabbat for several years without knowing it.

'What do you mean?'

'I mean a day of rest. Turning off the phones and computers. Everything.'

'Are you serious?'

'Yeah.'

'That's amazing.'

'Isn't it?'

His eyes are wide. I continue, emboldened. 'Until a month ago I knew nothing about Judaism at all. But everything I learn feels so comfortable, so familiar.'

He nods. 'You're recognizing who you are. Realizing what you've always been. You just didn't know it until now.'

'Yes.'

'It's a big thing you're going through,' Eli says. 'It's huge.'

It's a simple, even obvious statement, but Eli is the first person to reflect this back to me. Something lights up in my chest: I've been seen. Later I will understand the power in this, the psyche's desperate lunge toward an acknowledgement that has been withheld for so long in my family. But for now I'm just grateful.

'That's it,' I say. 'You're right.' I take a big swallow of beer and force myself to look at his ring. 'And your girlfriend? The one in the book. Are you still together?' I think of how she called him and he refused to pick up, and of how frustrated I felt on her behalf.

'I'm with someone else now,' he says.

'You dumped her?'

'Something like that.'

'And your *new* girlfriend?'

'She's away for a couple months.'

'Is she Jewish?'

'Nope.'

'Does it matter to you?'

'You ask a lot of questions.'

I flush.

'I'm just teasing,' he says, and reaches across the table to squeeze my shoulder. He chews, considering. 'No,' he says. 'It doesn't matter to me right now.' He pauses. 'But at some point it will. I'd like to raise my children as Jews.'

We look at each other. I can almost see the joint thought bubble in the air over our heads, the cartoon sketch of the brood of Jewish children we could produce together.

What a relief it would be having a partner who could serve as my personal guide to my ancestors' tradition.

After dinner we walk in the Annex arm in arm, like a couple from an earlier century, like we've known each other for years. We stroll along the leafy avenues, turn down an alley lined with back doors, the secret selves the houses don't show. I have the feeling there's something Eli wants to tell me. Several times he starts and then stops. Finally he turns to me. 'I'm leaving in January,' he says.

There's a thud in my gut. 'Oh?'

Up on College Street we hear a woman yell, 'José! Get back here! You little idiot!'

'For a six-month writing residency,' Eli says.

I don't need to ask where. I know with complete certainty that he's about to say 'Paris', and when he does, he sees the look on my face and peers at me, puzzled. 'What?' he asks.

'In the Latin Quarter, right?'

'How did you know?'

'I applied.'

'You're not?'

'They took me. But I decided not to go.'

Eli has expressive features, but a look crosses his face now that I can't quite read. Relief, or disappointment. 'That's weird,' he says. 'That we'd apply to the same place.'

I nod. 'At the same time. And both be accepted.'

'Why did you turn it down?'

I think back. 'I'm not sure. It didn't feel right.'

He screws up his nose. 'Weird,' he says again.

Eventually we find ourselves back on College Street, lit up like a carnival at night.

'Toronto is so busy,' I say. 'I'm overwhelmed.'

'It's a good city.'

'But it's so big. Nobody knows their neighbours. You have to make *plans* to see anyone.'

'We made plans,' he points out.

We have reached our bikes. Identical blue milk crates strapped on as baskets. We kiss briefly on the lips, the hip city-kids' kiss.

I watch him bike away.

Just a little crush, I tell myself. No cause for concern.

But as I cycle home, I notice the leaves are falling. The days are getting darker. I am crying all the time. And Degan feels far away, like a tiny boat far out on the sea.

EIGHT

I SPEND THE FOLLOWING MORNING at my desk, researching therapists. I've come to recognize the signs that I'm going to need one. I've left it later than I should have, though, and the Googling, the calling and speaking to candidates, the locating of their various practices on a map of the enormous city takes a lot of energy. Still, I am determined to find the right person. Somebody – as Dad would say – *good*. There is a woman named Eileen who lives close to our new apartment, but my psyche demands something even more subterranean, and I settle eventually on Charlotte, whose office I get to by subway, taking a long, steep escalator down, down, into the series of tunnels that run beneath the city, before emerging again, north, in the sunshine.

Charlotte is a proper British lady of indeterminate age, with a pin skewering the bun on the back of her head and stockings under her sandals. Her office is decked out in full Jungian regalia, with a sand table and a mandala on the wall. She sits in a rocking chair; where Ben would nod or murmur, Charlotte rocks.

Me: 'I feel so awful.'

Her: *Rock, rock.*

Me: 'I can hardly get out of bed in the morning.'

Her: *More rocking.*

She asks me what else is going on in my life. I tell her about our recent move, about my newfound attraction to Judaism.

Unlike Ben, she alights on my Holocaust history immediately, questioning me about it in detail. 'Your relatives died in Auschwitz?'

I nod.

'Is there a way you remember them in your family? With a *yahrzeit*, maybe?'

'With a . . . pardon?'

She explains about the memorial candle lit on the anniversary of a death. I shake my head: no.

'Why do you think you're so suddenly drawn to Judaism?'

I tell her how I identify with Dad's side of the family. I've always been a Pick. I do share some of my mother's qualities: her particular brand of remoteness, her fixation with maintaining a good appearance. I love, as she does, to go to an early movie or crawl into bed in the evening and read. But my personality traits are all from my father. I'm dramatic by nature, and don't care much what people think of me. Prone to bursts of vigorous activity followed by long inert spells of brooding. If you put me beside my Martin cousins on my mother's side, nobody would think we were related; whereas my Pick cousins could be my sisters.

This Pick resemblance goes back several generations. We four granddaughters are sturdy brunettes with an uncanny likeness to our great-grandmother Marianne, the one who was killed in Auschwitz.

I say to Charlotte, 'I wonder what else I inherited from her besides looks.'

The fifty-minute hour flies past. I leave with instructions to pay attention to something Charlotte calls 'the still-small voice within.' *Close* attention. And I am to sleep with a notebook beside my bed, and to write down my dreams, in as much detail as possible, as soon as I wake up in the morning.

That night I dream of Dad's dog Moushka, 'little fly' in

Czech. She has been skinned, all her fur removed. She whimpers in pain. Dad is holding her. The vet stands above her, about to end the suffering, his long needle poised.

The following Tuesday, I go back to my hometown to present a writing award I have judged for local high school students. My father takes one look at me and sees I am depressed.

'When did it start?' he asks.

I shrug helplessly. 'I'm not sure.' I falter. 'I'm taking this course. About Judaism,' I say. Tears start to slide down my cheeks.

'Oh, sweetie,' Dad says. 'I'm sorry.'

We are standing in the back hall. He has just come in from walking the dog; he's wearing a fluorescent orange lumberjack coat meant for hunting season. He has not bothered to do up his boots, and the tongues loll heavily forward.

'It's only an introduction,' I say. 'The basics. But I seem to be having a strong reaction to it.'

'I can see that,' he says. 'I can't say I *understand* it, but I see it.'

'I know it's not logical.'

'Here!' he calls to the dog. 'Lie down beddie!'

'This might sound weird,' I say, 'but it feels genetic. Like my body is remembering the loss of my tribe.'

I am thinking of Eli, the kind of instant recognition I felt when we met. Of my sudden desire to observe Shabbat with someone who has grown up doing so. Can these reactions be a biological imperative? Something in my genes suddenly asserting itself?

Dad says, 'It's funny, but I think I know what you mean.'

'How so?'

He lists the people he's most comfortable with in the world: his cousins and several friends from Czechoslovakia. 'They're all Czech, so I thought that was why I felt close to them. Hearing you talk makes me wonder, though.' He pauses. 'They're Czech, but they're also Jewish.'

I bite my lip, my face wet with tears.

'Do you remember anything?' I ask. 'About your parents practising?'

'They didn't practise,' Dad says. 'That's the point.'

I nod at the well-worn line.

'But my father's *mother* . . .'

'Ruzenka?'

Dad nods. He squints, concentrating. I can see he wants to please me, wants to offer up a detail. Any detail.

'I think she used to come for dinner on the High Holidays. And we would eat . . . latkes?'

'Even I know that latkes are for Hanukkah.'

Dad shrugs. 'I'm sorry, sweetie. They were just trying to forget it.'

He lines his boots up neatly, turns toward the kitchen. He pauses for a second, then looks back at me, his face suddenly bright. 'I did hear a story about my father,' he says.

'Oh?'

'Before the war, when the political tide was turning, lots of Czech Jews were converting to Catholicism. Dad apparently scorned this. He said – get this – he said that he wouldn't convert to Christianity if he was *the last Jew on earth.*'

Dad laughs at the irony. His father *did* convert, essentially, and spent the rest of his life celebrating Christmas and Easter. Still, my eyes widen at this revelation. There was a time when my grandfather vowed he would never renounce his faith?

To hear this second side of the story is like spotting a small light flickering far out at sea.

Someone in my family, at some point, cared deeply about being Jewish.

I have only a handful of memories of my grandfather. We called him Gumper, after my eldest cousin's first attempt at 'Grandpa'. I remember him waltzing with Granny beside their swimming pool in Quebec. He wore high rubber boots and work pants, but I could see, even then, that he knew how to lead a lady, just the right amount of pressure on Granny's lower back to move her where he wanted her to go.

And Granny wasn't an easy lady to lead.

The morning Gumper died, I wet my bed. I was ten years old, and I remember the surprise, the intense shame as I sniffed around in my sheets and realized what had happened. I bundled up the urine-soaked bedding and tiptoed in to tell my mother. It was very early, before dawn, and I was confused by the lamp already lit in my parents' bedroom. Dad was on the phone, in his green plaid flannel pyjamas, his face slack. 'I'll be on the next flight,' I heard him say.

'Where are you—' I started to ask loudly, but my mother shushed me. 'He's gone,' she said.

'Who?'

'Gumper.'

'Gone? Where did he go?'

'He died, sweetie.'

And just like that, the shame of the peed bed disappeared, eclipsed by something entirely adult, the implications of which I didn't understand.

Gumper was a sportsman who loved fly-fishing and hunting: we have silent video footage of him on safari in Africa, dressed in khakis, his motions jerky from the old-fashioned camera as he lifts his fist in a cheer. He also loved mushrooming, that quintessentially Slavic pursuit. At camp one summer I made him a toadstool out of clay, glazed it and brought it home for him in my trunk. I remember the pride on his face, and the pleasure.

Gumper was passionate, and wildly successful. The grandson of an itinerant merchant, by the time he came to Canada he was so distinguished that the local newspaper ran a headline about him: 'Jan Pick, millionaire manufacturer of Prague, will establish a factory in Sherbrooke.' His wealth and his smarts got Granny and him out of Nazi-occupied Czechoslovakia. They escaped to France, then to England, and finally on to Canada. On the day of their arrival in Sherbrooke, Quebec, the mayor assembled a welcome party to greet them at the station. But Gumper was too busy staring out the window of the train, looking for exotic Canadian wildlife, plotting his next hunting expedition. They missed the stop entirely and sped past in the blackness, getting off an hour later in the sparkling metropolis of Montreal.

Three years later — back in Sherbrooke — my father was born.

In the Holocaust's aftermath, babies were often given the names of relatives who had perished. Granny and Gumper had lost almost everyone, but they called Dad Thomas, after Thomas Masaryk, the first president of Czechoslovakia, their beloved and forsaken homeland.

NINE

ON IMPULSE, I MAKE AN APPOINTMENT to meet Rabbi Klein
again in person. I bike up Bathurst Street: it's under heavy
construction, the street clogged with orange pylons and
honking SUVs, their shiny flanks coated in dust. I've driven
past her synagogue before but have never been inside. The
front hall is twice the size of the church I attended as a girl,
brightly lit and hung with modern art. There's a tastefully
placed kiosk selling pricey Judaica, and a front desk manned by
a uniformed security guard. He checks my purse, for what I
can't imagine, then politely directs me up a wide spiral staircase
lined with framed portraits of all the synagogue's earlier rabbis.
The secretary shows me in.

'Have a seat,' Rabbi Klein says.

I sit down in a red armchair and start to cry right away.

'It's not you – it's me,' she says. 'I have this effect on people.'

I sniffle, smile wanly.

I have forgotten how gorgeous Rabbi Klein is. She has the
kind of beauty that is hard to nail down: it's not just her long
curls, or her dimples or creamy skin, but the way she holds
herself, the openness in her face. Her aura is both innocent and
refined.

'So,' she says. 'Catch me up.'

I lean back in the armchair and start talking. I tell Rabbi
Klein about the Doing Jewish class, how sad I feel reading the
textbook. I tell her about my conversation with my father,

about the Jews he feels most comfortable with in the world. I also find myself telling her about meeting Eli, and the validation he gave me that what I'm experiencing is meaningful.

'I'm just reading his book,' the rabbi says.

I nod. 'Judaism used to be invisible to me,' I say. 'Now it's everywhere.'

We talk for a while about the legacy of denial, about how the grief I am feeling isn't just my own but my father's and grandparents', as well. About how a secret, passed down the generations, grows until it's impossible to hold. About the sudden desire I have to fix the past, to undo the wrong that's been done.

'I think I might want to convert,' I hear myself say.

I pause. The word *conversion* makes me think of thunderbolts, of door-to-door salesmen peddling salvation and of women with their eyes rolled back in their heads. I hesitate. 'At least, I'd like to learn more about my options.'

From somewhere down the hall, someone knocks on a door. We hear it open, then slam closed.

The rabbi gathers her dark curls in a fistful at the side of her neck. 'Refresh me,' she says. 'Do you have a husband?'

'A fiancé.'

'And he's Jewish? Not Jewish?'

'Not Jewish,' I say.

A little frown wrinkles her forehead. 'How does he feel about all this?'

'He's supportive,' I say. Which Degan is. Absolutely.

'He wants me to be happy,' I say. Which he does.

The rabbi smiles a Botticelli smile. 'He sounds wonderful.'

'So anyway,' I continue, 'the people in my Doing Jewish class are all signed up for the Jewish Information Course this winter. I was thinking *I* might like to take it. That it might clarify things, shed some light. I wanted to ask –' I swallow, my throat all at once dry. '– I wanted to ask if you'd sponsor me.'

I'm surprised to hear myself say this. The JIC is a long and exhaustive class, and I've reached the hardest part in the novel I'm writing, the place where I really need to focus. I have no extra time at the end of my days, not to mention energy. But something else has taken over, an instinctual part of me I know to defer to, so I submit and wait for the rabbi's reply.

'Yes,' she says finally. 'I'd be happy to sponsor you. And Degan.'

'And Degan?'

'He'd also have to take the class.'

'Okay,' I say uncertainly. Still, I'm relieved. I've been warned that getting a rabbi on board is difficult, that it's their job to push you away as a test of your sincerity, so I'm especially chuffed. What was all the fuss about?

'The class starts in January,' she says. 'We're already halfway through the fall. But I like you. And you're obviously sincere.'

Good. Fantastic.

But I see there's something else.

'They probably haven't told you this in your Doing Jewish class,' she says.

I wait for it.

'No *beit din*,' she starts to say but stops again, realizing I don't know the term. '*Beit din* – literally "house of judgment". It's a Jewish court. A panel of rabbis.'

I nod.

She continues. 'No *beit din* here in Toronto would agree to create an intermarriage.'

I exhale, relieved. 'I'm not married,' I remind her.

'No. But you will be.'

I pause, not understanding.

'We don't want Judaism to be a wedge between you and your fiancé,' she says.

I am silent. How would it be a *wedge* between us?

'Degan is . . .' I pause. Didn't I already say this? I repeat it, just in case. 'Degan is incredibly supportive.'

'Is he interested in raising a Jewish family?' the rabbi asks.

I stare blankly. We don't even have a date for our wedding. Suddenly just the *thought* of a wedding is scary. But Rabbi Klein persists. 'Is he interested in *being* Jewish?'

This is like asking if our postman is interested in becoming the king of England. I continue to stare blankly, but no more help is forthcoming. And then it dawns on me. Slowly. She makes me say it myself. 'I can't convert unless Degan does, too?'

'Right,' Rabbi Klein says, relieved I have finally figured it out. 'We want to make sure you are on the same path. Together.'

And what if we aren't? I wonder.

⟨⁄⟩

I leave the rabbi's office in a daze. Biking down Bathurst Street, I almost get run over by a delivery truck; it whizzes past me, horn blaring. I feel there has been a mistake, that I didn't make myself clear. My family died in Auschwitz. My father *is* Jewish. Frankly, I am surprised that I can't just call the religion my own and have that be the end of it.

Degan also receives the news with incredulity. 'What's she saying? You're not good enough by yourself?'

I plunk my bag on the floor and wrap my arms around him, inhaling soap and warm skin.

'I guess,' I say, my face pressed into his neck.

'What does she—' he begins. 'What's her name again?'

'Rabbi Klein. Rachel.'

I lay my head on his shoulder but Degan takes a step back. 'It sounds to me like Rachel is saying you're not good enough for them.' He scratches his beard. 'No. They're saying *I'm* not good enough because I'm Christian.' He shakes his head. 'It's ridiculous.'

'The religion is very family based,' I say.

'And *your* family died in *Auschwitz*.'

'They were Jewish enough for the Nazis,' I agree.

'And how would it hurt them? To have you?'

I shrug. Mentally I do the math: right now, in our household, there are two people. And no Jews. If we have a baby, that baby will not be Jewish.

If I alone could convert, there would be one Jew in our home. In that scenario, if Degan and I have a baby, the baby will be Jewish. Two Jews where before there were none. Two *sincere* Jews, in the rabbi's own words.

It's hard for me to see the harm done.

❧

I do a bit of reading online. The Reform Movement's 1983 Resolution on Patrilineal Descent is clear. It allows for the child of a Jewish father and non-Jewish mother – a child like me – to be accepted 'as Jewish without a formal conversion, if he or she attends a Jewish school and follows a course of studies leading to Confirmation. Such procedure is regarded as sufficient evidence that the parents and the child herself intend that she shall live as a Jew.'

In other words, such a child is taken at her word. Couldn't the same concept hold for an adult who decides to apply herself?

The document refers to the Reform Jewish community of

North America but in practical terms seems to apply only in the United States. In Toronto, apparently, the maternal line is all that matters.

I do some more digging and discover that in biblical times Judaism was patrilineal: any child sired by Abraham (who had multiple wives and concubines) was an Israelite. The change came in the rabbinic period, and its impetus was the need to be certain of parenthood. You can never be *sure* who fathered a child: a woman might lie or might not be certain. Whereas maternity is obvious and indisputable. It's a sexist notion, but it isn't a surprise to me. What *is* a surprise is that my own religious identity is suddenly tied up with Degan's. Like runners in a three-legged race, we are bound together by someone else's rules. My fate will be his. Or his will be mine.

⌾

I sit in Charlotte's office with tears running down my cheeks. I unfold the crinkled piece of foolscap on which I have written a dream about my great-grandmother Marianne. As per Charlotte's instruction, I've included as much detail as possible. In the dream I am in a cattle car, walking backward toward my great-grandmother, but when she finally meets my gaze, she wears my own face. It's not that she looks like me; she *is* me.

I feel like a fourth grader reciting an awkward, exaggerated composition. The dream is full of all the things I try so hard to avoid in my writing: a hackneyed setting (an empty train!), obvious metaphors (my face where hers should be!). Still, as I read, the atmosphere in the room changes. Charlotte's chair rocks. The air is like soup, or some kind of weird clingy water. I strain to keep my mouth at the surface. I sense that the density, the deadness that threatens to pull me under, is related to the dream and to my history. 'What does it mean to you?'

Charlotte asks. 'That your great-grandmother looked at you with your own face?'

'Isn't it obvious?'

Still I resist saying it. The concept of the intergenerational transmission of trauma seems so fantastical, like saying that Marianne tripped on her shoelace seventy years ago and *my* ankle is sprained as a result. My happy childhood, my privilege: how could things that happened so long ago, to people I never knew, affect me?

Layers of fog close in when I try to engage the details of my history. I feel physiologically *unable* to remember the structure of our felled family tree, the many severed branches, who was related to whom and in what way. Perhaps it's a kind of defensive amnesia, a psychic version of a runner's cramp.

'I did some reading this week,' I tell Charlotte. 'About a therapist who works with second- and third-generation survivors. Their marriages crumble, their children are troubled. But they fail to see how their struggles are related to their parents' Holocaust experiences.'

'Sound familiar?' Charlotte asks.

My psyche bucks and heaves.

This has nothing to do with me.

This has everything to do with me.

Charlotte: *Rock, rock, rock.*

I think about the traits I have that I am almost unconscious of, traits that nonetheless govern my daily life. For example, last week there was a plastic bag with old apple slices and almond butter in the fridge. The almond butter was smeared on the inside of the bag, and extracting it would have been a hassle and made a mess. I threw the whole thing out. But the apples were good. If not *good*, then edible. I thought about the calories, about how long they could keep a body going. Even if the apples were rotten. How it would be possible to extract every ounce of almond butter from the bag. An apple filled with worms. It could be eaten. *Would* have been eaten. Devoured.

I threw it out, but I thought of it for hours.

Bread was Granny's downfall. She could never say no to dinner rolls, to the crusty baguette on the cutting board.

When she ate a chicken breast, nothing remained. The bones on her plate so light as to barely exist, pale and nearly weightless, picked clean.

TEN

MY LITERARY AGENT Anne has teamed up with a prominent British agency that will represent her authors in the European markets. One of the British agents, John, is in town, and on Sunday night Anne invites a handful of us to the Spoke Club to meet him. The room is dark and filled with beautiful men in suits. The writer Andrew Pyper asks what I want to drink.

'Scotch?'

He signals the barmaid.

Another writer, Michael Winter, approaches us, puts an arm around my shoulder. 'Can I get you a drink?'

'Your friend here took care of it.'

I look around at the room: Rob Wiersema, Russell Smith, Peter Norman. Michael and Andrew. Where are the other women?

The music is loud and the agent's accent heavy; we stumble through a conversation about Carol Ann Duffy. I am astonished to hear that some of John's clients are poets. Is poetry so valued in Britain that money actually enters the equation?

'Are you a poet?' John asks, his eyes on my chest.

'I am.'

Anne overhears this and jumps in. 'And a *novelist*. She's working on a new manuscript.'

'What's it about?' John asks.

I explain it is set in Czechoslovakia around the time of the Munich Agreement.

'Why did you want to write about that?'

'My grandparents were Czech.'

'What's your last name?'

'Pick.'

John says, 'Was the name shortened?'

'No. It's a Czech name. A Czech Jewish name.'

He doesn't pause, or flinch, or pull back. Soon we are shouting, over the thump of the bass, about his clients Colm Tóibín and Ian McEwan. I hear myself laughing. But inside I am scared: have I ruined my chances? He knows my secret. Maybe now he won't sell the novel. Britain is antisemitic. The whole world is antisemitic. I should have just stayed comfortably in hiding.

❧

Books about evil pile up beside my bed. Hannah Arendt's classic *Eichmann in Jerusalem*. The more recent *Becoming Eichmann*, a historical rebuttal to Arendt. Tom Childers's *The Nazi Voter*, recommended by my childhood friend Jordan, whom I've started emailing with again. I don't open the books. I return them to the library, check out more, but those, too, remain untouched. I want no mediating influence. If I am to understand these acts of inhumanity, I want to understand them on their own terms. Unvarnished, unadorned. I forsake theory in favour of anecdote. I force myself to read about the guards in the camps who would put live mice in the prisoners' mouths, then hold them closed. The mice would burrow down out of instinct, eating the hosts alive from the inside.

With women, a mouse was inserted into the vagina, which was sewn shut with thread.

I read about a woman who was pregnant when she arrived at Auschwitz. She gave birth in a dirty barracks to a beautiful baby girl. Dr Mengele, otherwise known as 'the Angel of Death', was curious how long a human infant could survive without nourishment. He bound the mother's breasts so she could not nurse. For six days her daughter suffered terribly. On the seventh day, the mother administered morphine to kill her own child and thus save her.

I gravitate to these unique tortures not out of voyeurism but because of their detail. After three generations of denial, I am trying to make the Holocaust seem real. To accept it. One million dead people are too many for my psyche. Two million, six million – a bland mass of incomprehensibility. But one woman forced to hold her own infant until she starved? That remains seared in my mind forever.

❧

November arrives. The nights fall quickly and completely, as though someone has thrown a bolt of black velvet over a lamp. Debra, the daughter of the minister from my class, emails to ask if I want to meet her at synagogue for Erev Shabbat, the evening service. I'm pleased by the invitation and accept. On my way in, I hear a woman screaming in the boardroom, 'I'm sure you have a right to criticize my country and my city, but I don't want to hear it! I DON'T want to HEAR IT!'

The service takes place in a small chapel upstairs. The space feels like someone's living room, with wooden beams and wall-to-wall carpeting, and a bimah, or pulpit, at the front where the fireplace otherwise would be. Rabbi Klein sits in a pew with her three small children. She passes one a blue sippy cup and puts a finger to her lips, signalling for the other two to be quiet while an older woman behind her talks. She looks up and sees me, and waves, welcoming. I wave back but lead Debra toward a seat on the opposite side of the room. I see the rabbi as untouchable, in the fashion of a famous rock star, and the relaxed atmosphere in the sanctuary as terrifying.

I grew up going to Anglican church – not every Sunday, but once or twice a month. I recall the stiff formality, having to get dressed up, the black patent Mary Janes that dug into the backs of my heels. The church basement, where the children made crosses out of Popsicle sticks and glue, was always cold. After Sunday school, we filed upstairs to join the adults. I braced myself against Dad's voice, singing 'Sons of God', loudly and off-key. I braced myself, but I was proud to be beside him.

In the difficult years following Gumper's death, he would put his forehead on the pew in front of him and cry.

Dad was on the board of directors of our church for several years. He sometimes still attends. If you press him, though, he'll admit he thinks Jesus was a 'spiritual person'. Probably not the Son of God.

Debra and I slide into our seats. The Shabbat service begins with *niggunim* – 'wordless melodies'. I hum a few bars, but my voice is dry in my throat. I am all at once sick with envy, seeing these families, the kids racing up and down the pews, the men wearing *kippot*, shaking hands, everyone breaking all at once into 'L'cha Dodi', the song that welcomes the Sabbath as if it is a bride. I feel comfortable here in a way that I never did at church. Still, I don't know how to belong. I close my eyes and try to let the Hebrew words wash over me, soothe me, but instead they are like tears: if I give in to them, I will never stop crying. It is a familiar, old kind of sadness. A sadness that has driven me to bad decisions in the past, that has at its core a desperate kind of hunger.

I think about Gumper. *Not if I was the last Jew on earth.*

The sermon is about the custom of putting a rock on a Jewish grave to mark it. I picture Gumper's tombstone, unadorned in the small Quebec cemetery, furred over with several inches of snow.

At the end of the service, wine is passed out to the adults, grape juice to the kids. There are big hunks of freshly baked challah for everyone. Debra, the minister's daughter, leans over and whispers, 'Makes the wafers look pretty meagre.'

I laugh. The sanctuary is warm; the lights are bright and children's voices fill every corner. For a moment it is okay to be alive.

We file out with the crowd. 'Good night,' I say to Debra. 'Good *Shabbos*,' I add for good measure.

'To you, too.'

And then I walk back into the autumn darkness. Dread hits me like an open palm. I double over. I can barely make it to my car.

❧

Degan comes home and finds me under the covers, with the shades drawn. It is eight in the evening. The dishes are undone, and there are clothes and jewellery strewn across the bedroom floor. He sits on the edge of the bed. 'I'm worried about you,' he says.

He reaches for my shoulder. I flinch from his touch.

'What's going on with you, babe?'

I shake my head, helpless to speak, my eyes filled with tears.

Degan leans down, kisses my forehead.

'It's so dark,' I finally manage.

There's a black glove pressing down on me, a hand at my throat.

We spend Saturday at home, quietly observing the Sabbath. On Sunday morning I sit at my desk and read, to keep up a semblance of routine, to try to keep myself afloat. I flip through the pages of a contemporary anthology on depression. One writer sees it as a philosophical problem pertaining to the nature of the self. Her essay is so abstract that you could be forgiven for thinking she suffers from nothing but an excess of intelligence; and yet, the list of drugs she has been on is two full lines in length. (I am surprised, on encountering the list, by how familiar the names are – Celexa, Effexor, Paxil – like in a child's list of fruit or farm animals.) The next writer sees depression as 'akin to being tied to a chair with restraints'; whereas a third seems so pleased by his condition you could no sooner wrest it from him than take a prized soother from a toddler.

I turn to Eric Wilson's bestseller *Against Happiness*. 'To sit long with our various alienations and our sumptuous paralyses and our nervous fears is to come indeed to a startling realization,' he waxes. 'Melancholy connects us to our fundamental self.'

Perhaps. Except, I can't help but think that his endorsement is for something quite different from the depression Andrew Solomon describes in *The Noonday Demon*, in which he is pinioned to his bed for weeks, able only to blink and to cry.

Freud addressed this discrepancy in his seminal essay 'On Mourning and Melancholia' when he wrote, 'Even in descriptive psychiatry the definition of melancholia does not seem to warrant reduction to a unity.'

From the kitchen I hear Degan turn on the radio. A Sugar Ray song, 'Fly', is playing. I latch on to the lyrics in the manner of a sinner reciting Hail Marys. In my mind the singer's longing to fly transforms instantly, to *I just wanna die.*

I sing the line under my breath, over and over all morning. It is as though, by repeating it, I am stacking sandbags to prepare for a flood. The truth is, I do *not* want to die. But by claiming the opposite, perhaps I can outwit the bad blood.

I do not want to die.

Well, only a little. There's a difference between wanting to die and wanting to never have existed in the first place.

❧

An hour later, I stack my books neatly beside my keyboard and lean back in my chair, arching to crack my back. It's still early – not yet noon – the weak sun limp against the windowpane. I hear Degan opening the fridge, then running the tap at the kitchen sink. I turn on the computer, check my email. I note the Hebrew date, then read about the month of Cheshvan. It is – surprise! – the bitter month, the month of spiritual darkness. It includes no Jewish holidays.

The month of Cheshvan is for identification with our ancestors.

On a whim, I go to my shelves and pull out a final book to add to my reading pile. Years ago, I stole it; it is the only thing I have stolen in my life. I remember walking out of the bookstore in St John's with complete entitlement, striding through the double doors with the hardcover under my arm for anyone to see. The book was called *Suddenly Jewish*. And the words rang in my head: this is *mine*.

ELEVEN

AT THE END OF NOVEMBER, my cousin Lucy stops through Toronto. She's the eldest of the four Pick granddaughters, a senior lecturer in the history of Christianity, in the divinity school at a big American college. She's also a world-class authority on Spanish medieval Jews. Luce takes me out to a French bistro on the nicer end of St Clair. I order a spinach salad; she orders the duck confit poutine. While we're waiting for our food to arrive, I explain the pain I'm experiencing, the visceral desire to reclaim what's been lost.

'I'm thinking about it all the time,' I say.

'I understand,' she says. 'I went through something similar.'

From across the restaurant we hear another patron: 'He'll *never* learn that Torah portion.'

We both laugh. I look at Lucy across the table, taking in her freckles, her hazel eyes. How she looks like me, how we both look like our great-grandmother Marianne. 'I'm taking a class,' I say. And then, on a whim: 'I'm thinking of converting.'

Her eyebrows go up. It's not judgment or disapproval, just curiosity.

'What would it involve?'

'The class. And then the *beit din*—'

She nods to show she knows the term.

'Would you have to go in the mikvah?' she asks, referring to the Jewish ritual bath.

'Yep.'

The waitress places our orders in front of us. Lucy has ordered well as usual. She prods her poutine with the tines of her fork.

'Granny had to go in the mikvah before she married Gumper. Because she'd been baptized.' She takes a bite. 'Granny *hated* the mikvah,' she says. 'She felt it implied that she was unclean.'

'She told you that?'

'She did.'

'Don't *all* Jewish women immerse before getting married?'

'Ones who practise, sure. But Granny never practised. I mean, she was baptized! So the mikvah would have been a requirement from the rabbi. Who Gumper's family would have furnished.'

'Because Gumper's family was more observant?'

I know the answer, but I defer to Lucy's authority. She had a decade of adult conversations with our grandparents while I was still a little girl.

'Yes,' she says. She lifts a french fry from the mess of duck and gravy, and chews, her face softening. 'Gumper was always so sad at Christmas.'

I cast my mind back but can't access any memories of Gumper at Christmas, only the kind of recollection that comes from seeing a photograph again and again. The shot that keeps appearing in my mind's eye now is of Gumper on Christmas morning. He's unwrapping a novelty licence plate, the type you might see on the back of a red convertible, inscribed with the French words *J'aime ta femme*.

'I love your wife.'

Who would have given him such a gift?

There's a rumour in our family that Granny had an affair. Several affairs. Dad remembers Gumper taking off his shoe and hurling it across the room at his wife. But in the Christmas photo, Gumper's head is tilted back, his mouth wide open as he laughs.

'It's Gumper who makes me want Judaism back,' I say. 'Thinking of what he went through, what he lost.'

'He *hated* Christmas,' Lucy says. 'The whole big show.'

Not if I was the last Jew on earth.

I put my fork down; it makes a small chiming noise against my plate.

'Maybe I'll convert,' I say, as though thinking of the idea for the first time.

Lucy asks, 'What does Degan think?'

I shrug. 'He's supportive.'

She smiles. Says, 'The only way to *really* get it back would be to marry a Jew.'

Eli's name pops up on my computer screen. It's a Friday afternoon, the autumn light waning outside my study window, the Sabbath coming slowly closer, a steamship filling more and more of the horizon. He writes, 'Do you want to have coffee?'

'Sure,' I answer. 'Let's.'

We have a subtle power struggle over where we will meet, who will be the one to travel across Toronto. I'm the one who ends up taking the bus south, and then the subway east to the Danforth. I sit on the bench outside the Big Carrot, where Eli is picking up some groceries.

My phone vibrates in my pocket. 'I'm inside,' he says.

I see him before he sees me, in front of the dairy fridge, the bushy hair, the wool sweater. He's not classically handsome, not exactly, but my body responds with sweat, an uptick in my heartbeat. I sidle up. 'Hey.'

There is broccoli in his cart – just the crown – and rye bread.

Almond butter, organic yogourt. The contents of his shopping cart look exactly like mine.

Eli turns to me and grins, puts a hand casually on my shoulder. 'Well,' he says, 'I hear you're engaged.'

'Who told you?'

'You did. By email.'

I exhale. 'I forgot.'

'Do you have a date for the wedding?'

'No,' I say. 'Not yet.'

Eli is paying for his groceries, not looking me in the eye.

'And they won't let you convert because your boyfriend isn't Jewish?'

I nod. The cash register dings and he pockets a handful of change.

'I've been thinking about it,' he says. 'It makes me so pissed.'

'Are you surprised?'

He shakes his head. 'Unfortunately not.' He pauses, runs a hand through his messy hair. 'They're like that,' he says.

As though he isn't one of them.

Outside in the autumn dusk, the street lights are coming on one by one. We walk down the Danforth, each carrying a bag of groceries. At Broadview we head south. The neighbourhood is affluent, the red brick houses wrapped in big front porches. Behind the gauzy curtains are domestic friezes: a man cutting onions, a small girl practising a cello. To an outsider, Eli and I would comprise another domestic scene: a couple carrying their groceries home for dinner at the end of a long week.

Eli touches my elbow. 'Look.'

I follow his gaze. It's only five o'clock, but the moon is already out. It shines, full and bright, like a fisherman's lantern, like a little portal to infinity punched in the darkness.

Degan gets panic attacks from looking at the stars; perhaps it's an existential fear of our human insignificance, maybe an inner ear imbalance – we're not sure. My instinct, developed over the seven years of our relationship, is to pretend I don't notice anything celestial. But Eli wants to give the moon its due. We stand in silence, shoulder to shoulder, availing ourselves of its exuberant beauty.

When we arrive at his house, he shows me in, shows me around. Thick, creamy carpets, antiques. I remark on the beautiful claw-foot tub in the bathroom and check my email on his laptop. I notice a framed photo on a coffee table by the window – a redhead with red lipstick and her arms thrown around Eli's neck. 'Your girlfriend?'

He nods. 'She's away for another month.'

Downstairs, he lights a fire. I watch the curl of his back as he bends over kindling and newspaper, listen for the hiss of the match. He straightens, turns to face me, wiping his palms down his thighs. 'I have some nice Scotch,' he says.

'Do I look like a girl who says no to Scotch?'

We settle on the pillowy couch, talk for a while about memoir as a genre, the writer's responsibility to the truth. There's an onus on the writer to get the essence right, we concur. But the order of events, the dialogue – a reader should understand that any book is creative.

'I'm glad I'm working on fiction,' I say.

'Will you ever write about your family?'

'I doubt it.'

'You should.'

I tell him about my visit with Lucy, what she said about Granny and Gumper's wedding.

The fire cracks and spits.

I sigh. 'I really want to go in that tub. Like, *really*.'

Eli's eyebrows rise. 'Upstairs? *My* tub?'

I laugh. 'The mikvah.'

'Have a bath,' he says. 'Make yourself at home.'

TWELVE

THE MORE DEPRESSED I FEEL, the stronger my longing for Judaism becomes. It is as though everything unmet in me, all my aloneness, has finally found a point on which to fixate. The elusive something that will make it all better shines like a new toy, the way a frosted glass beckons to a drinker.

The only thing is, I'm not sure if that's the story I'm in – one of addiction and desperation – or if I'm in another kind of story, one with a real happy ending.

I take up the reading of conversion memoirs as a mother-to-be takes up child-rearing manuals. I read *Stranger in the Midst* by Nan Fink, and *Turbulent Souls* by Stephen Dubner, the co-author of *Freakonomics*, whose Jewish parents converted to Catholicism. He wonders, 'Was it love that had inspired my return to Judaism? No, I told myself, not love . . . It was instinct. My noisy soul had demanded that I follow the flow of my blood.'

Yes, I think. Exactly.

La sangre llama.

'But that flow,' Dubner continues, 'had now led to my father . . . was my embrace of Judaism nothing more than an embrace of my dead father, a glorified nostalgia trip?'

This gives me pause. I, too, have always idealized my father. Would I have such a longing for something – for *anything* – on my mother's side of the family?

The details of my world are intolerable. I brace myself

against parking meters, dollar stores, the national anthem. Degan comes in and out of the scene like a mechanical toy doll, like an image on a faraway screen with the volume turned all the way down. I am losing weight. Food makes me queasy and I have a constant case of the runs.

At least I will look good in my wedding dress.

And when I think of that train of silk and lace trailing behind me down the aisle, it seems as heavy as history itself, with only me to drag it into the present.

THIRTEEN

MUM EMAILS: 'What do you want for Christmas? What does Degan want?'

I consider. 'We'll be celebrating Hanukkah over the holiday,' I finally write. 'Do you want to join us?'

Several days go by with no reply. Finally there's a single line from Dad: 'Sure, we can if you like.'

I tell Degan bluntly, 'I told my parents we're celebrating Hanukkah.'

'Of course you did,' he says. We haven't talked about what we've been calling 'the conversion conundrum' recently, but I know he knows how much this will mean to me.

I look at his expression. Such generosity. 'Yes, let's do Hanukkah this year,' he says.

⚬〜

Degan goes to work all day and listens to people's problems. To twenty-somethings who refuse to eat, and to others who mutilate their bodies. The office politics are like a hundred-legged sea creature. He comes home to an apartment buried beneath a mountain of dirty laundry. The minute I see him I start to weep. 'I'm sorry,' I say.

He hugs me.

'I had such a long day,' he says.

Degan tries to tell me about a client, a single mother, a

Somali refugee he wants desperately to help, who is being screwed over by immigration. But his voice is like traffic down the parkway that splits Toronto in half, the individual words indiscernible over the general noise. Weeks go by; I am completely unable to hear anything he says about his own life. He is paying two-thirds of our rent so I can write. The least I could do is put dinner on the table. What kind of wife am I going to be? I'm a failure before I've even started.

I think of Granny and Gumper. At the end of the war Gumper returned to Europe. He wrote letters home to Granny, love letters, unabashed. From Prague on June 13, 1946: 'I'm really longing to see you, truly I am! I see so many bad marriages here, and my constant hope is that ours will continue to be a good one. Otherwise, things always end disastrously.'

⌒

I arrive early for our next Doing Jewish class. Out in the parking lot a car alarm is screaming; the rabbi claps her hands and it stops, as though at her command. 'Okay,' she says. 'Let's get started.'

She looks around at us. 'Who knows which month we're in?'

She's appealing to the Jews who are here to support their partners in a potential conversion. They shift in their seats: the Israeli with the dreadlocks, the cluster of ball-cap wearing boyfriends.

'Tevet?' one of them guesses.

'No. Anyone else?'

Everyone in the class averts their eyes, nobody willing to risk an answer.

'Kislev,' the rabbi says finally. 'The month of trust. Also the month of?'

I raise my hand. 'Hanukkah?'

'Correct.'

Debra gives me the thumbs-up.

'*Which*,' the rabbi adds quickly, 'is a very *minor* holiday. A holiday for children.'

I busy myself with my notebook.

'Anything else about Kislev?' she asks.

The silences blooms and bursts.

'Kislev is the dark month,' she says. 'Both outside and within. As the days get shorter, our own inner darkness makes itself known.'

Rabbi Glickman invites us to close our eyes. To enter the blackness, the cold. My lids fall shut as though weighted by coins.

She begins to speak in a singsongy voice, like a yoga teacher might use in Savasana or a kindergarten teacher during story time. 'Christmas is such a big light,' she says. 'It's so over-powering. We need to fortify ourselves, to push back against it, to find our *own* way to light the darkness. Our own Jewish way.'

Lay off my holiday, I think instinctively.

I open one eye; the rabbi is looking directly at me.

I close my eye, chastened. But in my mind's eye my dukes are still raised.

'Now picture a menorah,' she continues in her singsongy voice. 'Perhaps the special menorah you had as a child.'

I exhale, refocusing. A menorah, okay. That was the one Jewish item we did have, at Granny and Gumper's house in Quebec. It was pushed to the very back of the highest shelf of a huge walnut cabinet Granny and Gumper managed to smuggle out of Europe. Nobody mentioned the menorah; it was never lit. And instead of eight branches, it had six.

Rabbi Glickman says, 'Picture the menorah. Envision the row of unlit candles.'

I do.

'Now light a match,' she says.

I imagine striking the flint, wait for the little flame to rise, but my brain refuses the image. The rabbi is instructing the other students to light the candles one by one. I try, try again. But again my mind balks. It knows the light is a lie.

We learn that Kislev, the dark month, is also the month of dreams. Almost all the dreams that appear in the Torah occur in Kislev. Back from class, I fall into a deep sleep while the first snow falls outside my window. I dream that my cell rings. When I answer, Eli whispers in my ear. *Come with me to Paris.*

I know him in my dream by his Hebrew name, Moshe.

Come with me, he whispers again.

Is this the still, small voice within? Or is it a test, a temptation?

On Friday afternoon my phone buzzes in my pocket. 'Let's meet up,' Eli says.

He sounds different from the dream. Buoyant, and matter-of-fact.

There's no discussion about who will be the one to cross Toronto.

An hour later I ring his doorbell; there's the sound of footsteps from deep within the house. After several minutes he appears, wearing a beige cable-knit sweater. There's a fire in the grate, and behind him our Scotch is on the table, already poured. I feel, for a moment, that I could actually step into this advertisement, which could be for booze, or J. Crew, or for some other life I'm meant to be living. Maybe this is my chance to leave my lead cloak behind forever.

Eli takes my coat, kisses me on the cheek. 'How've you been?'

'Not great.'

'Still feeling down?'

'You could say that.'

'Well, you look good.'

He ushers me into the glossy magazine.

We settle beside each other on the couch. I notice that the photo of his girlfriend, the one that used to be on the coffee table, has been removed. I put my feet in their wool socks up on the ottoman.

'It's been a long week,' I say, although of course it's been more than a week: it's been a month, a decade, a lifetime. Because this is the thing about depression, or *one* of the things that makes it so awful: you cannot, no matter the effort, remember life without it. You know, intellectually, that there have been periods of happiness. Of peace and ease. But knowing and believing are two different things.

'How've *you* been?' I ask.

'Good,' he says. 'Busy polishing my dreidels.'

I smile.

'I was thinking,' he says. 'My mum is having a Hanukkah party on Saturday.'

'Oh?'

I wait. Two seconds. Three.

'It might be interesting for you,' he says. 'Because of what you're exploring.'

A vision of his family home, the crystal chandelier ablaze, a long table laden with the traditional latkes and jelly doughnuts, rises up in my mind. His mother, a beautiful woman with the same olive skin as Eli, stands with a match poised over the menorah. She gestures me to her side, puts an arm close around my shoulder. She invites me to light the candles. As I do, she sings the blessing. My harmony weaves through hers, as though I've known this song my whole life.

'I'd love to come,' I say, jumping on the invitation before I can remember to try to sound aloof. 'Thanks!'

He grins.

I pull my daybook out of my purse to mark down the date. 'Just let me –' I say, flipping through the pages. Then I realize. The party falls on Degan's birthday. We're going to be up at my family's cabin.

'Oh shit,' I say. I check the date again to make certain. 'No. I've got plans.'

'Really?' Eli says. 'Can you get out of them?'

I rub my temples, digging into them with my thumbs.

'No,' I say. 'I can't.'

We're sitting close to each other, our hands just a few inches apart. I see out of the corner of my eye that Eli has stuck his index finger out, in my direction. I instinctively do the same. The tips of our fingers touch.

'That's too bad,' he says. 'I was hoping you could come.'

He turns and looks me in the eye. 'I'm happy to see you,' he says.

The heat rises to my cheeks. I want to meet his acknowledgement with my own, to tell him I am happy to see him, too, but all I can manage is 'Likewise'.

'Really,' he says. 'I've been thinking of you.'

It's hard to hold his eye. I want him to continue at the same time as wanting him to stop. The impulses push up against each other inside me, competing like sisters.

The sun is setting: for a second time I've found myself here at the beginning of the Sabbath. Eli leans over and touches my cheek.

My palms are sweating. I can feel my pulse at my neck, so close to where his hand is resting. I force myself to pull back.

'I should go,' I say.

He smiles and sighs. 'Yeah,' he says. 'You probably should.'

He lowers his hand to his lap. I immediately regret what I've said.

'Do you want me to go?' I ask.

He smiles again, a rueful smile. 'You probably should.'

⌖

I walk down the Danforth with my hands in my pockets. The lights from the storefronts cannot touch me. I think of Lucy's confidence: *The only way to really get it back would be to marry a Jew.* My chance is gone. My one chance lost. I can't see another.

On Sunday I go for a massage. The masseuse, Yona, is a Jew married to a Gentile. The first thing she told him when they got together was that their future children (I picture his eyebrows rising) would be brought up as Jews.

I take off my clothes and lie face down on the massage table. Yona doesn't ask how I am. I don't tell her. I lie like a corpse while she digs her fingers into my shoulders, my back, pulling and prying the secrets from my cells. Tears roll down my face and splash on the floor. It's the opposite of a burial. It's an unearthing.

⌖

After, I go out onto the street, my loose, pummelled muscles tensing against the cold. On impulse, I fumble in my pocket for my cell. There's a message waiting from Dad: 'Call me right away,' he says. 'It's urgent.'

I stand on the freezing sidewalk panicking, pressing the wrong buttons through my gloves. I breathe deeply, force myself to slow down. When Dad finally answers, I don't bother with hello. 'Is everything okay?' I ask.

'Sure!' he booms. 'It's fine! I just wanted to tell you something I learned about Gumper's mother.'

I let my breath out slowly. A cloud appears in the cold air in front of my face.

'Sweetie? Are you there?'

'I'm here,' I say.

The dog barks in the background. 'The thing I learned is about Gumper's mother, Ruzenka. It's about her last name,' Dad says.

'Bondy?'

'Yes. It's from the Sephardic name Bondia.'

'Oh?'

'And from *Bon dia* in Catalan.'

'Which means?'

'In English, "Good day". In Hebrew, "*Yom tov*".'

A smile comes over my face. I stomp my feet to warm them.

'So our name is a celebration. A happy day.'

FOURTEEN

OUR CLASS MEETS AGAIN, two weeks early, because people will be going away over the 'winter holiday' – which is code, I realize, for Christmas. I arrange to meet Rabbi Glickman before the class, to level with her. To tell her how hard it is that the other women in our class will be 'allowed' to convert, but I won't, despite being half Jewish already. Not 'allowed' because I plan to marry a Gentile.

'That's too bad,' she says blandly when I explain.

We find a table at the small café in the foyer of the community centre. She sits and motions for me to do the same.

'The other women,' I say. 'I don't think they are really interested in Judaism. They're only interested in getting married.'

'And isn't that a noble cause?'

I'm silent.

'Isn't it?' she asks. Her piercing gaze reminds me that Degan and I still haven't set a date for our wedding.

The waitress arrives and the rabbi and I both order lattes.

'So,' the rabbi says evenly. 'You're faced with a difficult decision.'

'Whether to convert?'

'Whether to get married.'

I pinch my earlobe between my thumb and forefinger.

She eyes me. 'Intermarriage is frowned upon,' she says. 'You do know that, right?'

I blink. Blink again. They want me to ditch my fiancé? I forced myself to walk away from Eli, from that beautiful scene in the glossy magazine – in other words, I've done the right thing – and this is the result?

'Can I have some sugar here?' the rabbi asks the waitress. She turns back toward me reluctantly. 'Do you know about *gilgul nefashot*?'

I shake my head: no. My eyes are wide.

'*Gilgul nefashot* translates to "rolling souls". It's a concept that applies to bringing Jewish souls back to Judaism. There are lost Jewish souls. They attach to someone who will eventually find a Jew to marry.'

'So it's all predetermined?'

But the rabbi won't bite. She repeats, 'When you convert, you are bringing a soul back to Judaism.'

I wonder if she's been listening to anything I've said. 'I'm not *allowed* to convert,' I remind her. 'Unless Degan does, too.'

A look of mild annoyance crosses her face, as though I have interrupted some well-polished speech. 'In your case, you'd be bringing *two* souls back.'

'But Degan doesn't want to convert.'

She shrugs. That part isn't her problem.

We walk in silence back up to the room where our class takes place. Rabbi Glickman greets the rest of the students and then asks if anyone knows what month comes after Kislev. People have been studying up: several hands wave in the air, Debra's included, but the rabbi chooses to answer her own question. 'Tevet,' she says. 'The month of goodness and bodily heat.' She pauses. 'Judaism has a notable lack of emphasis on sin. With regard to sexuality especially.' She pauses again. 'Unlike certain *other* religions.'

I lower my head to my notebook, brow furrowed.

Debra, the minister's daughter, refuses to be shamed. She raises her hand again. 'For example?'

'Well,' says the rabbi, 'for one, making love is considered a good thing. A sanctified part of Shabbat. In Judaism, the pleasures of the body are celebrated.'

I feel again the heat of Eli's hand on my cheek, the pulse of my skin under his touch.

'Between married partners,' she adds.

I flush.

'In Tevet,' the rabbi says, 'we ask ourselves how we can bring the *goodness* of the sexual impulse into our homes.'

I wait for the answer, but she doesn't supply one. She peers at us over her glasses. She is a woman with almost no extra body fat. Her close-cropped hair gives her the look of a bird.

'In the Torah,' she says, 'we are told about a human being's two inclinations: toward good and toward bad. These are not states but *tendencies*.'

'The *yetzer harah*?' one of the baseball caps asks.

'The *yetzer harah* is the impuse toward bad. And who knows the good impulse? The *yetzer*—?'

I remember my conversation with Dad. Bondy.

Bonas dia.

Good day.

Yom TOV.

'*Yetzer tov*?' I ask.

The rabbi nods, acknowledging me. We hold eyes for an extra moment, as though she is seeing me for the first time, re-evaluating her earlier opinion.

I think: My name shares something with the good impulse. With goodness itself.

'Yes. *Tov* means "good".'

Someone clears their throat.

Rabbi Glickman says to the whole class, 'Please put down your pens. What I'm going to tell you now is important.'

We do as told.

'In Judaism we are held responsible for the inner wrestling match between the two impulses. At any moment we can turn back toward good.'

'How so?' Debra asks.

'We are never condemned,' the rabbi answers. 'For example, if my daughter is naughty, I tell her that her *yetzer harah* got the better of her. And send her to her room until her *yetzer tov* is ready to come out.'

Giggles from my classmates.

'But really,' the rabbi says, unsmiling. 'Think of what this means. There's always the chance to redeem ourselves. *Always*.'

⌇

I approach Degan in the kitchen, where he is dipping strips of marinated tofu in a bowl of nutritional yeast.

'I wanted to tell you. I had drinks. With a man.'

'That writer? Whose book you read?'

'How did you know?'

He shrugs. 'I'm not stupid.'

He jiggles the bowl of yeast to distribute it evenly. 'What's his name again? Eli Bloom?'

'Bloomberg.'

I fiddle with Granny's ring, spinning it on my finger. 'I just wanted to say . . .'

I pause. What *did* I want to say?

'Never mind. Forget it.'

'Are you sure?'

There's a challenge in his voice, a crimped edge of fear running around his studied calm. I recognize the fused desire to both know and not know. I remind myself there's nothing for him *to* know. And check myself. Is there? There isn't. 'I'm sure,' I say. 'Yes. Don't worry.'

Degan looks up and holds my eye. 'Okay,' he says evenly. 'I won't.'

The alarm goes off and Degan stumbles out of bed; he has four clients to see before the first in a series of seminars on diversity he has organized. A homeless man is coming to speak about his experience with the federal health care system. The students, I know, will be blown away. Degan is doing something concrete with his life, something practical. *Tikkun olam* – 'repairing the world'. Whereas I sit at my desk every day, mired in self-focus and indulgence.

On the first morning of Hanukkah, I email Eli. 'Chag Sameach,' I write, pleased that I know the salutation. But as soon as I press Send, I realize my mistake: the Jewish day begins at sunset. Hanukkah doesn't start until this evening.

Eli doesn't reply.

I get up from my desk and wander around the apartment. I stand in the kitchen and look out the window at the schoolyard behind us. It's only December, but already the running track lies buried under two feet of snow. A man in a fluorescent green vest, some kind of city worker, huddles in the lee of a portable, trying to light a cigarette. Shielding it with his cupped palm, flicking the lighter again and again.

I'm overcome with dread at the thought of Hanukkah. I have a tin menorah and a box of candles that I bought in anticipation of the season. They are in a plastic bag under the sink. I have no idea what to do with them.

When Degan arrives home, though, he wishes me 'Chag Sameach'. I tell him about my despair, that I don't know how to celebrate the holiday. He's been cold since my revelation a few evenings ago, but still he comes to the rescue. 'We'll figure it out,' he says. 'It can't be that hard.'

We Google 'Hanukkah' to refresh ourselves on the story. We read about the Maccabees' battle to practise their faith; about the miracle of oil enough for only one day lasting for eight days in a row.

A miracle. That'd be good.

We Google 'The Blessing for Hanukkah' and listen to a bright-voiced woman who sounds like Barbie recite the words. After several listenings, we are able to sing along with her. We light the first candle. It is a mitzvah to publicize the miracle, to place the menorah in the front window for everyone to see. But something in me freezes as Degan pulls back the drapes. I swallow and swallow. My palms are damp.

'Are you okay?' Degan asks. He puts an arm around my shoulder. 'No one is going to hurt you.'

I swallow. 'I know,' I say, my voice wobbly.

'Here,' he says. 'Look. We'll put the menorah a few inches back from the window. People will see the light, but not what it is.'

But in the face of this compromise, I change my mind. 'No,' I say. 'Let's put it right up front. Where it belongs.'

The New Year is creeping up like a cat. I drive up to Israel's, the Judaica store on Eglinton Avenue, to look for a 2008 day planner. I want one that will anchor my daily life in Judaism, but when I see the rack of stationery and calendars, I realize my mistake: the secular New Year starts in January, but the Jewish one starts in the fall, with Rosh Hashana.

I get back in the car and drive to the big-box business store, where I buy a secular calendar. At home, I set about the task of making it Jewish. I write 'Shabbat' on every square marked 'Friday' and 'Rosh Chodesh' on every new moon. I boldly cross out 2008 and replace it with the Jewish year, 5768. Jews are still counting up from zero because their messiah has not yet arrived.

Their messiah? *Our* messiah?

It is a season of inordinate snow. We shovel all evening in the street lamp's cone of light, then wake in the morning with aching backs to find the small path we'd cleared gone. The big light of Christmas is everywhere, as Rabbi Glickman has warned, but up on St Clair, a chalkboard in front of a café advertises jelly doughnuts for Hanukkah. I sit down for a latte and hear a musician telling his friend about his set list. 'Klezmer music,' he says. 'They want Klezmer music.' And on my way home, I pass two women in Sorrel boots tromping down the snowy sidewalk. '*How* did I not *know* your mother was a survivor?' one demands of the other.

At the gym I run on the treadmill beneath fluorescent lights, sweating and straining and making no geographic progress, and then I walk the streets for hours, trying to keep my endorphins pumping, to extend the small reprieve my workout has allowed me. The entire population of Toronto treads along Bathurst Street, their faces turned down like shutters against the sleet. Everyone pushing past one another in a big race to the end of the day.

After the small pond of St John's, big-city Toronto affords every possibility, every food you could ever want to eat, every class you might consider taking. That evening, I go to the weekly contact improvisation jam. The practice is a kind of improvisational modern dance involving touch. You let your body follow its impulses, using the other dancers' bodies as support. There is no talk involved: someone sidles up, leans a shoulder into your back, and soon you are entirely entangled, a physical manifestation of the psychic encounter. I dance with a man whose name I don't know. I guess that he's Jewish by his looks.

Is this wrong?

Would he guess the same of me?

At the end of the evening, everyone stands around wishing each other a Merry Christmas. My dance partner introduces himself as Michael. 'Chag Sameach!' he says.

It is so thrilling to be taken as a Jew. I am paralyzed with gratitude and fear.

He says, 'Chag Sameach – right?'

But I can't quite accept it.

'At least you've got the shirt,' he says.

I look down. I'd forgotten what I was wearing. It's a T-shirt my childhood friend Jordan, the one who first called me out on the Pick Secret, brought me back from a trip to Israel as a teenager. Maccabee Beer: The Beer the Chosen People Choose.

FIFTEEN

I DREAM THAT DEGAN AND I are taking the JIC; that I am – we are – happily engaged in meaningful learning about Judaism. When I wake up, Degan is lying on his side in his blue plaid pyjamas, head propped up in his palm, looking at me.

'I had the best dream,' I say.

His face lights up. 'Oh?'

'Not *that* kind of dream.' I squint, rub my eyes. 'I dreamed we were taking the JIC.'

'The what?'

'The class. The Jewish class.'

He sighs. 'That's what a "good dream" means to you now?'

I run my tongue over my teeth.

'Can't you take it yourself?' he says. 'The class?'

'I'll ask,' I say. But I remember what Rabbi Klein told me, that the partners of all potential converts are required to sign up, as well. I think of the crowd of baseball caps and their gaggle of fiancées.

'For some reason I can't stop thinking about it,' I say. 'It feels like the next task the world is presenting me.'

From down on the street we hear the *beep, beep* of a snowplow reversing.

Degan rolls onto his back, exhaling heavily. 'It's one night a week?'

I hesitate. 'And a few extra weekends.'

I tell him about another couple Rabbi Klein mentioned,

Tom and Diane. Diane is Jewish, so their baby is, also. Tom is considering conversion. 'He's wrestling with the big questions, too,' Rabbi Klein told me.

'Why don't we get in touch?' I ask Degan.

He nods, noncommittal, yet I know the prospect of another man with the same quandary is appealing. But when an email comes back from Tom, he sounds confident that he will convert, like it's a done deal. 'Why don't we meet up at *kiddush* next Shabbat and talk?' he writes.

Isn't *kiddush* the blessing over the wine? Or the prayer for the dead?

Tom emails back, suggesting gently that it is a reception after the Saturday service.

I freeze, insecure in the face of his certainty. I don't reply.

Later, Degan approaches me from behind at my desk. He puts his hands on my shoulders.

'I'm working,' I say.

He backs away, his arms in the air as though he's in a stickup at a bank. 'Okay, okay. I just wanted to tell you I'll take the class with you.'

I swivel my chair to face him. 'Which class?'

'Which class do you think?'

'Really? You'll take it?' I pause. 'For me?'

His brow furrows. 'Not for you,' he says. 'Well, partially for you. But I'm also interested in it for my own reasons.'

I don't push my luck by asking what those reasons might be, although I know it is some combination of his desire to support me, and his intellectual curiosity. Degan's brain is insatiable; he can get interested in anything.

He can also lose interest just as quickly.

'Sign us up,' he says.

'Are you sure?'

'I said I'd take it!'

I recant. 'Okay! Great! I'll call the rabbi.'

∾

I bring him along to a meeting I have scheduled with Rabbi Klein that same afternoon. 'What do you want me to say to her?' Degan asks as we pull into the synagogue parking lot.

'Just be yourself. You'll be great.'

Truthfully, though, I'm as nervous as a teenager bringing home a first boyfriend. I feel a desperate desire for everyone to show their best side, to end up, against the odds, liking each other.

In the front foyer of the synagogue is a swarm of mothers dropping their toddlers off at the preschool. They are all Jewish, I think. The children, their parents. And then I feel a strange, undeniable relief. I don't need to hide.

We climb the spiral staircase under the domed ceiling, past the row of framed portraits of rabbis. It's been months since I've seen the lovely Rabbi Klein. Her dark curls spill over her shoulders like those of a Greek goddess, or a woman in a Pantene commercial. 'Chag Sameach,' she says.

'To you, too,' I say. 'This is Degan.'

They smile and shake hands, and we seat ourselves in the two red armchairs across from her. After a bit of small talk, the rabbi turns her attention to Degan. 'Tell me about yourself,' she says.

'Sure. Uh, where should I start?'

'Did you grow up in a religious home?'

'Anti-religious, more like it.'

'How so?'

'My mother was raised Catholic, but the brutal, abusive version. She spent my childhood teaching me to avoid religion. Socialism was her god. And charity. So *tzedakah* is very familiar.'

The rabbi gives a nod of acknowledgement at Degan's correct use of the Hebrew term. He's been reading up. Or perhaps he already knew the expression. He often surprises me with his breadth of knowledge. He couldn't fix a toaster to save his life, but he knows the intricacies of the stock exchange, the relationships among all the pre-Socratics, the play-by-play of the Battle of Britain.

'I've been a spiritual seeker all my life,' Degan is telling Rabbi Klein. 'In my teenage years, I would sneak off to church without telling my mother. I loved it. The community, the quiet reverence. For me, spirituality is a crucial part of our human existence. And church was where I first found that.'

I worry that he is going a little heavy on church, which he hasn't attended in a decade, but who am I to say? The whole charade is so ironic. It isn't that Degan is insincere, but that he feels forced to perform in order to dramatize his sincerity. We are performing an identity of people with spiritual sides, with aptitudes or readiness for Judaism. We're trying to make ourselves appear good enough, *Jewish* enough. According to the Nazis, I would already be Jewish two times over. Debra has emailed me a quote from the book *None Is Too Many*, its title taken from the Canadian government's immigration policy during the Second World War. Under a Nazi decree in Germany in 1933, anyone with as much as one Jewish grandparent was legally defined as a Jew.

One.

My family history for the past three generations has been a long performance of Christianity. Now it seems we will have to enact the opposite performance. In order to be accepted, we will have to perform a Jewish identity in much the same way my grandparents performed a Christian one.

Rabbi Klein says to Degan, 'Sorry if this seems like a silly question, but I just want to be sure. You want to take the class? The JIC?'

He nods. 'I'm up for it.' He touches his glasses where they rest on the bridge of his nose. 'Although I'm nervous about how much there is to learn.'

She gathers her long curls, holds them for a moment next to her neck. 'The learning is the easy part,' she says. 'Especially for someone as smart as you obviously are.' She lets her hair go. 'It's the identity reconstruction that's harder.'

I draw in my breath sharply. Degan's right arm is pressed up against my own; I feel his muscles tighten. *Identity reconstruction?*

'Of course, there's no pressure,' she says. 'Some people convert right after the class. For others it's a much longer process. This is a happy story. Please know I'm with you regardless of the outcome.'

'*I* won't be converting,' Degan says. 'I'm just supporting Alie.'

The rabbi smiles knowingly but doesn't say anything. Then, as we move to get our things, she asks, 'How is Hanukkah going?'

'Good.' I nod. 'We're fumbling along.'

As I'm zipping my coat, I tell her about the visceral fear of putting the menorah in the window, how the fear turned to excitement and back to fear on the edge of a dime.

'Yes, I can imagine. That sounds intense.'

She hands Degan his bag and picks up the synagogue's monthly bulletin, then leafs through it randomly, telling us about everything going on. Hebrew classes. Torah study. Then, all at once, she says, 'Oh! You know Eli Bloomberg!'

I freeze with a hand halfway into my leather glove, trying to remember how she knows this. I give as small a nod as possible in acknowledgement.

'He's reading here in January,' she says. 'You know he wrote this great book about his Hasidic upbringing and what happened when he began to question it?' She searches my face for a reaction. 'You do know him, right?'

Degan has turned his back and is busying himself with his scarf.

I point to the opposing page in the bulletin. 'And what's this? Shabbat Nation?'

She searches my face, then plays along.

'It's a Shabbat service for people in their twenties and thirties. You should go. I think you'd love it.' She doesn't know exactly how she's blundered, but she looks as relieved as we are to change the subject.

✑

One person's certainty makes room for another's reluctance. This is true of dynamics within a relationship, and true of the existence of the relationship itself. Degan's ambivalence about conversion lets me be the one to hold the certainty. I can be sure precisely because he isn't.

If I were with Eli, a born Jew, *he* would hold the strength around identity. What would have room to rise up in my psyche then? Fond reminiscences of Sunday school? Family memories from Christmas? A reverence for the elegance of the Holy Trinity as a symbol?

Am I denying myself the love of what's already mine?

I am writing a novel about a Jewish boy who is baptized. Meanwhile, I find myself going in the other direction. We Picks are like a swing. Forward, then back. Joining a group, leaving it for another. It is the stuff over which wars are waged, over which civilizations rise and fall.

And I'm not the only one practised in shape-shifting. Driving home, Degan and I debrief our meeting with the rabbi. 'I felt so uncomfortable,' he says.

'You did?'

'Like it was all a big show. '

'You seemed so present. So interested.'

He shrugs. 'I do that for a living.'

SIXTEEN

I CONSTRUCT AN ELABORATE FANTASY in which I attend *shul* with Eli's family. His mother invites me back to dinner after the service, and from then on I have a standing invitation, a place to make Shabbat every week.

The only way to get it back would be to marry a Jew.

Small hitch: I still have not yet met Eli's mother.

Second small hitch: I have only a few weeks in which to meet her before Eli leaves for Paris.

I call him on Friday to ask if he wants to go to synagogue. He doesn't pick up. I wait at home, too depressed to face the service alone. Degan has to work late. When Eli finally calls back, his message is a string of excuses: his phone died; he didn't have a charger.

He pauses. 'I went to yoga. And then . . .' More silence. 'And then I was tired,' he says.

When Granny died, she left an extensive will, her substantial assets distributed carefully among her progeny. Still, there were riches remaining, jewellery and clothes, and we four granddaughters were invited to divide those belongings among us. The cashmere stoles, the bracelets. But the thing I love most is a thin white handkerchief embroidered in blue with her initial.

A for Alzbeta.

A for Alison.

I cry into its cottony folds.

There are things I used to care about: That the bills were paid on time. That we ate the kale in the crisper before buying more. I once nagged Degan about ironing his shirt before work. I remember this through a fog of incomprehension, stunned that I would have noticed such a thing, let alone felt compelled to *do* anything about it.

Challah = carbohydrates. I eat the whole loaf before the Sabbath arrives.

SEVENTEEN

IN THE SEVEN YEARS of our relationship I've always made Degan a scrapbook for Christmas, a painstakingly detailed chronicle of our adventures together over the preceding year. I save ticket stubs and receipts, photos of where we've travelled, and cut and paste them into the story of us that we're writing together, that is always being written. This year I don't make the book. I – someone who is usually prepared months in advance – don't do anything to get ready for the holiday, have not bought a single present. I decide at the last minute to 'give the gift of time' to Mum and my sister Emily, inviting them out for meals on me. I rush out and buy books for Degan and Dad. I panic secretly that I don't have anything to give Eli, and then I remember: no yuletide gifts required for Jews.

On December 23, Degan and I drive to Sudbury to see his mother. The suburbs of Toronto slowly fall away, replaced by pine trees, and granite, and the inscrutable Canadian Shield. In Crystal Beach we stop at a Tim Hortons for coffee. There's a long line of travellers at the counter, kids in snowsuits begging for doughnuts, everyone en route to whomever they call family. On the radio, Emmylou Harris sings a haunting rendition of 'Silent Night'. Back on the highway: snow and bare spruce, an empty, gunmetal sky. Degan drives with his hand on my knee. Tears slide down my face.

Christmas is upon us. It's not the holiday itself that I mind, but the fact of not doing Hanukkah properly, as well; of having missed out on the parties – Eli's mother's in particular – and skipping synagogue because I couldn't stand to go on my own.

I imagine Gumper on Christmas morning in the years after the war, lost and bewildered among the presents.

Degan's mother has a tiny apartment, so we stay at a cheap roadside motel. At night we lie in bed without touching. Trucks rumble past our bed, down the long highway in the darkness. In the morning we drive south, back to my family, to celebrate Jesus Christ's arrival.

$$\varrho \frown$$

For potential converts to Judaism, December is the litmus test. It's simple enough to bid adieu to the Easter Bunny, and giving up Lent is only easy irony. But the big box of Christmas, with its wrappings and trappings, its stuffing and turkey and mistletoe . . .

When we arrive at my parents' house in Kitchener, an hour away from Toronto, Handel's *Messiah* is playing on the stereo. Coloured lights and pine boughs decorate the mantel, and bowls of candy canes dot every available surface. A red poinsettia perks its ears up by the sofa. The atmosphere is so comforting, so familiar, like a favourite pair of wool socks worn until the toes are full of holes. I know that a spiced beef will be waiting in the fridge, having soaked up the flavour of cloves for the past two weeks; I know before entering that the living room is sweet with the smell of the pine tree. Degan sings along with the stereo, ' "And He shall reign for ever and ever!" '

'I guess we should ask them to turn this off,' I say half-heartedly.

' "And ever!" ' he sings.

I laugh; Degan stops humming. 'I'd be sad to lose Christmas

carols,' he says. His way into life is through music.

Our family's traditional Christmas Eve dinner is a mixed grill. I pass on the pork chops. Mum, who has spent the day overexerting herself in the kitchen, asks, 'Are you kosher now?'

'No. Just not that hungry.'

My sister, Emily, arrived earlier in the afternoon. She is between boyfriends, so it is just the five of us. Over the meal, talk turns to the foundation of Christianity, the letters of Paul, who met Jesus on the road to Damascus. Degan swallows his mouthful of beef and creamed onions. The Gospels, he tells us, were written sixty or seventy years after Christ. At that time, there were other people similar to Jesus – other charismatic leaders with disciples and pedagogies – but their stories didn't catch on the way Jesus's did.

'You really know your Christianity,' I joke. 'Must be all those years you spent sneaking out to church.'

Degan has told me he really believed. Then, all at once, his faith wore off and he abandoned it. Easy as that. It's unnerving.

'Who wants a dividend?' Dad asks, his monetary word for a last small bite of dinner.

'I'm stuffed,' Em says.

A chorus of agreement.

Dad places his cutlery, monogrammed with his mother's initials, parallel on his plate and pushes his chair back. 'Speaking of church,' he says, 'who's coming?'

Dad's maternal grandparents died in Auschwitz. His paternal grandmother, Ruzenka Bondy, of the *yetzer tov*, made it out. She came to Canada, where, as our family lore has it, she became a pillar of the United Church. She taught her grandson – Dad – that the particulars of faith matter less than having faith in general: a prayer practice, a community with whom to worship.

Dad learned from Ruzenka that faith is in the doing.

'Anyone?' he asks again. 'Church?'

Mum says she is too tired and has potatoes to mash for tomorrow's Christmas dinner. Emily doesn't want to go, either.

'Degan?' Dad asks, appealing to the only other man in the family.

'Sorry, Thomas. I'm beat.'

Mum gets up to clear the plates.

'Alison?' Dad asks.

I pause. 'Did Gumper ever go?'

Dad scrutinizes my face. 'Where?'

'To church.'

'He did. To the United Church, with his mother, Ruzenka.'

'Really? Why?'

'Why *what*?' Dad looks mildly impatient.

'Why did he go?'

'Why do you think?'

'I don't honestly know.'

'What's your hunch?'

'My hunch? He went so people would think that they were Christian.'

It is ten o'clock on a snowy Christmas Eve. The dishes are cleared and coffee has been poured. The one or two cars passing by in the street make angel wings with their headlights.

'Sure,' I say finally. 'I'll come with you.'

⌇

Dad and I mount the newly shovelled stone stairs into St John the Evangelist, the big Anglican church where I grew up, where I attended Sunday school and made crosses out of Popsicle sticks and glue. At the age of eleven, old enough to reason, to consciously make decisions, I studied for Confirmation here and committed myself to Christ's teachings for life.

At the entrance to the sanctuary, there's a row of mailboxes for the members' families. I locate the *Ps*, then the box marked Pick. I put my hand in, feel around. From the far back corner I fish out a name tag. Alison, it reads. How long has it been sitting there, waiting to be claimed?

Although Anglican in denomination, St John's is Catholic in formality. The huge stained-glass windows show Christ suffering through his stations. The pews are cushioned with red velvet; the organ's brass pipes shine. Growing up, I remember the church as a bastion of wasp pretention, but looking around I see that the congregation has changed. We find our place between a Chinese couple with a small son and two black women who look to be sisters.

One of my fondest memories of Granny is being at church with her on Christmas Eve, when she would sing the carols in a selection of the various languages she could speak: 'Silent Night' in German, 'O Come, All Ye Faithful' in Latin. High above us in the balcony now, the choir opens with the English version, their voices clear, like birds calling out across water. In all my years of attending church on Christmas Eve, I have never *not* been overcome by this. The haunting melody has always brought me to my knees. Sure enough, shivers spread across my neck and down my arms as the words ring out: 'Come and behold him, born the King of angels' – gathering us in, one and all.

The Gospel is read from the centre of the aisle. The minister gives a sermon about going to Jerusalem and being greeted not by an innkeeper, but by guards with submachine guns at what seemed like every turn. Dad crosses himself when the priest does. In the intercession, he takes his glasses off, kneels with his eyes closed. I notice, though, that he does not repeat 'Lord, hear our prayer' along with the rest of the congregation.

It's been so long since I attended church that the words of the prayers take me by surprise: 'We are not worthy so much as to gather up the crumbs under thy table.' I have forgotten this emphasis on sin, so harsh in contrast to the beautiful carols, this emphasis on the inherently wicked nature of humanity. 'Grant us therefore, gracious Lord, so to eat the flesh of thy dear Son Jesus Christ, and to drink his blood, that our sinful bodies may be made clean by his body.' Judaism, I think, is more forgiving.

I lean over to Dad and tap him on the shoulder. 'Did Gumper take Communion?' I whisper.

He opens his eyes. 'No,' he whispers back.

'What about Granny?'

'No.'

I nod. Dad closes his eyes again. After a minute I nudge him a second time.

'Do *you*?' I ask.

'Yes,' he whispers back, without hesitation.

The quiet organ music filters through the church's lofty rafters. 'I take Communion because I like the tangible feeling of receiving something from God.'

He wants me to know he likes the ritual, but he doesn't believe in the miracle.

⌒

I decide to follow Granny and Gumper's example, to eschew the central part of the service, but at the last minute I change my mind. The choir has moved on to 'O Little Town of Bethlehem'. I join Dad and the long line of townspeople – parishioners – shuffling up the aisle to the altar. The bench is plush and pillowy beneath my knees. I lower my eyes, and feel the minister's presence moving down the line of bowed heads in my direction. When it's my turn to be blessed, he places the host in my crossed palms and says, 'The body of Christ, given for you'.

The wafer dissolves on my tongue.

I think of the Catholic school where Dad was raised, of the thin sheets of dough dotted with holes where the hosts were punched out. The nuns would send them home with the children, in cookie tins.

Dad is kneeling beside me, his shoulder pressed against mine. I can tell he is pleased to be here together. Or perhaps I'm the one pleased to be with him.

'The blood of Christ, given for you,' the minister tells me solemnly.

I tip the cup to get a good swallow.

It's after midnight when Dad and I pull into the driveway. Something glints from the front window of the house. I look, then look again. The menorah, with six candles lit. Degan has placed it there in my absence.

On Christmas morning, we sleep in. Emily, Degan and I open our stockings together, drawing the ritual out, item by item. Santa has outdone himself, as usual. Stamps, socks, nail polish, subway tokens, SmartWool socks, a little gizmo that inflates and heats water so you can have a hot shower on a camping trip. Granny used to say that every Christmas had a theme – books one year, music the next – and as we move on to the wrapped gifts, this year's theme emerges. I receive Claudia Roden's *Book of Jewish Cooking* from Mum. Beautiful Shabbat candlesticks from Degan. Dad gives me a bound copy of our Pick family tree.

We 'take a break', which is tradition in our family, as though the opening of presents was some kind of sporting event, and move to the dining room table, which Mum has set to look like the cover of a home decorating magazine. The first course is a throwback to my girlhood in the seventies: grapefruit cut in half and dotted with a maraschino cherry. When we're done eating, we call my Pick cousins, who are celebrating together in the Netherlands, cooking a big traditional Christmas dinner.

Later I find an email from Eli: 'Happy day of Jesus. Remember, he was a Jew. And a rebellious one.'

EIGHTEEN

ON BOXING DAY, I PLACE MY Doing Jewish textbook on the table between Mum and Dad. 'It's Hanukkah,' I remind them. 'There are a couple of pages in here you can look at if you're interested.'

Dad takes the book – he's game. I sit beside him on the sofa as he reads, listening to his small grunts of interest. Occasionally he reads a section aloud: '"It is customary to exchange *gelt*, or chocolate coins covered in foil wrappers.' He pauses. '*We* did that! With Granny and Gumper.'

Mum pipes up, 'So did *we*. For Christmas.'

Meaning chocolate coins aren't necessarily Jewish.

Dad reads a sentence about the tension surrounding Christmas trees in interfaith households. As though it has nothing at all in the world to do with us.

In the evening, everyone goes out. My sister is visiting an old high school friend; my parents have a cocktail party with those members of their 'Tuscany Group' who don't winter in Florida. Degan, God bless him, has had enough of my family and decides to go see a movie by himself. Dusk falls; I'm alone. I take my stash of candles out of my suitcase and try to remember which way to insert them into the menorah. Left to right? Right to left? There is a mnemonic, but I can't make it stick in my mind.

I arrange the candles haphazardly and carry the menorah gingerly to the front window. I imagine our neighbours across the street seeing it, the ones who are also members at St John's, the ones whose daughter was in my Confirmation class. I picture various members of my mother's tennis club driving past.

The ledge on the windowsill is narrow; the flames lengthen, coming dangerously close to the gauze curtains. I move the menorah to the dining room table, but the table is too far from the window and nobody will be able to see it from the street. With no good solution – I can't be responsible for the house catching fire! – I abandon the project, blowing out the candles and retreating to the couch in the family room, where I read quietly about the war in Nigeria and pray the New Year will be better.

❧

Sometime later, I feel a hand gripping my shoulder. 'Wake up,' Degan says. 'We forgot to light the menorah.'

From the kitchen, I hear the sounds of the rest of my family returning home from their evening's activities. Emily stomps the snow from her boots. 'I'm going to walk the dog,' Dad says.

Degan calls out to him. 'Do you want to join us in lighting the menorah first?'

There's a pause. I can picture Dad looking to Mum, Mum shrugging as though to say: *It's up to you.*

Emily calls brightly, 'I'll join you.'

Dad says, 'Sure. We will, too.' I picture Mum looking to Dad to be sure, then wiping her wet hands down the front of her apron.

We gather in the living room. Degan remembers the mnemonic for the candles: Refill from the right. Light from the left. As he arranges them, he notices they have already been lit

– evidence of my aborted mission – and raises his eyebrows at me. I shrug.

He leads us in the blessings, having somehow already memorized them. I watch my parents from the corner of my eye, vigilantly checking for disapproval, but see none. After, we all sit around talking. About the struggle I am having with finding acceptance, about the historical precedents for Judaism's closed nature. Dad jokes, 'If they won't let you join, I'll put in a good word for you with the rabbi.'

❧

The next day Dad and I go over the Pick family tree he has given me as a Christmas gift. One of my ancestors bears the name Israel. Direct proof. And yet, part of me still finds it difficult to believe, as though the whole thing is an elaborate fiction. A story that belongs to somebody else.

After lunch Dad produces a shoebox of old family photos I've never seen. I extract one of my grandparents after the war, sitting around a table with people who look like business tycoons, diplomats. Bow ties, pearls, fur stoles. The gentleman beside my grandmother has his arm around her. She holds the hand of *another* man, an entrepreneurial type sitting at the head of the table. My grandfather – so handsome! so Jewish! – sits across from them. What was he thinking?

J'aime ta femme – 'I love your wife'.

I pull another photo from the box, of Granny's mother, Marianne. She stands with a man in ski pants in front of snow-covered mountains, her cheeks flushed from exertion, her full lips rouged.

'Who is she with? Is that her husband, Oskar?'

Dad shakes his head. 'It's someone else. He shows up in lots of the photos. A lover, maybe.'

I peek at the image again: Marianne has her face tipped up toward her portly companion. Her eyes are locked with his. They are both laughing.

I flip the photo over. On the back is written 'Marianne (Mitzi) Bauer'. And *Stuckerl*.

'*Stuckerl?*' I ask Dad.

'I think it was another nickname.'

I ask Dad what it means.

'"Candy",' he says. '"Little sweet thing".' He pauses, looking at the image again and then at me. '"Piece of work".'

⌒

I check my phone, wondering if Eli has called, but there's no message. My lead cloak settles over me as I pack up the piles of Christmas gifts, preparing for the trip back to Toronto. My mother expresses herself most clearly through the material. In addition to the mass of Judaica, I have received a computer and an expensive down jacket. My stocking alone would feed a small African country. All I can think about, though, is the lamp for seasonal affective disorder that Santa has somehow forgotten. About how I will now need to order it myself. About how long it will take to ship to Toronto, where I can sit under it and (hopefully, please God) start to feel human again.

As soon as I'm back in Toronto, I look online. The first site I land on promises relief from minor depression – as mine would be labelled, despite how I experience it. There are hundreds of models – desk lamps, wall lamps – in various colours and styles. I choose the first I land on, enter my credit card information. I settle in for several weeks of waiting.

⌒

That night I dream of a desert, a vast expanse of sand. I am small and inconsequential at the edge of its echoing vista. Far away, at the last reach of my vision, is a boulder.

There's a voice in my ear: 'Go out to the farthest rock where Jesus went.'

I turn but cannot see who or what has given me the instruction. I strain to see the boulder, shimmering under the blistering sun.

The voice comes again: 'Go out to the farthest rock where Jesus went.'

It echoes. After that, there is silence.

NINETEEN

CHARLOTTE SITS IN HER CHAIR with her legs crossed, a clip in her hair, her glasses on a chain around her neck.

'That's a very big dream,' she says. A long silence follows, during which we can hear the soft *thunk* of sleet against the window. 'What do you think it's about?' she asks finally.

I pause. 'Well, the obvious. That I'm wrestling with my religious identity.'

'And?'

'The boulder was so far away. I could see it, but I still have far to go.'

'Isn't that the title of the book you're writing? *Far to Go?*'

I pause. 'Yes. But . . .'

'But what?'

'I don't really think . . .'

'The subconscious mind is incredibly astute,' she says.

She has lit a beeswax candle – I catch the smell of its waxy sweetness. She searches my face. 'Jesus, too, withdrew at certain times to contemplate his identity. He went out to the desert and was tempted by Satan.'

I give a half smile and spin Granny's wedding ring on my finger. 'What exactly did he contemplate?'

'Whether he was half God.'

'Same here!'

But Charlotte doesn't laugh. She says, 'In psychological terms, Jesus is a symbol of rebirth. Of redemption.'

'Even for a Jew?'

'Regardless of the tradition of the dreamer.'

'So I'm being reborn?'

She makes a noncommittal noise in the back of her throat.

I tell Charlotte that it feels like my skin is pulled back, like all my nerves are exposed. Everything is cold, or made of glass, and it is too bright – I start to cry.

'Even the beautiful things hurt,' I say through my tears. 'Especially the beautiful things.'

Charlotte recommends 'being small'. I have a good brain, she says, but it is also my defence. It is possible that what I am going through right now is not something I can understand.

But I want to understand. Eli, Judaism: I need to make sense of it to make the pain go away. Tears are streaming down my cheeks as I speak. 'I know it's just projection—'

'Yes,' she interrupts. 'But a projection is all there is. It's the mind's only way to bring subconscious material into consciousness.'

I look at her blankly.

'Not "just" a projection,' she says, making quotes in the air around the word *just*. 'A projection is extremely intense and powerful.'

Charlotte suggests again that I should submit. Be still, bear it. Let the despair really wash over me.

'And in the meantime?'

'Tend to your home,' she says. 'Do laundry. Make soup.'

'Make soup?'

Rock, rock.

I have a book of poetry about to come out, launch invitations to send, student papers I've ignored, six million things tugging at my sleeves.

I could lose myself entirely in that crowd of needy hands.

Charlotte's point is taken. I will make soup.

After the session I lie down with Degan on the evening bed, snow piling up in the street outside our window. He sings me a beautiful song about a poor boy, cold and hungry at the side of the road. Partway through, I realize the boy is Jesus.

'Do you want me to stop?' Degan asks.

I press my face into his chest and shake my head. I don't want him to stop. Degan and Jesus: the ones I already have.

The week between Christmas and New Year's is a strange kind of limbo. The main event finished but the resolution not yet arrived. My parents' wedding anniversary falls during this stretch of time. They've been married for thirty-five years. Several lifetimes.

Degan asks again if I'm ready to set a date for our wedding, but despite my feeling close to him, something in me balks. 'Let's look at our calendars in January,' I say, trying to stall.

We go downtown to the Boxing Week sales. Degan picks up some new clothes for work: a sweater vest, a casual blazer. At the checkout counter he grabs some boxer shorts. When we get home, we find they are patterned with Christmas trees. 'I'll take them back,' he says.

Later, at contact improv, I lie limply in the centre of the polished studio floor. A woman with blond braids and leg warmers rolls me over onto my side. Pokes at me with her big toe. Leans in with the full weight of her shoulder. The more she tries to engage me in the dance, the heavier my body becomes. I move off to the side of the dance floor and rest against the heaters, watching. Slowly the dancers get started.

The ones become twos, the twos become fours and fives. Soon there is a big pile of bodies in the centre of the room. Legs sticking out, arms at odd angles. I try not to think about Auschwitz.

⌒

I read *Suite Française* by Irène Némirovsky and the remarkable *Austerlitz* by W. G. Sebald. I read both volumes of Art Spiegelman's graphic memoir *Maus*. *The Reader* by Bernhard Schlink and, for the second time, Styron's *Sophie's Choice*. Styron's daughter has written a memoir about her father's depression, what it was like to grow up in the shadow of such a literary lion, and I gobble that book up, too. I read *The History of Love* by Nicole Krauss, an American writer who is exactly my age. The pathos in these books is so palpable, as is the tragedy of the characters' lives. My own novel feels stilted and unformed. I have not understood the insidious loss of the Holocaust. Or rather, I have understood all too well but am unable to render a new impression of a subject matter that is so well-worn.

⌒

I wake in the middle of the night and tiptoe across the soft carpet, upstairs to my computer. There's a green light beside Eli's name in gmail. 'You're up late,' I write. 'How're things?'

'*Comme ci comme ça*. You?'

'Meh,' I write. And then: 'You're leaving soon, hey? Let's get together. Sunday?'

I'm still hoping he'll introduce me to his mother, but I can't tell him that, can't quite let him know what I imagine he could give me.

I press Send and sit at the computer answering other emails, waiting for Eli's reply. After ten minutes the green light beside his name turns red and then blinks off altogether.

The next morning his answer is there: 'I saw your note. I'm not trying to blow things off. I'm leaving the country in 10 days and have a ton of stuff to do. I'd like to see you.' A space. 'But I'm busy on Sunday.'

While reading this last line, something blooms in my chest, a bright spreading stain of awareness. I'm looking in the wrong place. I'm looking outside, when I know full well the answers I need are inside me. It's just so much harder to find them there.

Shabbat arrives over and over, like a present tied with a bow. We now call it '24 Hours Unplugged, Jewish Style'. On Friday evening, Degan guards the hearth while I go out into the darkness, to synagogue. At the car I turn back and see two high flames from our candles: one for him and one for me.

The temple at Holy Blossom is filled with adults. It's still 'winter' break, and the families with children must all be away skiing or in Florida. I sit beside Debra. I have managed to memorize the chorus of 'L'cha Dodi', the liturgical song sung at dusk to welcome the Sabbath bride, but when the time comes, the congregants bust out into a tune I don't recognize.

There are, I will learn, as many ways to sing 'L'cha Dodi' as there are Inuit words for snow.

One thing remains consistent: in the final verse, we all stand to welcome her, the invisible bride whose presence means the Sabbath has begun. Debra gestures to a woman who happens to be entering the sanctuary; she's wearing a purple cloche hat and discreetly stuffing her cell phone in her purse. 'There she is!'

'You know her?' I ask.

'Of course. The Sabbath bride.'

I laugh but am grateful when the verse ends and we sit back down. All the standing: it's exhausting.

The rabbi's 'sermon' is a colloquial lecture on a book about Yiddish he's been reading. He tells us about the expression *Nisht getoygen, nisht gefloygen,* which translates roughly to 'It doesn't fly; it doesn't even get up'. Meaning that something is completely unbelievable.

The rabbi uses the expression in reference to the Christian belief in transubstantiation: how the bread is literally transformed into the body of Christ during Communion, and the wine to his blood. The ridiculousness of this idea.

The congregation dissolves into laughter.

I lean into Debra, catching her eye. I can tell from her face that she, too, is hurt, but she braces herself. 'Remember,' she whispers, 'it's a defensiveness born of persecution.'

I think of the list of Jewish expulsions that Jordan has sent me. Beginning in the year 19 CE: Rome. The Frankish Kingdom. Germany. England, France. Warsaw. Spain. Sicily. Lithuania. Portugal. Prague.

'And then,' Jordan wrote, 'you get to the nineteenth and twentieth centuries, where the history is better known.'

Around me the congregation is still laughing. I think of Debra's words: 'It's a defensiveness born of persecution.'

I know that she's right. Still, an incredible loneliness rises up in me. I remember back to the minister on Christmas Eve, to the thin wafer on my tongue: 'The body of Christ, given for you.'

Did I feel it was *literally* the body of Christ? No. But I felt welcomed by the symbol, included. Gathered in. Whereas here I feel totally alone.

At a time of spiritual crisis, it is best to do nothing. To float.

To rest. To ask for guidance. But when I finally make it home and collapse into bed, I find myself unable to pray. I am between Gods, as others are between relationships or careers.

TWENTY

I RETURN TO THE SYNAGOGUE the next day to hear Eli speak about his book. It's my last chance to see him before he leaves for Paris. I know with a newfound certainty that he can't give me what I want. That a Jewish partner would be a shortcut, a hindrance rather than a help. Still, I'm stubborn. I refuse to let him go without some kind of resolution.

The event is held on the top floor, in a spacious solarium from which you can see the sparkly lights of the city spread out below you. When I arrive, fifteen minutes early, the place is already packed. Eli stands at the podium in a leather jacket that he doesn't remove despite the stifling heat. I try to catch his eye, but he's riffling through his papers, glancing around at everyone but me.

He gives a little wave, a half smile at a table of young women.

Rabbi Klein has the task of introducing him. She is as gracious as ever, listing his accomplishments, literary and otherwise, and welcoming him to the stage. Eli opens with a prepared speech. He talks about what it was like to write *Help Me*, and about the mixed reaction he's had from the Jewish community in general and the Orthodox community in particular. He is poised, but from across the room I can see his pages shaking slightly in his hands. When he's finished, the floor is open for questions.

A young woman in heavy eye makeup and track pants with

Juicy written in sparkly cursive on the rear stands up. 'That part you read about Israel, and the fence between Israel and Gaza. Did you mean that the fence is *bad*? Because the fence has meant way fewer suicide bombers.'

Eli waits a beat.

'It isn't good or bad,' he says. 'What I was really trying to say is that we need to get past good versus bad.'

An older man with a red *kippah* perched on the top of his head jumps in. 'Ambivalence is fine, but aren't there some things that are clearly right or wrong? Like the question of Israel's right to exist? Hamas denies even this, if I'm not mistaken.'

The questions have veered toward the political, toward the small portion of his book that deals with Orthodoxy in Israel. Eli uses the sleeve of his leather jacket to wipe perspiration from his forehead. He hesitates, then says, 'Again, I think it's more complex than right or wrong. Especially when it comes to issues of land ownership. Which, of course, should resonate with us here in Canada.'

I cheer silently, but the questioner's face is blank.

'Because of what we've done with our Native Canadians' land,' Eli clarifies.

But the man won't be diverted. 'Hamas denies us. Am I right?'

Eli sighs. 'Yes,' he says. 'But not *us*. Israel. And they deny it within their own historical context.'

The man's eyes widen. 'You agree with that?'

A voice from the audience shouts, 'We *are* Israel!' There's a smattering of applause.

Eli flushes. He ignores the comment from the audience and addresses the man in the red *kippah*. 'Of course not. I just . . . Honestly? I don't have an answer for Hamas,' he says.

After the question period, Rabbi Klein stands back up to

thank Eli. She says, 'Eli, you have helped open our hearts. We agree with much of what you say. And your words are beautifully written.'

She is generous and kind in her acknowledgement that he's been controversial.

❦

After, there's a long line of people waiting for Eli to sign their books. I join the queue. Several people ahead of me is a striking woman with dark eyes and glossy brown hair. She's a head taller than all the other women in the room, and when she stands next to Eli, they look like two of a set. For a moment I think this might be his girlfriend, returned from wherever she's been travelling, but I remember: his girlfriend is a redhead.

The woman reaches the front of the line. She and Eli speak intently. He leans in, touches her elbow. I fiddle with my phone, pretend to check my messages. The crowd clears out, but their conversation continues. Eli says something to the tall woman, and a storm of emotion crosses over her face – first sadness and then something close to rage.

I take a few steps back to give them space.

The solarium is now almost empty. Soon I'll have no choice but to go. I want the chance to say goodbye, but I can't very well stand here while they get into an argument. I reach for my bag; Eli looks over and sees me. He gestures me over.

I hesitate, but he gestures again. 'Alison, this is Shayna. Shayna is a musician. Alison is a writer.'

We eye each other warily.

The woman – Shayna – sighs. 'What do you write?' she asks, clearly out of obligation. I mutter something about my novel-in-progress.

'And you?' I ask. 'Do you play the . . .'

But I can't think of the name of a single instrument.

'I'm a singer,' she says. She's pulling on her jacket. 'And a kindergarten teacher,' she adds.

'But mostly a singer,' says Eli, making a face to indicate how good she is.

Shayna pulls her long hair back and ties it with an elastic from her wrist. 'If you'll excuse me, I have to get going.'

'So long,' she says to Eli. 'Have a great trip.'

'Thanks,' he mumbles, but she's already disappeared out the door.

Eli and I turn to face each other properly. He looks happy to see me, relieved, although perhaps just in comparison to the conversation he's been having.

'You were great,' I say.

'You thought so?'

'I did,' I answer sincerely.

'You look tired,' he says.

'Why, thank you. And you do, too.'

He laughs. 'These things take it out of me.'

'So you're off,' I say. 'To Paris.'

'For better or for worse.'

'I'm guessing for better.'

He shrugs.

'Are you excited?'

He looks like he's weighing his options, deciding how much of the truth to tell. 'I'm ready for a change of scene. It's been a hard fall,' he says finally.

'No kidding.' I pause. 'Why didn't you just tell me you didn't want to see me?'

'Tonight?'

'All month.'

He appears surprised. 'I *did* want to see you.'

I raise my eyebrows. 'I left a lot of messages,' I say. 'I really needed some help. With all the Jewish stuff.' My eyes fill with tears. I blink, but they fill again.

'Didn't I help you?' Eli asks. He leans in, genuinely concerned.

I'm silent.

He smiles, then his brow furrows. I can see he's arriving at some kind of realization, but I don't know what it is. I fiddle with my ring. 'You should marry a Jewish girl,' I say. 'So you don't have a messed-up kid like me.'

'That's *exactly* what I've been thinking,' he says. He pauses, realizing how his words sounded, and we both burst out laughing.

'Not that you're messed up,' he says.

'Clearly not.'

'Clearly not at all.'

We laugh some more. Then his face grows serious. 'I'm sorry, Alison,' he says. 'I'm sorry I couldn't help you more.'

And as he says this, it becomes clear to me for the second time: it wasn't his job to help me in the first place. I don't know how I missed seeing it earlier. There was nothing he could have done. A trip to synagogue together would have changed nothing.

'I'm jealous of what you have,' I say. 'That's what this all comes down to.'

'*Had*, you mean.' He's referring to his disenchantment with the Judaism of his youth. But we both know that Judaism, in any of its forms, is there for him should he ever want it back.

'I'm angry about what's happening to you,' he says. 'I hope you know that.'

'I do.'

But another revelation makes itself known to me: he *is* angry at Judaism, but for reasons of his own. We've both been using each other. In the same way that he's been a focus for my desire for Judaism, I've been a focus for his anger at it.

'You're the perfect convert,' he says. 'They should want you.'

I smile. 'Yes. They should.'

He's looking over my shoulder at the last group of people, chatting in the far corner of the basement. 'Can you hang on a sec?' he asks. 'I'm just going to say good night to my mum.'

'Your mother is here?'

'She is. Do you want to meet her?'

'Yes!'

Maybe it's not too late, I think, picturing her arm around my shoulder as we light the Shabbos candles. But when we cross the room, she isn't among the few remaining guests.

'I guess she went home,' he says.

This feels like the biggest loss of all.

We get up slowly, digging around in our bags for our mittens and scarves. Out on the street, more snow has fallen. Our boots squeak on the sidewalk. The street lights wear halos in the night.

'Oh,' Eli says, 'I almost forgot. I brought you your Hanukkah gift.'

He looks me in the eye, a little nervous suddenly, and pulls a book from his bag. I recognize the title. It's about a train that carried Jews to safety during the war, a topic very close to the one I'm writing about. 'For your research,' he says.

'Wow,' I say. 'Thanks.'

I give him a hard hug goodbye.

Eli flags me a cab, holds the door for me. I get in, give the cabbie my directions. At home, before going inside, back into my life with Degan, I stand on our porch in the cold and flip open the cover of the gift.

'For Alison, on your journey, and the light along the way,' Eli has written. 'With love from one Jew to another.'

PART TWO

The future is made of the same stuff as the present.
– Simone Weil

ONE

OLD HABITS DIE HARD. The Jewish calendar begins with Rosh Hashanah in September, but I can't deny the secular New Year, the unblemished promise it holds. On the first day of January, I pack our station wagon with books, my journal, my tall winter boots. Driving toward the Allen Expressway, I note that the street lamps on Eglinton Avenue are adorned not with Christmas decorations but with tinselly menorahs left over from Hanukkah. Several hours later I arrive at our family cabin to deep snow and the sound of the river down in the valley, carving its way through the darkness. Standing at the front door, I jiggle my key in the lock, above me a wild profusion of stars. Inside, I move through the rooms, turning on the baseboard heaters, electrical filaments crackling to life all around me. The cabin smells musty, like dust and mothballs. I build a fire and curl up on the couch in my sleeping bag, quiet and calm against the world. I'm reading the most beautiful novel about loss that echoes down the generations. I think of the breakfast tray I loved to bring to Granny when I was a girl, with a poached egg in a delicate porcelain egg cup and fingers of toast to dip in the runny yolk. I think of Granny's mother, Marianne, whom I look so much like. *Stuckerl* – 'piece of work'. Smiling into the camera in her old-fashioned bathing suit. She's gone forever. I think of my father, to whom I can't find the right thing to say.

When I was little, I prayed every night before bed. Mum or

Dad would come to tuck me in. My prayers consisted primarily of a list of people we'd ask God to bless ('God bless Mummy, Daddy, Emily, Gumper, Granny, Lucy' and so on). This was followed by a singsongy leave-taking by my parents, a string of instructions blended into one long word: *night-night-sleep-tight-don't-let-the-bedbugs-bite-God-bless-see-you-in-the-morning!*

God bless. See you in the morning.

I think of the faith in this message.

I remember once trying to reinstate 'God bless' with my family. I was home for a quick visit. I got up from the dinner table and said, 'I'm bagged. Going to crawl into bed early. 'Night. God bless.'

'Good night,' they answered mildly, looking at me curiously for a half-second too long.

I tried it over several successive evenings and heard 'Good night' and 'Love you' but never 'God bless' in return. The words have fallen out of fashion in our family, like crimped hair or bell-bottoms.

Tonight, when I'm done reading, I make my way down the cabin's dim hallway and get into the big double bed. I pull the down comforter up to my chin. From the window I can hear the rush of the river, close by but invisible in the darkness. I fold my hands, close my eyes and try to pray. But I find myself unable to conjure up God, *any* God, even the God-in-everything that is normally so palpable in solitude.

It wasn't Christ I prayed to as a girl: it was a vague idea of 'God' as a man with a beard in the sky. But now I ask myself: what does the Jewish God look like? I strain for an image. All I can summon is my childish notion of the unshaven grandfather, only now he is also wearing a black hat and spectacles.

I recall a passage from the book I've been reading: '"When a Jew prays, he is asking God a question that has no end." Darkness fell. Rain fell. I never asked: "What question?"'

❦

I stop in to see my therapist Charlotte on my way home from the cabin three days later.

'How are you?' she asks.

'Tired.'

'Have you been sleeping?'

'More than usual.' I calculate the hours from the previous night: thirteen. And I could have gone longer.

There is nothing I like better than sleep: not TV, not chocolate. What does it mean that I instinctively group sleep with mindlessness, with escape? In sleep there is a remove that I find endlessly appealing, a chance at oblivion that renews itself daily, like this winter's never-ending snow.

Sleep nourishes, sure, but it also absolves, removing the demands of the daily, the duties and tasks, and the pesky need to exist.

I tell this to Charlotte.

No response. Only rocking.

The radiator clanks like a ghost in chains.

She purses her lips. 'Maybe you're sleeping so much because you have a lot of dreaming to do,' she says.

I stare blankly.

'Your dreams are helping you work out your relationship to your ancestors. To your great-grandmother Marianne. A relationship that's too painful to hold with your conscious mind.'

'We celebrated Hanukkah,' I tell Charlotte, trying to change the subject.

'"We"?'

'Degan and I. My sister. My parents.'

'That sounds significant. Was it healing?' she asks.

I nod my assent. But as I do, the opposite feeling asserts

itself, that there is no healing possible. How have I not realized this before?

I'm quiet, gnawing my lip.

'What are you thinking?' Charlotte asks.

'I'll never heal it. Will I?'

She cocks a thin eyebrow.

'I've been lunging after all things Jewish,' I say. 'People, classes, rituals. Thinking that the cure for the Holocaust lies in the practice of the religion itself. That by finding my way back there, I can somehow save Marianne. But there *is* no cure for the Holocaust. Is there?'

Charlotte looks at me. 'No,' she says. 'There isn't.' And then: 'I've been waiting for you to make this distinction.'

I grip the chair's wooden arms, suddenly fuzzy-headed, dizzy. 'What distinction?'

She peers at me over her glasses, then speaks slowly, enunciating her syllables: 'The distinction between the Holocaust and Judaism.'

The idea that sleep is a psychic defence is hardly new, but I'm struck still by its immediacy, the way my eyelids begin to droop at the first hint that a conversation may turn controversial, that someone is about to say something I might find difficult. 'Did you hear what I just said?' Charlotte asks.

She uncrosses her stockinged legs, crosses them in the opposite direction. I shake my head: no.

She hesitates, uncertain whether to reiterate. She believes I have to come to the big revelations myself. But she *does* speak, and when she does, I can barely hear her words for the scream of the static behind my eyes.

'You *cannot* save your murdered relatives,' Charlotte says. 'No matter how Jewish you become, they are never coming back.'

TWO

WHEN I ARRIVE BACK at the apartment, a big stack of mail is waiting for me on the hall table. I tear open a cream envelope to find the outline for our upcoming Jewish Information Course. Degan and I read it over, aghast. Not only is there a three-hour class every week, there are tests and a final exam. Hundreds of pages of reading. 'You really want to do this?' he asks.

Faced with the schedule, my resolve is only sharpened, my desire to convert strengthened. I feel a pure, unclouded kind of knowing.

'Because looking at this –' He shakes the paper in the air. 'Do you see how many holidays there are? What does a religion need with so many holidays?'

'They must feel there's something to celebrate.'

'A package came for you, too,' Degan says. He gestures to the corner of our hall of mirrors. The box is bandaged with masking tape in the manner of an Egyptian mummy, but a corner of the label is peeking out. The SunBox has arrived.

Degan holds the box steady while I tear off the tape and remove the giant pieces of Styrofoam. I pull the lamp out, all awkward angles, its long neck bent like some exotic bird. I hesitate for a moment with the cord in my hand and then plug it in. The light that bursts forth is brassy and bold, with the confidence of a cheerleader or a canvassing politician. We stand next to it, mesmerized. It's seductive, viscerally undeniable. I don't care if this is the placebo effect: I immediately feel better.

We move the lamp into the bedroom and stretch out on the futon like sunbathers on a white sand beach. 'Do you *feel* that?' I ask, gesturing to the lamp.

'I do.'

But he sounds uncertain.

'Really?'

'Totally.'

I look at him, expecting to see a sly grin, but his face is slack, his brow heavy.

'How are you?' I ask.

'Okay.'

'You seem down.'

'I'm okay,' he says.

'How was your week?'

I wait for him to answer, but he appears wary, as though he's not sure I'll stick around to listen.

I roll onto my side and prop my head up in my palm, facing him. 'No, really,' I say.

'Well, if you really want to know, I'm kind of sad.'

I look at his face again. The blue-black circles under his eyes. The first bits of grey in his stubble. I reach for his hand.

'I used to believe our love was a pure, big love,' he says. 'Exempt from the world.' He searches my face, and I nod to show he should continue, that I want to hear whatever he has to say.

'Now I feel abandoned by you, with the depression, the fixation on . . .'

I wait to hear 'with the fixation on Eli,' but instead he says, 'Fixation on Judaism.'

I exhale.

'I'm worried that if I don't convert, you'll leave,' he says.

If part of me has considered this, that option is now entirely dismissed, as though by being pulled up into the light of day, its ridiculousness can really be seen.

'Don't be silly,' I say, but my tone is gentle, to let him know I can see how he got this idea. Rabbi Glickman's words echo in my head: 'You're faced with a difficult decision.'

I want to convert. Degan's station means I won't be allowed. But I find, replaying my conversation with the rabbi, that the decision is not difficult at all.

'I want to get married,' I say.

It is as though, in speaking the words, the conclusion arrives fully formed. It is not so much that I've resolved the issue with Eli, but rather that I see there was never any issue in the first place. There was only me trying to sort out my history in the worst way possible, which was also the best way I knew how. How could I have been so confused? When I think how easily I might have lost Degan, I almost weep with relief.

I look up at him; his face shows a mixture of confusion and love. 'I want to get married,' I repeat. 'Let's set a date.'

'Soon?'

'Sure,' I agree. 'Soon.' I don't want to wait. 'Let's do it,' I say. Degan laughs. 'Okay!'

'Okay?'

'Okay.'

We make love to seal the deal.

❧

After, we lie in bed in the candlelight. Degan reads aloud from Abraham Joshua Heschel's famous book *The Sabbath*: 'The higher goal of spiritual living is not to amass a wealth of information but to face sacred moments.' How long has it taken me to face this moment, to give myself to it completely?

The next day we are quiet in our wonder. We write a draft of our wedding invitation and include the date: May 19. What kind of wedding will we have? One that honours the complexity of our lives. I thrill at the thought of a *chuppah*, a Jewish wedding canopy that symbolizes the home we will build together as a couple, and the home we will build with all of Israel.

In the early afternoon I crawl back into bed, turn out the lights and try to nap. I can hear Degan upstairs, singing Gillian Welch, and Ryan Adams, and a song he wrote about the rainy ocean town where we used to live. The guitar trails off and I hear the clink of dissonant strings as he leans it up against the desk. He comes down and finds me shivering. Pulls back the covers and gets in, wraps his arms around me. He begins to sing softly into my ear, a beautiful song about a man picking his guitar while his lover lays low beneath him.

I realize he is singing about me.

'Did you just write that upstairs?' I ask.

'No.'

'Where did you write it?'

'Right here.'

'Now?'

'For you.'

⟡

The cliché applies: the more I learn about Judaism, the less I know. Still, it occurs to me that in our ignorance, in the absence of an entrenched family tradition, Degan and I now have a unique opportunity: to make a *new* tradition, our own, to give to our children. We are acquiring the tools. The language, the history. Our love will build the rest from there.

In the wake of the huge decision to move forward with the

wedding, part of me expects that my psyche will recoil, that I will feel numb or afraid, but instead I feel love and intense relief. I sleep in Degan's arms on the sofa while he reads a book about Prozac. When I wake, he's gone out to meet a friend: there's an envelope propped up beside me with a heart drawn on it. A Degan heart, so lopsided it looks like the letter *B*.

B for brave, for bravo, for best.

I am with the best man for me.

We learn in class that Adar is the month when joy increases; it takes hearing this for me to realize I'm actually feeling better. I buy a new desk, with a roll-out tray for the keyboard so my shoulder won't hurt when I work. My editor writes to say that she will have a copy of my new poetry book any day – and instead of shame and dread, I feel excitement. I choose books on the Holocaust to review for both the *Globe and Mail* and the *Walrus*, and accept two offers to judge literary contests, which I regret when I see the bulk of manuscripts. With my own book and the upcoming wedding, I'll have enough on my plate.

The upcoming wedding!

Degan seems funny and smart again – which is to say, I emerge from my dark haze and can see him as he is. I want to get married, finish my novel and have a baby.

THREE

I DECIDE TO TRY OUT SHABBAT NATION, the Friday-evening service Rabbi Klein recommended so many months ago. It is held in the same solarium where Eli gave his talk, against the glittery backdrop of Toronto's skyline. By the time I get there, things are under way; several bearded men in white linen shirts are up on the makeshift stage. Their instruments are exotic: a kind of harp, a long bamboo tube. In the middle of the cluster of linen-clad men, a tall glossy-haired beauty is letting loose a bright ribbon of song. I look at her, look again. Finally I recognize her as the woman who was arguing with Eli after his presentation. Sarah? No, Shayna.

'I'm a singer,' she'd said.

No kidding.

Shayna beams at the participants, seated in a circle of plastic chairs, and motions for us all to stand. People shift nervously in their seats. She comes down from the stage and takes us, one by one, by the arms, still smiling. She instructs us to put our arms around each other and sway, and we willingly do it, wanting to please her. She must make a dynamite kindergarten teacher.

I look around the circle: men with colourful, Guatemalan-style *kippot*, and women in long, flowing skirts. There are toddlers running around behind the bimah. The proceedings wind down into a *kiddush* of sushi and wine. I cannot get enough of the challah, dense with yeast and white flour.

My mouth is full when Shayna approaches me. 'We've met,' she says. 'Where?'

Her height matches her presence. Up close, she seems even taller than on stage; she must be six feet.

'I think it was—'

'This always happens to me,' she says. 'Why can't I remember where I've met you?'

I try again. 'I'm pretty sure—'

'Weird,' she says. 'Isn't it?'

'I guess. But—'

'I always like a mystery!'

She grins, popping a piece of sushi into her mouth, and I take my chance. 'We met after Eli Bloomberg's talk.'

Shayna's face changes, a slight reconfiguration of features, which I can't read. She chews carefully, her palm flat against her chest, as though to prevent herself from choking. 'Oh!' she says, when she has managed to swallow. 'Right. You're Eli's friend.'

I nod.

'I just had an email from him,' she says. 'Sounds like he's happy to be away.'

I have just received an email saying the opposite – that he's having trouble adjusting to the residency in Paris, that he misses Toronto and his friends – but something tells me to keep quiet. There's a strained silence. Shayna finally says, 'I should go help the guys pack up the instruments.' She gestures behind her to one of the bearded men trying to cram an oversized pair of cymbals into a wooden box. 'It was nice talking to you.' She pauses. 'I'm sorry. Remind me of your name?'

'Alison.'

'Right. Good Shabbos, Alison.'

I have been taken as a real Jew.

'Good Shabbos to you, too,' I say.

When I arrive home, the apartment is dark. I go into the kitchen, turn on the light and look at the calendar on the wall. It is January 20, the date my great-grandparents Oskar and Marianne were deported to Auschwitz.

⟡

The following week the Jewish Information Class begins. The first meeting takes place in a small, hot classroom in the elementary school wing of the synagogue. The walls are covered with Hanukkah decorations and tourism posters of Israel. Degan and I try to wedge ourselves into the child-sized orange plastic chairs and schoolhouse desks, our knees doubled up underneath them. Around us, other couples are attempting the same contortion.

Debra is the only single person. I wave to her on the other side of the room.

A heavy-set woman with a flop of red curls enters and introduces herself as Harriet. She is wearing a purple track suit and matching lavender UGGs. 'Welcome, everyone,' she says brightly. 'Shalom.'

I have been warned against this particular teacher in no uncertain terms. A prominent editor at one of the city's biggest publishing houses took the class with her fiancé, and it almost split them up. 'Try to get another teacher,' the editor advised me. '*Any* other teacher.'

Yet despite having known that Harriet would be our teacher this session, I want to start as soon as possible. Degan has agreed to take the class, but he's prone to changing his mind. And the road to conversion – if that's where I'm headed – is long. Besides, Harriet seems friendly enough. 'Shalom!' she says again, in case anyone missed it the first time. I don't see what the problem is.

We go around the desks introducing ourselves. 'I'm Andrew,' says a big man with earrings and a shaved head. 'I'm here to support Lindsay in her path to conversion.'

His bride-to-be, a bleached blonde, blushes, although I can't tell if it's in response to the conversion or the impending nuptials.

The man to Lindsay's left says, 'I'm Ari. I'm here to support Layla, who hopes to convert before we are married next June.'

His fiancée flushes in turn.

The class, it turns out, consists entirely of couples engaged to be married. '*Mazel tov!*' Harriet says, over and over again. As we continue around the circle, I notice that the Jewish partner is almost always the man; I realize that because of matrilineal descent, these men want their fiancées to convert so their children will be Jewish. The only exception is Tom and Diane, the couple Rabbi Klein told us about. Their baby has fat cheeks and a slick of drool on her chin. A Jewish baby. Because her mother is Jewish. Her father is studying to convert.

Diane catches me making faces at the baby, sticking out my tongue to try to make her smile. 'What's her name?'

'Tamara,' she whispers.

I can't tear my eyes away.

After the introductions, we launch into our first Hebrew lesson. Harriet draws several characters on the board. 'The first letter of the aleph-bet is what?' she asks.

'Aleph!' the Jewish men recite reluctantly, collectively. They can already speak Hebrew. I see immediately how this will work: each potential convert, each bride-to-be, will have her own personal tutor.

We take a short break, during which the Jews in the class compare notes on summer camps and day schools, and then return for the lecture portion of the evening. Harriet comes back into the class stuffing the last part of a banana into her mouth. 'How do you become a Jew?' she asks.

She answers her own question: 'Only one way. You're born a Jew.'

She places her hands on her belly. 'The way to become Jewish if you're not born Jewish is to be born Jewish,' she says smugly, pleased with herself.

I look around the class. Furrowed brows. Does this mean there's really no way in?

The answer to Harriet's 'who's on first' riddle is eventually revealed: the mikvah. Through immersion in the Jewish ritual bath, you can be reborn as a Jew. There's a collective sigh of relief from the partners of the potential converts. Harriet giggles over the class's anxiety, her earlier conviviality having taken a fast turn to the passive-aggressive.

Now that we've established anyone can – theoretically – become Jewish, she says she will tell us a little more about the course. 'It will be rigorous,' she says. 'You will have to attend synagogue. You should live as Jews in your home.'

Here she looks at the clock: there are two hours left.

'Live as Jews,' she reiterates. 'Go to synagogue.'

She keeps us until ten in the evening, finding new ways to make the same point.

Degan drives home. He can barely keep his eyes open. 'I don't know about this,' he says.

One week down and twenty-nine more to go.

FOUR

THE FOLLOWING FRIDAY there's a special contact improv workshop with a teacher visiting from another town. When I arrive, the studio is freezing, with frost on the inside of the windows. 'We just turned on the heat,' Michael says.

'Shabbat Shalom,' I say in reply.

'Oh,' he says. 'I didn't grow up with that.'

I try again with his friend. 'Good Shabbos, Ariel.'

Ariel looks blank. 'I'm not really religious.'

The next morning I go home to Kitchener for a spontaneous visit. I mention to Mum and Dad that Degan and I are considering a *chuppah* for our wedding ceremony. Dad wrinkles his nose. Mum turns back toward her cooking. She is making borscht. The heel of the cabbage sits discarded on the cutting board. How many calories, I wonder reflexively. How many people could the pile of refuse feed? The bright red skins of the beets. The compost bin under Mum's sink could make soup for probably fifty people. I try to stop myself, but soon I am thinking about the hunger of the children in the camps; about what it would be like to have a child beg for food and have nothing to give – although here my mind trembles and capitulates to fiction. The scene in *The Shawl* by Cynthia Ozick when the toddler escapes and runs toward the electric fence. The titular scene in *Sophie's Choice* when the Nazi guard forces her to choose between her two children.

If she refuses to choose, both will be killed.

For the moment, at least, my psyche protects me, allows me to see these as scenes in books, not as actual events in history, events that have something to do with *me*.

*   *   *

Writing and depression feel unrelated to me, like stars in separate constellations. When I'm in the throes of the darkness, I never think to draw a line between the two. And when I'm feeling sunny, despite knowing the correlation – that artists of all stripes are more depressed than the general population, that a higher percentage will take their own lives – the relationship seems intellectual, abstract.

In certain historical periods, conversations about melancholia emphasized creativity over depression. And it's true that at the start of any project, during the process of generation, I am often flooded with the bad blood. Yet, paradoxically, the act of writing also feels like an island to rest on, an oasis of hours, even a single hour, in which I experience pleasure. And it occurs to me that the relief I experience when writing is not just about holding the darkness at bay but about ordering it, controlling it. As I writer, I can take the horrors of the Holocaust – for example – and place them within the strictures of plot, character, tension. I can render them believable, and imbue them with a moment of redemption – not in terms of the outcome of the story but in terms of narrative tension. Ah. *This* is how it ends. And we close the book and set it aside, satisfied.

Maybe writing fiction serves a dual function: letting the author excavate her psyche while at the same time functioning as a kind of psychic shield. A writer digs up the contents of her unconscious mind, and then attributes it to someone else – not to a family member or friend, mind you, but to a character.

Which is to say, someone who does not even *exist*, someone who comes from the imagination entirely.

☙

In the midst of my first depression, I moved to Montreal to take a course at McGill on the Holocaust. My nights were dogged with dreams of Nazis; I spent my days eating Mr Christie Pirate cookies and putting on weight. It was during that semester that I first really registered that someone in our family had *survived* Auschwitz. Gumper's cousin Vera lost her husband and both her children, aged five and ten. Later, after the war, she moved to New York. Granny and Gumper visited her occasionally, but they never invited her to their home in North Hatley. Probably because they couldn't 'risk' an openly Jewish relative.

I decided to go meet Vera myself, to interview her for the research paper I needed to do for the class. Predictably, perhaps, I've forgotten almost everything about the meeting other than the psychic exhaustion I experienced; the intense desire to know coupled with an even more intense desire to *not* know, to cling to the ignorance that my father had, it occurred to me then, been wise to foster.

Only the briefest impressions of that visit remain. Vera's apartment had a huge candle in the main room. I didn't know then about the *yahrzeit* candle, a memorial candle a Jew lights on the anniversary of a loved one's death, but I understood immediately and implicitly that this was what it was for. It was on fire around the clock, and I knew, too, that Vera thought of her lost family all the time; that the flame did not stand *in* for memory so much as accompany her every moment of every day in the gruelling task of never being able to forget.

Vera was short and stooped, with gnarled knuckles and the

telling blue number tattooed on her forearm. She had a suitcase of photographs of her dead children that she brought out to show me as part of our interview. It sounds implausible, all these years later, the suitcase – why would she not have put the photos in albums or in frames? – but for whatever reason, she didn't. The suitcase was the small, compact kind meant for travelling overnight on a trip you planned to return from shortly. It held hundreds of loose photos. Vera showed them to me cautiously, wanting me to see these images of her children, to possess them even, while at the same time barely able to stand letting me hold them. This was fifty years after her children's deaths.

Still, she allowed me to leave that afternoon with the gift of two postcard-sized black-and-whites. In the first, Vera's daughter, Eva, who was five when she was killed in the gas chambers at Auschwitz, smiles into the camera. The entire field is filled with her face: the chubbiest cheeks you have ever seen and a halo of wild brown curls.

In the second photo her son, Jan – ten when he was killed – appears as a young child. He stands on a cement pier, wearing a bathing suit with straps, like something you might expect to see on a Russian weightlifter. His small tummy protrudes. His hands – the knuckles still plump with baby fat – rest on his hips. He looks sideways at the camera, the slightest of smiles on his face. The look is not quite pride, but almost – a look of confidence. He knows he is wanted; he knows the world will treat him well.

These two framed portraits hang in my hall now. I look at them every day. I look at them, but I cannot really see them. When I try, my mind again capitulates to fiction.

I pull out *Sophie's Choice* and flip through the pages. I find the scene where the narrator must choose between her children:

'You may keep one of your children,' he repeated. *'The other one will have to go. Which one will you keep?'*

'You mean, I have to choose?'

'You're a Polack, not a Yid. That gives you a privilege – a choice.'

The distance fiction provides lets me imagine the scene rather than reject it, lets me graft my own experience onto it so firmly that I am almost not surprised to come across the name of Sophie's boy: Jan. The same as Vera's son.

And her daughter, Eva.

Sophie's children, Eva and Jan.

Vera's children, Eva and Jan.

I picture Vera on the platform, faced with this impossible dilemma. I picture little Eva, with the fattest cheeks in the world. Her face, by then, would have been gaunt and pinched. And Jan, his small tummy, his unwavering trust in the world. How could you choose?

And then I remember: Vera had no choice. Both her children are gone.

FIVE

AS I WRITE MY NOVEL *Far to Go*, Dad embarks on his own research into our family history. We exchange a steady flow of emails each morning, me asking questions and him answering them. Soon he begins his own attempts at documenting what he learns, including an idea for a book recounted from the point of view of Granny and Gumper's shared passport.

The passport left out on a desk, its pages riffled by the wind.

Later, Dad sends me drafts of his chapters. Accompanying the thorough research are small boxes of text, containing the fates of various relatives.

Ella was gassed, meaning suffocated, to death on Marh 8, 1944, at Auschwitz. May Ella's soul be bound in the bond of eternal life.

And:

May he rest in peace and not be forgotten. Alfred was murdered, at Svatobořice in 1942 at the age of 78 . . . those bastard Nazis.

For my part, as I work on the novel, I am also taking a second set of notes, more personal, about my depression as it relates to our family. As I write, however, I am assailed by doubts about my own qualifications to tell this story, as though my father and my older cousins have a lease on 'truth' because of their increased years. As though my dead relatives have taken the truth to the earth and my opinion is entirely irrelevant.

A photographer from New York comes to interview me as part of a project on hidden Jews. I confess my uncertainty to her. She assures me that my version is not inferior, only different. It is mine. I counter that it is inferior precisely *because* it is mine – which is to say, I have learned my position in the family. I feel an oppressive, relentless psychic weight, a nagging voice that I have to somehow override each time I set pen to paper.

Every family has its own mythology; adding a writer to the mix means that the mythology becomes externalized, that a trace of it exists physically, in the larger world. The material version – the book – accrues the sheen of truth, despite the fact that it is just one of many possible stories. Who am I to claim the official version?

In reading William Styron's depression memoir, *Darkness Visible*, and his daughter Alexandra's *Reading My Father* (there is an essay by Styron's wife, Rose, as well), you notice the divergence between the stories but also the overlap. The books act as a documented inheritance; a reader can follow the lineage directly, tracing a line from origin to output, a crude furrow in the dirt from cause to effect. Of course, William Styron is not the bona fide origin, only a juncture in the river, and his daughter recognizes as much, going back a generation further to expose what she comes to see as her *grand*father's undiagnosed depression. The decision where to begin a family story is arbitrary. There is always a previous generation to excavate, like a never-ending series of lost civilizations buried deeper and deeper in the sand.

But a shovel only digs so deep. And a story, any story, has to start *somewhere*.

SIX

GRANNY AND GUMPER settled in Sherbrooke and summered in nearby North Hatley, an affluent hamlet populated in July and August by cottagers from Montreal and the American South. Granny and Gumper would eventually build their own house there and live in North Hatley permanently, but in the summer of 1945 they began by renting a cottage – belonging, as fate would have it, to the family of famed literary agent Andrew 'the Jackal' Wylie. The cottage is still there; its shuttered windows, its big colonial wraparound porch overlooking Lake Massawippi. This is where Granny was sitting, her glass of rye beside her, when the telephone rang one lovely July afternoon. Sailboats dotted the water below her. The war was over. Gumper had returned to Europe to see what he could find out. He was calling from across the ocean to report on his findings.

We don't know what words were spoken, what information exchanged, only that after Granny hung up, the phone rang again. It was Miss Cinnamon, the county operator. She was breathless. 'Mrs Pick, Mrs Pick. Was it okay?'

It was the first transatlantic phone call she had ever placed.

As I continue writing my novel, Dad finds a cache of letters from Gumper addressed to Granny in Canada during this time. The letters are in Czech. Dad sends them off to the translator and they come back one at a time. In our family, we collectively hold our breath. We are all amazed by what Lucy calls Gumper's 'schmaltzy-ness', the way he dotes on Granny. 'I look at your photo every night,' he writes, 'and talk to it when I first wake up in the morning.'

I add this line to my novel, ascribing it to a secondary character.

Partway through the correspondence is a document titled *Report from England*. Under the heading 'Conditions in Czechoslovakia', sandwiched between sentences about the efficiency of the postal service and the equal efficiency of the trains, is the blunt sentence 'Unfortunately there is no trace of the Bauers and we must assume they are no longer alive.'

'The Bauers' are Oskar and Marianne. Granny's parents.

'No longer alive' sounds so much safer than 'dead'. So much safer than 'murdered'.

Even Dad is shocked by Gumper's curtness. 'How could he have referred to Granny's parents' murder in such abstract terms?'

We are afforded a glimpse sixty years back in time, to the early days of the family strategy: Minimize. Deny.

Freud's seminal essay 'On Mourning and Melancholia' considered the difference between the two states. In mourning, he suggests, a loss is felt consciously, keenly, whereas in some cases of melancholia, a loss has been experienced, but the analyst cannot see clearly what it was. Freud supposes that the patient, too, while beset by longing and sadness, cannot consciously perceive what it is he has lost.

In our family we didn't even try.

It's possible, of course, that Granny's mourning process was completed years before my birth. Possible that I'm surmising, speculating about something I cannot know. My reluctance rears its head, my fear of saying the wrong thing, of saying anything at all. In this area of interpreting my family history I possess a marked lack of confidence, an uncharacteristic undermining of my own observations, so it pains me to say what appears quite obvious: that no grief process occurred; that instead of mourning there was an attempt to halt the unbearable trauma in its tracks; that the denial of Judaism was not just a tactic to adapt to the New World, with its antisemitism, but to erase the existence of the pain itself.

When I learned our family secret – first via Auntie Sheila's words over my head and later from Jordan on the playground – I was full of questions. Over and over I asked Dad how my grandparents could have done what they did; how, after what they'd gone through, they could have denied who they were. And I was told, over and over, that their denial of Judaism was a forward-thinking decision, one meant to buffer against future eventualities. If my grandparents weren't Jewish, they could join the clubs they wanted to join, could socialize however they desired. Their children would be protected against prejudice both small and monumental.

Yet I see the decision not just as forward-thinking but as reactionary. If you weren't Jewish, Jewish history did not apply to you. If you weren't Jewish, there was nothing to mourn.

❧

After reading Granny and Gumper's correspondence, I insert a series of letters into *Far to Go*. The relationship of these fictional letters to the real letters from my family's history is ambiguous, in the way that the relationship between a writer and the world she creates always is. The letters are written between various characters; major, minor, offstage.

A writer has to understand her characters deeply in order to make them come alive. A character is a splinter off the self, sure. A shard of the author's self, lived or unlived, repressed or desired or disdained. Still, a character is a fiction, a fabrication: she grants me the chance to avoid speaking in the first person.

Characters exist in the symbolic realm, which, it does not escape me, is also the realm in which my family lived, their lives not so different from those in fiction or the lives of actors in a play. Acted with authenticity and enthusiasm, a bang-up performance, but a performance nonetheless.

It occurs to me that this performance, and the secret it protected, has been a boon to my writing. I work at my book as though taking dictation, the novel's symbols appearing on the page as though dug up like prehistoric weapons perfectly preserved in mud and clay. Rail as I might against my grandparents' silence, there is something about it that helps me now, that lets the well-trod, *trampled* terrain of the Holocaust feel fresh. 'Make it new' is Ezra Pound's famous dictum – antisemite that he was – and I am able to make it new precisely because it *is* new. Not to anyone else, but to *me*.

SEVEN

THE BOOKS EDITOR from a Toronto magazine emails to ask me to a movie. I take it as a friendly gesture – we've crossed paths at several book launches in the past weeks, and each time ended up talking about this particular film. But when I get to the theatre, I find him sloppy drunk. 'How *are* you?' he breathes, reeking of his poison.

'I'm depressed,' I answer, too tired to lie. Because of course the joy I felt in the month of Adar has faded; the sliver of black slipped back in.

The editor leans over and grips my arm. 'That makes you a good Jew.'

The lights go down; he tries to hold my hand. I shake him off, lean forward in my seat with my arms hanging over the empty chair in front of me. I bury my fingers in the popcorn. I am repulsed by his breath and his desperate eyes, and enraged by what he seems to expect. But I stay for the duration of the movie, frozen in my seat. At the end, he asks about the book I'm working on. This, I realize, has been the purpose of the exercise, his end of a transaction that I haven't let myself be conscious of. He wants to spend time with me; I want a review in his magazine. I'm disgusted with myself, and too ashamed and angry to make the pitch.

'It's about the Holocaust,' I say with a sigh, which is exactly what I've vowed not to say, having internalized the idea that people are sick of the topic, that the last thing we need is another book on *that*.

'I grew up with the Holocaust,' the editor says. 'My father's parents came from a family of Polish Jews who all died.'

The editor becomes immediately interesting to me again, his transgression entirely forgiven. I see every Jew, every survivor, as a potential saviour, thinking they might know something I don't, might be the one with the piece of information that allows me to understand the nightmare.

I try to engage him in a conversation about his history. 'I don't want to talk about it,' he says.

Degan gets home from work and we drive up to the synagogue for our class. We jam ourselves into the tiny desks and start in on our lesson. We learn that a new vowel, vaguely similar to the English *o*, can appear with or without a line beneath the dot, although the rule to distinguish the scenarios remains unclear to us. Tamara, the baby, has the best pronunciation in the class, babbling out the new vocabulary from her sling on Diane's chest. After the break, Harriet tells us it is 'Jewish Partner's Night' and sends the crowd of baseball caps away into an adjacent room. They will be talking about the responsibilities of being supportive to their converting partners.

'Where's my supportive partner?' Debra pouts.

And I find myself wondering the same thing. Where is the person who will guide *me* in this process, bring me home for Shabbat, correct my Hebrew? I am the one coaching Degan on the difference between the two- and three-dot vowels as he crams in the minutes before class. I don't judge him: he's doing this for me; he's giving up a night every week when he'd rather be doing a hundred other things. But I, too, would like someone to relax into.

As a teenager, I didn't think about marrying a Jew. Jordan would kiss anything in a skirt, but we all knew that one day he'd make a Jewish girl his bride. We listened to a lot of Moxy Früvous in high school, getting out of our car at abandoned intersections in the middle of the night to dance to 'King of Spain' while the traffic light turned red, then green, then red again. We listened to Neil Young and Paul Simon. I loved the songs 'America' and 'American Tune', and the opening line of 'Hearts and Bones', with its reference to wandering Jews. I liked the melody, and how it named me clearly. Pick, from the acronym pic, *perigrinus iudei confessionis*, Latin for 'traveller of the Jewish faith'.

Sometimes I would imagine I could find a Jewish boy. He would be the one, and I the one-half. But I didn't think about it seriously. It might happen. Or it might not.

❦

Suddenly, though, it again feels crucial – just as it did during my obsession with Eli. I tell Degan as much in the car on the way home. 'If I were single, I would only date Jewish men,' I say, staring out the window with my arms crossed in front of my chest.

Degan swerves out of the turning lane. 'You're kidding me, right? I go to that ridiculous class with you and this is what I get in return?'

'You said you weren't taking the class for me,' I retort.

'You're serious.'

I'm silent.

He slams his palm down on the horn. A minivan speeds past, the driver giving us the finger. 'Fucking unbelievable,' Degan shouts.

I see that I've gone too far, but it's too late to take my words back.

'This is about that writer, isn't it?'

My stomach sinks. 'Which writer?' I ask. But I know full well who he's talking about.

'Eli Bloom.'

'Bloomberg,' I mutter.

'Oh! I got his name wrong! Please accept my apology.'

I see immediately what is happening. All the long months when Eli posed a real threat, Degan had to pretend otherwise. He didn't want to lose me. But now that the threat is gone, it's safe for his rage to appear. I brace myself and inhale, choosing my words carefully.

'It isn't about him,' I say. 'It has nothing to do with him. You know that.'

'Don't tell me what I know.'

I swallow.

Degan says, 'He'd make a good Jewish husband, though, you have to admit.'

'It's not . . .' I falter. What can I say? 'I'm sorry.'

'You're *sorry*? And you want to screw Eli?'

'I didn't mean it,' I say. 'I really, truly, didn't mean it. I just . . .'

His jaw is clenched. 'Then why did you say it?'

'I don't know. It was stupid.'

'I don't know if I can handle the class,' he says, his anger taking a turn.

Without the class I'm lost.

'That woman,' he says, referring to Harriet.

'I know. But we need to look at the bigger picture.'

'What bigger picture?' he challenges.

'The class is just another hoop to jump through.'

He's silent. He has no desire to jump through any hoops and we both know it. I press my eyes shut. When I open them, he's looking at me, his face softer.

'What makes *me* mad is that you should have been in there with the Jewish partners tonight.'

'What do you mean?'

'I mean, I think you're Jewish. Already. Now. You're just realizing it for the first time.'

I nod and reach for his hand. An uneasy truce.

'I really am sorry,' I say.

When we get home, Degan shovels the walk while I get ready for bed. He crawls in beside me. We fall asleep, and wake in the middle of the night clinging to each other. We make love roughly, violently, trying to cover up the unanswered questions.

EIGHT

CHARLOTTE DOES NOT SEEM SURPRISED to hear we've been fighting. 'As a wedding approaches, the stakes in a relationship get higher,' she says.

'The funny thing is, Degan wasn't as worried about Eli before, when he might have had cause to be. And now he's worried for no reason.'

'Are you still thinking about Eli?'

'No. I'm not.' I weigh my words and find them to be true. The sentiment flakes a bit on the surface, but the core of it is genuine.

Charlotte says, 'Perhaps it's now safe for Degan to acknowledge his worry. Now that the real threat is gone.'

'That's exactly what I was thinking,' I concede.

Charlotte crosses her ankles demurely. 'So if Eli is out of the picture, who will be your Jewish guide?'

I pause. I can't tell if she's being rhetorical.

'I'll be my own Jewish guide?' I say, in a little kid voice, shrugging and looking to her to see if this is the answer she's after.

'Is that what you want?'

'I asked you first.'

She smiles. There's a light layer of concealer caught in the creases around her mouth, but her words are pure, unadorned. She's asking me what help I need.

'I've been trying to muscle through it,' I say. 'Alone.'

'Because you want to do it alone or because you feel you have no other option?'

I shrug again. 'Isn't it obvious?'

'No, actually. It isn't.'

'Who's going to help me? My father certainly isn't.'

'Should he?'

'*Shouldn't* he? He's the parent, right? Aren't I supposed to be able to look to him?'

'You're angry at him.'

'I'm *not* angry at him,' I snap.

She nods, her face placid. I have a flash of what it would be like to slap her. I puff out my cheeks and slowly let the air out. 'Maybe I am angry,' I say. 'But I don't want to be. I get it. At least, intellectually. He didn't grow up with it. He knows nothing about it. I know way more than he does.'

'Does that also make you angry?'

My eyes fill with tears.

'Helpless,' she suggests. 'Sad.' It is unlike her to supply me with the words. I nod, biting my lower lip.

'Make room for the feeling,' she tells me.

I give in and let myself cry, hard and gasping, for several minutes, leaning over with my face in my palms. Then I look up and shake my head. I take a deep breath, glance around the room. 'I feel better,' I say, and laugh. The heavy dread is gone. 'That's all it takes? To, uh, what did you say? Make room for the feeling?'

'Sometimes.'

I pull on my right earlobe. 'I always feel that if I start to cry, I won't be able to stop.' As I say this, I remember Granny Pick saying the same thing. My inheritance.

I look to Charlotte, my face scrubbed clean. 'The thing about the Jewish guide,' I say. 'What should I do?' Only very occasionally do I allow myself to ask her advice directly.

'You'd like to find someone – someone *appropriate* – to help you navigate the new cultural Judaism you're discovering.'

I nod to confirm.

'Why don't you ask for a guide?'

'Ask who?'

She sweeps her hand through the air above her head and raises her eyebrows.

'You mean, like, ask the universe?' I giggle. 'Like, put it out there?'

'Yes,' she said. 'Or however you'd like to think about it.'

I nod. Why not. How could it hurt?

At home in bed I fold my hands discreetly under my pillow. To be seen – by Degan, by myself – in a real prayer position, on my knees (which is the Christian prayer position anyway, I realize), would be too much. But I close my eyes, and this time when I try to picture God, the image that comes is a country sky, dark and full of stars. 'I would like a friend,' I whisper. 'Dear God, please bring me a Jewish friend.'

❧

On Sunday morning I gather up my water bottle and my knee pads and walk through the slush to the contact jam. I wave at Michael from across the room and warm up with a woman with spiky red hair and a purple body suit. We tumble around a little, crack each other's backs. The relief of physical communication below the busy level of my head.

Toronto is a big city, but, like any place, circles overlap. The writers and musicians, the painters, the dancers. I'm not surprised to see Shayna, Eli's friend with the beautiful voice, stretching out her long legs against the banister.

She sees me, too, and gives a little half wave. 'Alison, right?'

I walk the few metres to where she's standing.

'Do you come to the jam?' she asks. 'I haven't seen you before.'

'Not always. Often. But we know each other from—'

'I remember,' she says.

This time the pause is comfortable. We lean against the wall, watching as dancers begin to assemble their bodies into complex puzzles. Ariel flounces past in dinosaur pyjama pants, waggling his fingers in my direction. Shayna takes up her stretching again, unfolding her long limbs the way a grasshopper might. 'How's it all going?' she asks, holding her heel in her hand, extending her leg while bracing herself against the wall.

'Good,' I say. I scrunch up my face. 'I can't remember what I told you last time, but I'm studying for conversion. My fiancé and I.'

She lowers her leg and looks at me properly for the first time. 'You're converting?'

'Maybe. We'll see.'

'Is your fiancé Jewish?'

'No.'

'Wow,' she says. 'That's brave.'

'Thank you?'

She laughs.

'No, I'm serious,' she says. She looks me in the eye to make sure I hear what she's saying. 'Most people who convert are marrying someone Jewish.'

I feel the blood rush to my face, feel that exquisite mixture of pain and pleasure that comes from being seen when you're vulnerable.

'It's a problem that he's not,' I say. 'The *beit din* doesn't want to create an intermarriage.'

'What do you mean?'

'If they convert me and I then marry a Gentile . . .'

She squints. 'They know your dad is Jewish?'

I nod unhappily. Shayna sighs. 'We have a history of turning people away.'

We rest our eyes on the dance floor in front of us, the mass of moving bodies. Someone grunts with pleasure or exertion; someone's bare foot squeaks across the floorboards. I hear something that sounds suspiciously like a fart, but nobody comments or apologizes.

'If there's anything I can do to help,' Shayna says.

Up close, I see the space on her forehead where her eyebrows have been plucked.

I nod, and she qualifies her offer: 'I mean, I'm pretty busy. But I'd like to help you. If you need anything.'

I do, I think. I need a friend like you.

I picture her speaking her mind with Eli. I picture her onstage, letting loose her brilliant spool of song.

'I grew up very . . .' She pauses. 'I grew up very Jewish. There weren't many Jews in Peterborough, so my parents really emphasized it. School, summer camp, family life.'

There's another silence, then she asks, 'Do you have somewhere to go for Pesach?'

I blink.

'Passover,' she says.

'Oh, I don't know. I haven't really – *we* haven't really—'

A man with dark dreadlocks approaches and taps her on the shoulder. 'Dance?' he asks, raising his eyebrows.

'Sure.' She turns back to me and smiles. 'Stay in touch, Alison,' she says.

⌀

Something about the conversation with Shayna, the simple fact of her, encourages me. A prayer directly answered, as though God has waved a magic wand and granted me the perfect answer to my wish. I suggest to Degan that we start to practice Shabbat in earnest. 'Sure,' he says.

'That was easy.'

We abandon '24 Hours Unplugged' like a too-small T-shirt: tossed in the corner and forgotten. On Friday afternoon I check my email for the last time. My cousin Lucy writes that she has been invited to teach in Israel. Would I think of joining her for a visit? I'm not ready for Israel, but I thank her for the offer.

In response to my question, she hesitates, but she agrees to hold a corner of our wedding *chuppah*. If we have one.

She signs her email 'Shabbat Shalom! (for tomorrow).'

In my Inbox, as well, are six other emails from my publicist, an urgent message from my website provider and a new sluice of requests for writerly help. I shut the whole system down.

There ought to be an expression for the precise kind of relief that accompanies turning off the computer for a full day. Shabbat would be worth it for this alone.

I do as our textbook says and 'prepare the environment', which means I wash the dishes and wipe the kitchen counters for the first time in days. I make my new favourite curried chickpea soup from the Rebar cookbook. Then I go to the gym and run hard on the treadmill for forty-five minutes. I come home and shower; the calm in the apartment is palpable. The sun is setting. The new day beginning.

Degan gets back from a hard day with clients. 'Shabbat Shalom,' he says.

I'm ravenous after my workout, but when I suggest skipping the change box devoted to charity and going straight to the meal, Degan says, 'No! *Tzedakah* is the most important part.'

We bless the light, the bread, the wine. We eat slowly and talk about our wedding, about our future children and about ritual. A child who grows up with Shabbat will know comfort and stillness, will know at least one way to God. We make a game out of practising our Hebrew, and brainstorm who might hold the other poles of our *chuppah*. We make love without protection. A baby. It feels not only possible but fated.

Bashert.

Later, before bed, I remember to check the mail. I stand on the porch in my slippers, moonlight in my hair. A manila envelope is sticking out of the mailbox. The return address is McClelland & Stewart publishers. The first copy of my new poetry book, *The Dream World*. The culmination of years of work has arrived in an envelope so light that it might contain nothing. A chapter ends, a new one begins. I hold its thin weight in my hand.

NINE

MUSIC NIGHT IS A TRADITION Degan and I started in St John's – one night a month when our writer friends come bearing instruments and we abandon the books we are writing in favour of song. On Thursday, the doorbell rings at nine. It's a fellow poet, a guitar case strung over his shoulder. Other poets and novelists fill the porch behind him. The harmonicas and mandolins pile up. We drink, and sing Johnny Cash and Willie Nelson and early Neil Young. The din escalates; the ashtrays fill up on the back porch. The music turns current: the Decemberists, AA Bondy. More guitars arrive, and Degan pulls out his keyboard.

The evening peaks around two in the morning when, for a brief moment, there are forty people stamping their feet and hollering along with Bruce Springsteen that they are sick of sitting around trying to write their books. The floorboards vibrate; a bookshelf collapses. Several people take this as a cue and pack up their instruments. There are last cigarettes on the back porch while cop cars drift by below us in the street.

At four in the morning there are five of us left.

'Look what I've got.' Someone pulls out a handful of white pills.

'Advil?' I ask.

The friend grins. 'Ecstasy.'

To say I'm not a drug person is an understatement. One drag of a joint makes me curl up like a grub from paranoia. But our friend says, 'This is so different from pot. So much better. So clean. Just trust me.'

'Ecstasy,' Degan says. 'Is it, like, sexy?'

'Sorry, pal,' says the friend. 'It's totally not. If it's cut with speed, it might feel sexy. But this, the pure stuff . . .' She shakes the pills in her palm like dice. 'This ecstasy is purely existential.'

Maybe because of how hard the winter has been, or because of how relieved I am that it's finally over, I obey without question. I swallow my pill. Degan swallows his. Around the room, others follow suit. We slump on the sofas, waiting for the drug to hit.

'I don't feel anything,' I complain. I pause. 'But my teeth are kind of tickly.'

Degan picks up his guitar, plays a few bars of 'California Dreamin''. The words are so beautiful: a windswept street, brown leaves blowing down it at dawn. Tears stream down my face. Then, just as quickly, they dry up. The flip side of grief is a blazing, blistering gratitude for being alive. We lie around grinning at one another. An hour passes. Someone scratches their leg. Two more hours pass. The little voice in my head that constantly narrates my life (better change my hair appointment, I'm not looking alert enough, I wonder what Julian thought about what I just said) stops. Entirely. It is replaced with a cavernous, cool emptiness, a calm that drifts slowly across my field of vision like snowflakes seen through huge, distant windows.

The warehouse of my self has been ransacked, but there's no need to do anything about it, no useless searching for the culprit.

'They did a study,' someone says.

An hour passes.

'They did a study where they gave Zen monks pure ecstasy.

The monks said you would practise for *years* to get even a taste of this.'

The minor feuds between writers in the room, the jealousies, are abandoned. We dance, then forget our feet and fall back onto the couches, smiling. Visible darts of light beam from the corners of our eyes. Technically, I know, it's just an inhibition of serotonin uptake. But after the darkness of these long winter months, I want always to live in this light.

The next day I wake up and grope around on my bedside table for my watch: 5:25. How can it be so early? We just went to sleep. Then I realize it's 5:25 in the afternoon.

I roll over onto my back and cover my eyes with my forearm. It takes me several minutes to force myself up out of the bed. My T-shirt is plastered to my back with sweat. I get in the shower: the drops feel like sparks on my skin, each one distinct, each alive. The water is simultaneously boiling hot and freezing cold. I towel off; in the mirror my eyes are wild and my pupils enormous.

I've made a date. When my old school friend Jordan heard what I was going through, he suggested someone I might contact, a cousin of his father's named Aaron, who lives in Toronto and has a big interest in Judaism and the Holocaust. Their family is Czech, the same as mine. Aaron's number had sat crumpled in my pants pocket for weeks; when I finally fished it out, I figured it couldn't hurt to try. I called and we set up a date for Shabbat dinner. Tonight the date has arrived.

I dress hurriedly and scrawl a note for Degan, who is still passed out on the sofa. A taxi whisks me uptown to Forest Hill. The houses here have big lawns, and Saabs parked in the driveways, and pillars like Southern plantations. An uneasy silence buffers the neighbourhood; not even Toronto's omni-present ambulance sirens permeate the insulated atmosphere.

Aaron, a balding man in his fifties wearing a shirt and tie, greets me at the door. 'Shabbat Shalom,' he says.

I wait to take his cue about shaking hands in greeting; he doesn't reach out to touch me.

'Isn't your fiancé coming?' he asks.

I flush. 'He had to go out of town,' I fib, picturing Degan prone on the couch.

Aaron hesitates for half a second, then says, 'Okay! Next time!'

I take off my shoes and enter the front hall, my feet sinking into inches of plush carpet. A huge crystal chandelier beams light in every direction, like the rays of a child's crudely drawn sun. I blink rapidly, trying to regulate the brilliance flooding my eyes. Aaron shows me into a dining room. There's a long table covered in a white linen cloth, around which fifteen people are seated. I had been under the impression this was just a small dinner. 'Everyone, this is Alison,' says Aaron.

Everyone murmurs hello.

It's clear that they've been waiting for me, sitting around the table for God knows how long, unable to begin until I arrived.

I have not eaten anything other than potato chips in twenty-four hours and the smell of chicken soup wafting in from the kitchen is almost unbearable. Saliva pools in my mouth. My jaw aches from hours of clenching my teeth. Jaw clenching, I suddenly realize, is the reason ravers chew soothers. I'd never clued in before.

I'm introduced to Aaron's wife, Sylvie, who I mistake for his daughter at first and who wishes us a Good Shabbos in a fabulously thick New York accent. The other guests include the owner of a huge hamburger chain and the head of a big

Liberal think tank. I don't catch anyone's name. I am unable to turn my head to match faces with labels. It is stuck facing forward on my neck, as though with Krazy Glue.

The candles have already been lit. Next is the hand-washing ritual. We move single file into the kitchen, where a special two-handled goblet has been placed beside the sink, along with a tea towel embroidered with the Hebrew blessing. The rest of the crowd speeds through the process; when it is my turn, I look to Aaron. I have just met him; we've exchanged maybe two hundred words. But he seems to know I need help. He recites a line of the blessing; I repeat it after him. He recites another line; I repeat that. We are looking in each other's eyes; the call and response is like saying wedding vows. Heady and intense. I turn away from him to hide the size of my pupils.

Back at the table, the blessing is said over both plain and whole wheat challah. Apparently there is also a difference between egg challah and water challah; one tastes better but leaves more crumbs. Aaron says to the assembly, although I get the sense it's for my benefit, 'There is a blessing for everything. If you were *really* religious, you would do nothing all day but say blessings.'

'For example?' I ask.

'There is a blessing for going to the bathroom, to thank God for giving you a body that works.'

The Hamburger King, a small man with watery eyes, says, 'No small thing! A body that works!'

Aaron scoffs. 'You don't say it? The bathroom blessing?'

'I do. At least once a day.'

'Are you kidding?' Aaron asks. 'Really?'

I can see that Aaron doesn't like being caught out as deficient in terms of his observance.

I sit with my tongue thick in my mouth while words fly like coloured ribbons snapped high over my head. Half the guests are American, and talk turns to the American primaries, Obama versus Hillary Clinton. 'Would the American people ever vote in a black president?' someone asks.

And someone else answers, 'No. If Obama gets the Democrats, then John McCain will take the presidency.'

The son of the Hamburger King, it is revealed, once went on a date with Monica Lewinsky.

The meal starts with bowls of clear chicken broth, a single sprig of dill suspended in the centre. We polish off the salad of walnuts and cranberries and go into the kitchen to serve ourselves for the main course. A Filipina maid is loading the dishwasher. This would be considered forbidden work for a Jew on the Sabbath, but it's okay for a Gentile to do it in a Jewish home. I help myself to melt-in-your-mouth meat the texture of pulled pork. But of course it can't be pork. It's beef brisket.

Back at the table, a second maid hovers in the corner. Something about her strikes me as odd. I manage to sneak another look and then I see: she is made out of papier mâché. A life-sized, looming model of a maid.

The dummy is tilted precariously toward the table: my pupils yawn wider. I look again and could swear I see her wink. I think of Marta, the hired help I am writing about in my novel – and the woman around whom all the action turns.

As we eat, I am enticed by Sylvie – God, I love that New York accent! – to tell my story to the assembly, which elicits a deluge of name-dropping and story after story of Jews who were raised Christian. The journalist Katherine Ashenburg has written an essay about it. The cardinal of Paris, it turns out, was a Jew.

Aaron, at the head of the table, has been quiet throughout. But now he turns to me. 'I've just come back from Israel,' he says.

I feel I am expected to give a particular response but am unsure what it is. I shift in my chair.

'I was there on a mission!' His mouth is smiling, but his eyes betray a deadly seriousness. 'I'm a Zionist. Unabashed.'

'So the mission was . . .' My voice trails off.

'The mission was, and *is*, to bring lapsed Jews back to Judaism. *Baal teshuvah* – it literally means "master of return". Bringing *secular* Jews back to the religious element.'

I clear my throat. 'That's interesting.'

Aaron calls me by name – 'Alison,' he says, and I sit up as though being called on at school. 'Alison, I believe in the idea of a Jewish soul.' He puts his cutlery down. The table has fallen silent. 'I don't just believe it. I *know* it to be true.'

I want to trust this, but I don't quite dare.

'How do you know?' I ask.

'I just do.' He looks me in the eye. 'And I can see that you have one,' he says.

I draw a sharp breath. How can he tell? We've only just met. I'm silent, composing myself. The rest of the table falls away into political debate – I hear the names of congressmen, senators. It is just Aaron and me again, our eyes locked.

'A Jewish soul?' I say.

He nods. And this time I allow myself to believe him.

At the end of the night I give Aaron a copy of my first book, *Question & Answer*, which contains a series of poems about Granny's life after the Holocaust. I've brought it along at his request. 'Shall I sign it for you?' I ask.

'Yes, please. But not now.'

'I can just—' I dig around in my bag. 'I'm sure I have a pen.' I squint; the light from the crystal chandelier is not as glaring as it was when I entered. The first hint of darkness is filtering in at the corners of my eyes.

'We'll do it the next time we meet,' he says.

I suddenly clue in. 'No writing on the Sabbath.'

He smiles. 'No work of any kind.'

He has the demeanour of a joker, but I see he is serious: the chandelier is on a timer so they don't have to turn it off manually, which would also technically count as work. I make a mental note to wait until I'm out on the street to call myself a taxi.

I thank Aaron profusely and go down into the night. The chemicals are leaving me quickly now; dread nuzzles at my neck. That familiar, silky black snout. I open my eyes wide and try to see the blinding light again, but its absence is as palpable as its fleeting presence was. As big and as empty.

When I arrive home, Degan is out, but there is a plant with a single pink blossom propped up on my keyboard, and a note: 'Good Shabbos, my love.'

TEN

MY MOTHER LOVES NOTHING MORE than to clip articles from the newspaper and send them to her daughters in the mail. Flood insurance, flu immunization, the dangers of eating tomatoes from a tin: they are notes of caution, dispatches of disaster narrowly averted. When I open today's mail, I find an article about the photography exhibit at McMaster University, Roman Vishniac: A Vanished World. Its subject is Eastern European Jews in 1938 and 1939.

Mum has included a short note: 'Do you want to go?'

It takes us several weeks to arrange a time that works for her, Dad and me. On the way there we stop in at Mum's parents' house in Hamilton. My Martin grandparents are both ninety years old, and have been married for sixty-six years. I give them a copy of my new book, *The Dream World*; I've dedicated it to them. Poetry is foreign to them, but they are pleased, I think, by the tribute.

In some ways I belong to the Martins, to our raucous and spirited family gatherings. My Martin cousins Lindsay and Heather were two of my best friends growing up. Still, as I sip tea and help Gramps with his puzzle, I wonder again about my general lack of interest – at least in terms of my own creative work – in this side of the family. It is not for lack of stories: my great-great-great-great-grandfather on the Martin side was the founder of the modern-day Humane Society. He was known as 'Humanity Dick' – a nickname bestowed by his friend King

George IV. Humanity Dick's life included all manner of intrigue: political office, romantic scandals, shipwrecks. A new biography has been written about him; I have not even made the time to read it. Gramps lent me his copy and I return it now, sheepish, with nothing to say.

The Vishniac exhibition is smaller than I'd expected. The photos show Hasidic Jews, rabbis with long beards and tefillin strapped to their foreheads. The children look raggedy and hungry. Dad calls me over to a picture of a skinny man with a box of wares displayed at his feet.

'This was us.'

'What do you mean?'

'Four generations ago your Bondy ancestors were peddlers. And on the Pick side, three generations ago.'

'Really?'

He nods. 'These are our genes,' he says, pointing at the photos. 'The genes that make me a go-getter. Proactive, resourceful, successful.'

Perhaps because of the secrecy he grew up with, Dad is acutely attuned to antisemitism, to any sort of stereotype or generalization about his people. Now, though, he says, 'If you want to talk about race, well, each race develops traits. The Jews were cheap – because they had to be!'

Uneasy with this line of thinking, I change the topic. 'Do you think it would have been important to Gumper to marry a Jew?' I ask.

'Why do you ask?'

'No reason.'

'Yes,' Dad says. 'Of course.'

I hear Mum behind us, facing one of the photos, humming the same three notes in rapid succession.

'And you, his son? Did Gumper want *you* to marry a Jew?'

'Of course not!'

So I'm not wrong in being a little confused.

'And he wouldn't have wanted *you* to get married under a *chuppah*,' Dad says. He pauses. 'And neither do I. If you want my opinion.'

I swallow. Digging around in my bag, I pull out a book I have recently read, a graphic memoir called *I Was a Child of Holocaust Survivors* by Bernice Eisenstein. I show Dad the opening quote, from Deuteronomy. 'It's powerful, isn't it?' I ask.

He reads the quote aloud: ' "Only guard yourself and guard your soul carefully, lest you forget the things your eyes saw, and lest these things depart your heart all the days of your life, and you shall make them known to your children, and your children's children." '

I watch his face: it's slack. I notice that his hair, which I used to think of as grey, has now turned predominantly white.

'So?' I prompt.

'It's powerful,' he concedes. 'But I don't see what it has to do with me.'

I take a deep breath. The connection is so obvious that I'm at a loss even to articulate it. I venture, 'I don't quite buy Gumper's transformation. Is it possible for anyone to change so deeply? How could the man who said he wouldn't convert if he were the last Jew on earth suddenly make such a radical shift?'

'The historical context was powerful,' Dad says.

'Yes. But there must have been a part of him that longed, a little part, well hidden away.'

But Dad won't give an inch.

ELEVEN

I CONSIDER THAT I AM WRONG. Maybe none of this applies to me, to us, at all; maybe I'm a dog barking at imaginary squirrels. I know how to check. Back at home, I pull out the tape of Gumper's cousin Vera; she was interviewed for Steven Spielberg's Shoah Project, a massive documentation of most of those still alive who lived through the Holocaust. I've had a copy of the tape for years but have been unable to bring myself to watch it. But now is the time. I'm finally ready.

I prop myself up in bed with Degan's laptop and slide in the disk. The opening shot is Vera's enormous, gnarled hand, the knuckles I remember from when I first visited her, holding a piece of cardboard with her name written on it. Vera Feldman. The camera pans up to her face. Grey curls, lipstick, round eyeglasses. There is something childlike in her awareness of the viewer; she sits up straight, tentative but smiling. Heart-breaking in her willingness.

She tells the interviewer slowly about her privileged girlhood. Her house in Malá Skalice had a bowling alley, a tennis court. I know from her daughter-in-law that Vera once owned 'a suit to match her racing car'. Imagine.

She tells the camera haltingly that there were only two Jewish families in Skalice; they went to nearby Náchod for the High Holidays. Her grandfather was religious 'in his own way'. There was no Jewish community where she lived, but Jacob, who was Gumper's grandfather, too, taught her what she needed to know.

As the subject of the 1930s comes up, Vera bites her lip, tears up.

'In May of 1933 my son, Jan, was born,' she says.

Jan – or John, in English – was also Gumper's name. She looks back at the camera and continues. 'In 1938 my daughter, Eva, was born.'

A pause to let the date sink in.

'Jews from Germany started coming to our town in '33, '34, '35,' Vera says. 'They told horrible stories.'

'Did you believe them?' the interviewer asks.

'Yes!'

But then Vera tempers her answer. 'We helped, we gave money, but part of us did not want to believe.'

'And did you believe the same thing could happen in Czechoslovakia?'

Vera inhales, aghast. 'No,' she replies, as though she has been asked whether she believes in the Tooth Fairy.

Vera describes the slow deterioration of Jewish rights. First they could have no servants. Then there was a curfew.

They had to give up their radio.

They were forbidden from owning a dog.

Eventually the Nazis took Vera's husband. He was gone several months. When he returned, he had lost thirty kilos. He had been beaten so badly that both his eardrums were broken.

'Then,' Vera says, 'on September 17, 1942 we were taken away from our children.'

The unseen interviewer does not extend condolences. There are no soothing sounds, no murmurs of empathy. The goal of the project is just to get every fact down.

They were removed to an internment camp in Moravia,

Vera says. The interviewer makes her stop and spell the name of the camp, which she does ploddingly, mechanically. She and her husband could have been anywhere; the important point was that little Jan and Eva were not with them. Vera and her husband were housed in a stable; there was nothing to eat. The beatings were awful. They were with her parents; her father was diabetic.

Vera tears up as she says this. I hold my breath.

'They took away his insulin,' she tells the camera, weeping. 'They beat him. They took away his insulin and beat him.'

Daddy.

'He couldn't stand it. He died.' Tears running down her face. 'It was the eighth of November. I was with him. After the war I tried to find out what happened to the commander. Tunz was his name. I hoped he'd died, but all the Nazis fled. Maybe he's living here,' she says, hopeless, gesturing around herself to refer to her apartment building, the state of New York, the whole country.

I pause the video and email my cousin Lucy. She writes back right away, saying that the Central Database of Shoah Victims' Names has a file on Hermann Bondy: 'beaten and starved to death. D. Nov. 8, 1942, age 66.'

Hermann was married to Ella Kafka.

Yes, *that* Kafka. Vera's mother, Ella, was Franz Kafka's cousin.

When I press Play again, Vera is talking about the literary legend. He used to stay in his room whenever anyone visited, so nobody ever got to talk to him. And Vera remembers going to his funeral and crying because his mother looked like a witch.

Later, Vera and her husband were sent to Theresienstadt, a fortress town that was just a stop on the way to Auschwitz for most Czech Jews. They arrived there in December of 1942.

The interviewer asks about how they got there: did they have to walk?

'Yes, yes,' Vera says, impatient, but by some miracle their children were there, and that was all that mattered.

There was very little food, of course. Some of the Czech gendarmes helped to smuggle in supplies. Vera had a mysterious high fever. Finally it was discovered she had three broken ribs from being so badly beaten in the previous camp.

Vera's husband was put in a military barrack. The overcrowding made everyone sick. Gumper's best friend dubbed the general sickness 'the Terezinka', but Vera knows the individual diagnoses of the ailments her family suffered from and tells the camera. Her husband caught infectious hepatitis. Little Eva caught scarlet fever. Jan got pneumonia.

They did not die from these conditions – although that might have been preferable to what came later.

TWELVE

THE FOLLOWING DAY Dad has a meeting with an old client in Toronto and we decide to have lunch. I wait for him at the Second Cup inside the Jewish Community Centre at Bloor and Spadina. He arrives twenty minutes late, the collar of his long down coat caught awkwardly under the strap of his backpack. 'I went to the wrong Second Cup,' he shouts.

I put a finger to my lips to show he should lower his voice.

'I had to get out my computer and look at your email again,' he continues, still shouting. 'If you want some good people-watching, go to the Second Cup across the street!'

He tries to take off his backpack, but his arm gets caught. 'There was a man,' he yells, as I help him untangle the strap, 'a man with a big beard and dirt on his face. But he was wearing a suit and tie!'

'A homeless man?' I ask.

Dad nods. 'He looked really neat!'

I know he is thinking of our ancestors, the peddlers.

We walk along Bloor Street to the restaurant in companionable silence. A car swooshes past, throwing up a spray of slush. I pause, squint into the bright winter sun, shielding my face with my eyes. When we pass the other Second Cup, Dad cranes his neck. I know he's looking for his homeless man.

'I brought you that book,' I say. 'Remember the one I told you about?'

'No,' he says.

'*I Was a Child of Holocaust Survivors*. With that beautiful Deuteronomy quote, about teaching your children.'

'Oh,' he says. 'No, thanks.'

I swallow.

'Why don't you want to read it?' I ask, unable to drop the subject.

'It has nothing to do with me,' he says.

There's a roar as a snowplow passes; this time we step sideways and dodge the slush. The bright sun glints off the plow's mirror, throwing out a rainbow prism. A skinny teenager dekes around us, hands in his jean-jacket pockets, his music playing so loudly we can hear the *thunk* of the bass from his ear buds.

'But when I'm in Baltimore next week,' Dad says, 'I'm going to that Holocaust memorial.'

'Why the memorial and not the book?'

'The thing about the Holocaust was its *scope*. The sheer numbers. But one individual story . . .'

'Isn't important?'

He shrugs.

'I guess I thought you might have something in common with the author.'

'Like what?'

'You're the same age,' I say feebly.

'And?'

'Well, your stories are very different, but the psychology of growing up in the shadow of the Holocaust—'

'Her parents were in the camps?'

'Yes.'

'Mine weren't.'

'I know.'

'In the camps, out of the camps,' Dad says. 'That's a significant difference.'

I fumble in my purse for my sunglasses and use them to cover my eyes. He is my only link to our family's past; he opens and closes on a whim, entirely unpredictable.

And I take after him entirely.

The restaurant is full of businesswomen in tailored suits, texting and picking at salads. We order steak frites and share a glass of wine. Over dessert I work up the courage to ask again if he will read the book, not for himself but as a favour for me.

'You're still thinking about that?'

'I found it very moving. Maybe it would help explain what I'm going through.'

Dad eyes me. 'Of course, sweetie. I'd do anything for you.'

I should have known this was the way to ask.

He pays our bill, and we traipse through the sunny street back to his car. We turn down the side street where he's parked; he stops in his tracks. 'Shit!' he exclaims.

My hand flies to my heart.

A girl shovelling the sidewalk jumps, then backs away from Dad, her eyes wide.

'A parking ticket!' Dad yells. 'The buggers!'

I exhale. A *parking ticket*?

He goes to inspect the sign, which states, clearly, there is no parking during the day. 'I'll take them to court!' he shouts.

The girl stows her shovel, then goes inside her house and closes the door behind her.

Dad continues to pace, looking up at the sign and wringing his hands. When his back is turned, I place the book on the passenger seat of his Volvo. I pat its cover once, to wish it good passage.

THIRTEEN

A WEEK LATER, I go away to speak at a conference on the life of Bronwen Wallace, a remarkable Canadian poet and short story writer in whose memory an award for emerging writers is given. On the drive home, I pass a United Church with a sign outside advertising Sunday-morning services. I think: *I will not go to church anymore.* I think: *I am finished with church.*

But although my wedding is imminent – a few short months away – I am no closer to solving the dilemma of what comes next in terms of conversion.

Degan meets me at the door of the apartment. I feel a rush of pleasure on seeing him after my time away. We print out a list of wedding guests and look online for a professional photographer. While he downloads Mendelssohn's 'Wedding March' for me to listen to, Degan laughs at the cliché. He wants me to consider whether it's something I might want to process to.

'What do you mean, "process"?'

He grins. 'Walk down the aisle.'

He has read about someone whose *chuppah* was covered in the handprints of their families and friends. A lovely idea, we agree. Even if no rabbi would marry us, nobody can stop us from doing as we please in our ceremony. We decide that Degan will break a glass underfoot once we are married, as per Jewish custom.

We huggle on the couch – hug + cuddle – and try to

memorize the Hebrew letters we've been assigned for our latest Jewish Information Class. To our untrained eyes, the letters look maddeningly similar. For example, there are two sideways *C*s. One makes the quintessential guttural Hebrew ch, as in the composer Bach or the bread eaten on the Sabbath, challah. The other makes a k sound, as in the philosopher Immanuel Kant. How will we remember the difference?

The k sound, *kaf*, has a single dot in its centre. It looks, we decide, like a Cyclops. And the curled-up edges of the *C* look like little girls' hair. So the Cyclops must be female.

We search for a name that begins with the k sound, and come up with Kitty Sherbatsky from Tolstoy's *Anna Karenina*. When we see the girl Cyclops, the hard k of Kitty Sherbatsky will remind us of the hard k in *kaf*.

Obviously.

Degan tells me about the class I missed while I was away. Harriet taught 'the *shva*', a baffling bit of punctuation indicating a pause that occurs mid-word in some places and not in others. He recounts being dragged up in front of the class to recite prayers.

'You're a trooper,' I say.

'You're away cavorting with the writers and I'm stuck here singing and dancing in Hebrew.'

He does a little vaudeville imitation, shuffling and tapping his feet.

I laugh at the thought of my pale British boy dancing at the front of the class. 'What?' he asks.

'Nothing.' I giggle some more.

Try as we might, we cannot make sense of the *shva*. We pour over Degan's class notes. Finally I email Harriet to ask for help.

She writes back, 'That's what you get for being absent!'

I reply, apologizing, and invite her to my upcoming book launch.

She answers, 'Yikes! It conflicts with our class! I definitely won't be attending!'

Degan wonders if we should start over in September, with the other teacher everyone raves about.

◦

I meet my mother in Guelph at the wedding caterer's. The caterer says she will take care of plates, chairs, chair covers, centrepieces. The wine will be 'continual pour'.

'What about a riser?' asks Mum.

'Like a podium?' I ask. 'Why would we need one?'

'You want everyone to hear you,' Mum says. 'Especially if you're going to be standing under that thing.'

By which, I know, she means a *chuppah*.

After the meeting I stop by my sister's house to plunder their communal costume box. Shayna has emailed to ask if I want to be her date for Purim, a minor holiday sometimes called the Jewish Halloween. I find a black slip dress and a bright red wig, and decide to go as a devil. I call Shayna on my way back into the city. 'Do you have any horns?'

She laughs. 'No. And I didn't have a costume, either – I forgot to grab something from the dress-up box at school like I usually do – until I bumped into a friend on the street. Just an hour ago. I described the angry witch living in my chest these days. Guess what she pulled out of the trunk of her car?' She doesn't wait for me to answer. 'Bloomers. A broomstick, a yellow dress, a perfect black hat. And makeup. A full witch costume. From the *trunk* of her *car*.'

I laugh. 'I'll be there in twenty minutes,' I say.

When I get to her apartment, Shayna pours us glasses of port. The space is small and cozy, with brightly coloured pillows and strings of beads hanging in the doorway; Shayna has to duck to move between the rooms. In the kitchen there's a Jesus magnet on the fridge. The Son of God is nailed to the cross, with a selection of accompanying magnetic outfits: a pink tutu, a wrestler's leotard, a black T-shirt with a skull and crossbones.

It's the first time Shayna and I have spent time together just the two of us; we talk fast as we pull on our costumes, making the quick confessions that women divulge to build intimacy. Me about depression, her about being single.

'What's up with the angry witch?'

She sighs. 'I'm just sick of being alone.'

I make sympathetic noises while applying my mascara. I try to be present, empathetic, but not too eager. I don't want to scare her away.

'Has there been anyone recently?' I ask.

She's bent over her long, willowy leg, applying clear nail polish to a run in her stocking; she looks up. 'Well, as a matter of fact, I did meet someone a few months ago. But it didn't work out.'

She's gazing at me questioningly, her pointy black hat upright. I get the sense there's something I'm supposed to say, but I'm not sure what. And then I get it. It lands like a boulder at my feet. 'It was Eli.'

She's silent.

'Was it?'

She nods unhappily.

'Yes,' she says. 'We had a thing.'

'Oh!' I pause. 'When?'

'Around New Year's,' she says.

My face goes slack as I calculate the timing.

'Shit,' she says. 'No.'

I grimace.

'Something happened with you, as well?'

'No,' I say. I adjust my wig. 'Well, sort of.'

'What do you mean?'

'It was just emotional. But—'

She interrupts. 'When?'

I grimace again. 'Same time. Just before New Year's.'

Shayna straightens; her eyes widen. 'Are you kidding me?' she asks.

'Sadly, no.'

'I don't fucking believe this,' she says. 'I don't even... *really?*'

I'm quiet.

Her face clenches and for a second I'm afraid I've lost her, but she throws an arm around me to show it's not me she's mad at.

'He's such a... he's such... I don't even know what to call him.'

'I have a few ideas,' I say.

She laughs; the taxi honks down on the street.

'That's us,' she says. She raises the bottle. 'More port?'

She fills my glass; I drink it down.

We descend the steps arm in arm, Shayna in her black hat and me in my devil wig. Newly allied in our indignation and our power. People are staring at us, trick-or-treaters in the wrong season. The turbaned taxi driver, presumably Sikh, asks why we are dressed this way. 'It's a Jewish holiday,' Shayna answers.

No fear, no shame, no need or desire to hide the truth.

I recognize these feelings within me only in contrast to her lack of them.

The cabbie drops us off at a tiny, modern Orthodox *shul* on a residential street in the Annex. Again Shayna has to duck her head to get through the doorway. It's as if we have entered a carnival: a solid wall of shouting and laughing, kids and adults alike dressed up as golf clubs, Turkish kings, Madonna. I was worried I would stand out in my fluorescent wig, but the opposite is true: I blend in perfectly.

We slide into our pew. A man dressed in drag waves at Shayna and fluffs his curly wig in our direction. He is moving down the aisle, pouring shots of vodka. The centrepiece of the service is the Purim *shpiel*, a comedic skit that enacts the Book of Esther. The motley crew that climbs onto the bimah has to perform over a steady din of voices. I can only discern vaguely what's going on. Vashti is a drag queen. Queen Esther wants a career. The readers who don't put their mouths close to the microphone are drowned out completely. The words to the song they have written – 'Going to the mikvah and we're gonna get married' – are projected onto a screen overhead. The bad guy is called Haman. He's devised a plot to have every Jew in Persia killed. When you hear his name read aloud, you boo or shake a rattle.

Someone from the congregation shouts, 'They want to kill the terrible Jews! But we'll show them!' The whole room hisses and hollers out their existence, their refusal to ever be erased.

I think of my family, how we hide.

I feel myself backing away from the idea of the wedding *chuppah*. I don't deserve one. These people are too brave for me. Too strong.

The service ends with prayer, and while there is still talking and laughing, most people open their Siddurs, or prayer books, and follow along. There is a lesson here, after all: Esther revealed herself as a Jew, and her honesty is the point on which the plot resolves.

Shayna leans over and points out our place in the prayer book. I've learned enough letters in class to slowly follow along. I ask her which word is Adonai, or God. It consists of two little hooks, implying that it cannot be pronounced. The word *God* like a soft breath of air.

I turn to look at Shayna.

'What?' she asks.

'Nothing.'

'No, what are you thinking?'

'Eli brought us together,' I say. 'We were first introduced at his reading.'

She scoffs. 'We would have met somehow.'

But I'm not so sure.

The book of Esther is one of two books in the Hebrew Bible that do not mention God's name. The explanation is that God is *behind* it all, that only God could make such a wacky series of events turn out well.

FOURTEEN

THE DAY AFTER PURIM is Good Friday, but I take no notice, my head still filled with the razzle-dazzle of the synagogue.

Although we haven't been in touch for a while, Eli sends a long email about how relieved he is to have moved onto another writing project, nothing to do with Orthodox Judaism. Nothing to do with Judaism at all. He felt guilty, he writes, after *Help Me*, as though somehow he was betraying the faith. 'To be honest it really made me sick.'

This is the first I've heard of him feeling this way.

He doesn't mention his girlfriend, or his love life.

When Degan gets home, I tell him I'm waffling about the *chuppah*. I'm thinking of the rowdy Jewish pride at the Purim service, about the contrast between it and my own family's history of hiding. 'Maybe we shouldn't have one,' I say.

'Why not?'

I tell him about Mum's comments, that we'll need a riser to stand on so people can see us under 'that thing'.

'Well, no offence, but your mother . . .'

'It's not just Mum,' I say. 'I need conviction to make that kind of statement. And I'm not sure I have it.'

'Maybe I have conviction.'

He winks and I smile.

'Let me think about it,' he says. 'Now that you're waffling, I feel more attached.'

On Tuesday Dad calls. 'I'm thinking of coming into the city tomorrow evening. What are you up to?'

'It's Gumper's *yahrzeit*,' I say. 'I'm going to synagogue.'

'*Yahrzeit?*'

'The anniversary of his death.'

There's a pause while he calculates the date. 'Oh,' Dad says. 'So it is.' He pauses again. 'Do you mind if I come?'

I hear shuffling in the background, followed by clicking. 'Good girl!' he shouts at the dog.

'Of course not,' I say. 'I'd love for you to come.'

'Maybe I will.'

'To synagogue?'

I want to be sure he has fully understood.

'Am I Jewish or am I not Jewish?'

I can hear his grin over the phone.

❧

The morning of Gumper's *yahrzeit* I wake from a dream of two boy rabbis, my father and my uncle. But in the dream they appear as charcoal sketches, empty, with nothing filled in.

I write the dream down – Charlotte will like this one! – then I get up and brush my teeth, make coffee. Degan goes into the bathroom but leaves the door open; I can see him dabbing his shaving brush in the soap.

'What are you up to today?' he calls.

'Oh, you know. Just taking my father to synagogue for the first time in his life.'

Degan looks up, his chin lathered. 'Seriously?'

I cry when he leaves for work, but mostly out of nerves.

An hour later there's an email: Degan must have written as soon as he arrived at his office. 'I love you,' he writes. 'You're in my thoughts, as is your grandfather. I wish I could be with you for the service today.'

He suggests gently that I clean up our apartment a little before Dad arrives. 'Even passing the vacuum over the front hall will help,' he writes. And instructs me how to change the vacuum bag.

I do the dishes. Wipe the counters. Make our bed properly, with the corners folded down. After, I go out into the March sunshine, remembering the Mourner's Kaddish, the prayer for the dead that will be the centre of the *yahrzeit* service: *yit'gadal v'yitkadash sh'mei rabba* – 'May the great Name of God be exalted and sanctified.' I take some shirts to the dry cleaner's, drop a copy of my new book off to a friend for her birthday, all the while repeating the only line I know by heart: *yit'gadal v'yitkadash sh'mei rabba.* Running on the treadmill, reciting it in my head in time to my pounding feet. In the shower, cooking, preparing to welcome my father. Thinking of Gumper and the prayer that does not mention death, that is affirmation of life itself.

In a few short months our apartment has sprouted a profusion of Judaica. Waiting for Dad to show up, I hide the Shabbat handbooks and the *tzedakah* box in the kitchen for fear of overwhelming him. I flip a stack of Jewish-themed books so the titles on their spines aren't showing. This is a tenuous dance, and I want Dad's support. It occurs to me that I will see him wear a *kippah.*

'You've never been to synagogue before, right?' I ask when he arrives, trying to sound casual.

'Just once. For a funeral.'

I put the kettle on. 'Whose funeral?'

'Dr Fischer's.'

'Your old therapist?'

Dad nods. I take this in.

His therapist was Jewish. Of course he was.

'I'm not sure if you'd remember,' I say, 'but part of that funeral would have been the prayer for the dead.' I explain about the centrality of the Kaddish. The kettle whistles. I move it off the element. 'Maybe we can practise it,' I say.

Dad looks strained. 'Now?'

I nod. 'Before the service.'

Dad clears his throat. 'If Gumper were here, he'd think we were silly.'

He clears his throat again. 'No. He'd be touched. But he wouldn't show it.' Dad pauses. 'What's really touching is that *you're* interested,' he says.

'I'd like to practise the Kaddish,' I repeat.

'In English?'

'It's in Aramaic.'

Dad looks confused.

'In Hebrew,' I say, for simplicity's sake.

I see immediately that I have crossed a psychic boundary. Dad's jaw tightens, and he clears his throat several times in rapid succession. 'Don't say it in Hebrew,' he says. 'Gumper wouldn't like it.'

I acquiesce and we read the prayer together in English. Dad's face is flushed with the effort that I know he's making for me. There's a long silence when we finish.

'Shall we light the candle now?'

Dad shrugs. 'It's up to you,' he says.

I touch the match to the wick. The flame rises. 'Would you like to say a few words about your father?'

Dad is clearing his throat with urgency now, as though afraid he will choke. 'Last night I had a dream,' he finally manages. 'I was hunting with Gumper. He was flushing pheasants, rattling the bushes so they would fly up into full view, but I was scared and didn't take a shot.'

On our way to synagogue we stop at Costco to exchange a printer. In the parking lot we see several Orthodox men with black hats and beards. Dad ogles them. 'This Costco is way better than the one in Kitchener! Better people-watching!'

We arrive early. 'There's a school in the synagogue?' Dad asks.

The kids are just getting out of class, and the halls are full of teachers and parents. The faint smell of peanut butter sandwiches.

I nod.

Dad says, 'It's a busy place.' He stops a teacher to ask how many members there are.

'Seven thousand?' she guesses.

'Wow. A lot more than my church.'

Downstairs in the main sanctuary he looks around, evaluating. A huge stained-glass window throws splotches of pink light over the rows of polished oak pews. I can see he likes the place. Feels at home on a gut level. There is money here, and reverence, but not the stiff formality of Catholicism.

We nod hello as people shuffle in: silk scarves, dark suits, a lone woman in a blue track suit and Nikes.

The service, held in an alcove off to the side of the sanctuary, is almost entirely in Hebrew. We sit and stand, sit and stand, understanding nothing. But then the reader begins to recite the names of the dead. We recognize the names of prominent Toronto Jews: Barbara Frum, Bora Laskin. Shivers break out along my neck and arms as the reader moves through the list. The names are listed alphabetically, and as we move into the *P*s, I worry that Gumper has been forgotten. But then the reader says it, sombre and sincere: 'Jan Pick. May his memory be for a blessing.'

After the service, I turn around and am surprised to see Aaron and Sylvie in the pew behind us. Their own synagogue is Orthodox, but I emailed them about the yarzheit and they decided to come. I introduce everyone. Aaron and Dad shake hands, the Jew who goes to church and the Jew whose mission it is to bring lapsed Jews back into the fold.

'We're going for dinner,' Dad says. 'Would you like to join us?'

Aaron smiles. 'I could suggest a good Kosher Chinese.'

Dad agrees. It's settled.

At the restaurant I eat my dumplings in silence, fumbling with my chopsticks while Dad tells Aaron and Sylvie about Granny and Gumper's arrival in Canada. 'It was 1941.'

Sylvie raises her eyebrows. She asks, in her New York accent, 'Did they come as farmers?

'No.'

Her eyebrows go up even farther. 'Almost no one got into Canada in 1941.'

'Maybe their passports were forged,' Aaron says. 'Maybe they entered as Christians.'

Dad shakes his head. 'Their documents are stamped with "Israelite".'

'Did they change their name when they arrived?'

'It was always Pick. An acronym, from the Latin, standing for "traveller of the Jewish faith" – *perigrinus iudei confessionis.*'

'This must all be a lot for you to absorb,' Aaron says to my father.

Dad lifts a dumpling expertly to his mouth. 'Not really,' he says. 'I'm happy to support Alison.' He points at me with his chopsticks, as though singling me out from a crowd. 'But for me it's nothing more than curiosity. I was telling a friend about coming to the service today. As I was speaking, the feeling went out of me. I felt suddenly empty, flat. I don't really care about the religion.'

I hear the far-off churning of a dishwasher in the restaurant's kitchen. We are quiet. I wonder if Aaron and Sylvie are thinking what I'm thinking: that a sudden numbness signals not an absence of feeling but a deluge of it.

❧

I come home and find the *yahrzeit* candle still lit. Degan is asleep, his form obscured by a pile of pillows and blankets. I move the candle to my desk, beside the SunBox, and write for a few minutes in its sadder, smaller light. There's an email from Shayna, asking how the service went. I reply that it went well, and write to tell Rabbi Klein the same thing. She answers right away: 'Good on you for making the moment happen.'

I crawl into bed beside Degan but am awake into the early hours. The *yahrzeit* candle's light dances wildly on the ceiling. When I finally manage to fall asleep, I dream that it is not Gumper but Dad who has died. There is no content to the dream, no storyline, only a sea of blistering grief. I wake to the truth that one day he will leave me forever.

A wave of dread comes over me then, in the middle of the night; there is something unfinished between us, something more that needs saying.

FIFTEEN

ON THURSDAY AFTERNOON I have an appointment with the woman who is making my wedding dress. The skirt still needs hemming, and adjustments made for the fact that my right breast turns out to be larger than my left. She tries to reassure me this is normal; I'm unconvinced. But out of the pile of silk and thread and lace, something beautiful is beginning to emerge.

Later, Dad calls to say they are talking about my poetry book on the radio. Three panellists, a whole half-hour show dedicated to *The Dream World*. 'They're referring to you as "Pick",' he says, guffawing.

His voice goes serious. 'Granny would have been so proud,' he says.

Granny loved nothing more than being seen, being known to the world, and I think how she would have phoned everyone she knew. We have a video of Dad and Lucy interviewing her. 'Nobody ever calls me,' Granny huffs, fluffing her hair, while the phone rings off the hook in the background.

The interview is entirely different from Vera's, focusing on the logistics of escape rather than the details of imprisonment. Granny gossips about affairs, infidelity, and chastises my grown father like he's a child: 'Your shoes are always dirty. Every time you're here I have to use the . . .' She flicks her manicured fingers at the carpet, unwilling to say the words *vacuum cleaner*.

'I know,' Dad apologizes off-camera. 'I was on the island

yesterday.' He's referring to a piece of land Gumper owned for pheasant shooting.

'It's full of mud there. Dreadful! Look at it.'

'Okay, okay, *okay*,' Dad says.

'Just look at it!' she scolds.

In the interview, as in life, Granny shies away from discussing her inner experience. But there are so many things I'd like to ask her: What did she long for? How did she feel about marrying my grandfather?

Just before their wedding, Gumper's father died. They went ahead, but his aunts all showed up dressed in black and crying. The honeymoon to the ski resort in Italy had to be called off. Granny didn't resent the intrusion, though. She had loved Gumper's father, too. He had shown a special interest in her, almost courting her alongside Gumper, taking her out on the town just the two of them. 'Very modern,' she confides to the camera. 'He wrote me poems on postcards. I wish I'd kept them.'

Granny's lavish watch, which I will wear at my own upcoming nuptials, was made entirely of diamonds and sapphires, a gift from her father-in-law.

~

Degan gets home from work and we drive through the warm green evening up to the north of the city for what is called, on our course outline, the Passover 'workshop'. The neighbourhood is opulent in the worst kind of way, full of houses that Granny, who had wealth and good taste in equal measure, would have called 'monstrosities'. Some are built from utilitarian concrete, with sharp points of glass or steel pointing out at odd angles. Others have enormous porches and pillars out front, as though Jews had colonized the American South.

The houses inspire a rant from Degan about the meaning of *tzedakah* – 'righteous giving' – and how inequality remains unaddressed in Jewish Toronto. We pull up to the temple, enormous and ugly in keeping with its surroundings, and cross the parking lot with a blond girl from our class. 'This is the strangest place,' Degan says. 'Don't you feel like you've landed on the moon?'

An awkward pause follows. 'This is my temple,' the girl says.

Inside, we pay five dollars, put on a name tag and enter a cavernous room that reminds me of the preaching hall in the documentary *Jesus Camp*. There is a young rabbi at the front, plugged into a mic so she can walk around and gesture with her hands. Our class has joined up with the Thursday-night class, and it takes all eighty of us several minutes to find our seats, eight at each round table. I look around and wave at Diane, with baby Tamara asleep on her chest. Once everyone is settled and the whispering and shuffling have ceased, the rabbi, a skinny brunette with a slight overbite, beams at us. She throws her arms in the air like some Southern Baptist. 'Welcome!'

The microphone squeals in protest, and a loud peal of feedback echoes through the room.

She frowns and fiddles with the wires. 'Can you hear me now?' she shouts. We nod unhappily.

Satisfied, the rabbi begins in earnest. 'You will SEE . . .' she says. 'You will SEE . . .'

There's a long pause, as though we are about to see the face of Adonai himself, before she completes the sentence: 'You will see some FOOD items on your table.'

We look down dutifully. I notice for the first time that each table has been furnished with a Seder plate, featuring a limp sprig of parsley, an egg, an orange and several paper muffin cups filled with suspicious-looking goopy substances.

'Who can TELL me . . . WHO can tell me the MEAN-ING . . .' the rabbi says, throwing her arms wide as though to indicate the scope of the heavens.

The meaning of what? Of life? Of death?

'WHO can tell me the meaning of the EGG?'

Total silence. I brace myself for a long and painful night, as though for a visit to the dentist.

'Nobody?' she asks, incredulous. She tries again.

'What about—' She pauses, her eyes closed, her face tilted to the heavens. 'What about the green vegetable? What is the BEST green vegetable to have on your Seder plate?'

I recall how our last class with Harriet focused entirely on the fact that there is no best anything, no one correct way. All Seders are based on custom and geography. Harriet managed three straight hours reiterating this point in different ways.

At a far table someone's hand goes up. 'Horseradish?'

We hear little Tamara gurgle.

'No!' the rabbi shouts, triumphant. 'WHO knows why not?'

Nobody knows why not, but someone else suggests that romaine lettuce might be the best. 'Yes,' the rabbi proclaims. 'And do you know WHY?'

She does not wait for an answer but carefully elucidates the merits of romaine: it is *sweet* at first, with a bitter aftertaste, and reminds us that the Egyptians did take the Jews in at first; that the story wasn't all bad, only the ending.

We slowly and painfully work our way through the other items on the Seder plate. The orange is to welcome women and 'lesbian folk'. The pink cup is Miriam's cup, to go along with Elijah's, and it is filled with water as opposed to wine, for a reason that is never made clear. The exercise requires several hours. In all her endless pontificating, the rabbi says one thing that really strikes me: 'For those of you on the verge of marriage and children, now is the time to learn. Now is the time to get good and COMFORTABLE, so you can give your children a sense of wonder and awe, a sense that THIS is what we DO.'

After the interminable lecture, we split into groups for the 'participatory' component of the evening. One group will be talking about designing your own seder. Another group will be doing a 'craft': colouring a piece of fabric for a matzah cover using fat markers suitable for five-year-olds. Degan and I choose to attend the music session. Maybe we can take back a song for Music Night with the writers. We are ushered into a room where orange plastic chairs are arranged in a circle around a bongo drum. 'Singing and dancing in Hebrew!' I whisper.

Degan shuffles his feet.

Our workshop leader enters: Rabbi Glickman. 'Shalom!' she says brightly.

Tamara lets out a loud squeal in reply. Tom and Diane pretend to shush her, but their faces betray delight in their daughter's precociousness. Two Jews and a Jew-to-be. A perfect family.

We make our way through a book of songs, one for every part of the seder: Sanctifying the Name of God. Washing the Hands. Eating the Green Vegetable.

The customary song 'Dayeinu' – meaning 'it would have been enough' – is a long list of things God did for the Jews.

We shake the maracas Rabbi Glickman has distributed and belt out the words in a rough approximation of Hebrew that I imagine would be incomprehensible to a native speaker. After the long lecture, it's a blissful kind of release; people stand, and dance self-consciously, and then begin to dance in earnest.

Degan shimmies toward me, his earlier mood lifted by the music, his head and shoulders tipped back. 'I forgot to tell you something,' he says under the din of the singing.

'What?'

'At work last week someone told me I'm a snobby wasp on the outside, but inside I have a warm Jewish soul.'

At the end of the evening, when we're getting our coats, Rabbi Glickman approaches us.

'How are the wedding plans going?'

I hesitate. 'We're trying to decide if we should get married under a *chuppah*,' I say.

She nods. 'What kind of wedding are you having?'

I describe what we've been discussing for the ceremony.

She says, 'It sounds strange. To have a Unitarian wedding when you're on the way to becoming Jewish.'

I look at Degan. Are we on the way to becoming Jewish?

'Not Unitarian,' I say. 'Interfaith.'

'Interfaith how?'

'We're not sure yet.' I decide to appeal to her authority. 'What Jewish elements should we include?'

'You could get married under a *chuppah*,' she says right away, and then pauses. 'You *could* get married under a *chuppah*. You *could* break a glass. But I don't know if I would.'

'Why not?'

'You're not Jewish. What kind of message does it send?'

'That I'm half Jewish?' I'm unable to keep the irritation from my voice. 'We're paying tribute to the multiplicity of our religious backgrounds.'

Rabbi Glickman straightens her spine, squares her shoulders, as though about to deliver a soliloquy. 'Another option would be to get married now and have a Jewish wedding later. When you're actually Jewish.'

I'm silent, but inside me a voice shouts: *No – this might be our only chance.*

SIXTEEN

PASSOVER IS UPON US, one of the greatest of all Jewish holidays, and the most celebrated. After scheming and shame-filled emails and thinly disguised begging, we've managed to get ourselves invited to two separate tables: Jordan's parents in Kitchener for the first night and Shayna's parents in Peterborough for the second.

In the car on the way to my hometown Degan and I talk again about the *chuppah*. 'I don't think we should have one,' I say.

I expect him to put up a fight, but this time he just shrugs. 'Okay.'

'I thought you were attached?'

He looks at me over his newspaper. 'There are other things that are more important to me.'

It's hard to tell whether I feel disappointment tinged with relief, or the opposite.

We leave the car at Mum and Dad's and walk the few blocks through the leafy neighbourhood to Jordan's parents' house. When Jordan and I were teenagers, we dubbed this area 'the laundry district' because of the warm smell of soap and steam escaping in the darkness as we carried on our nightly escapades. Jordan and his wife, Ilana, are at the door to meet us, with their two beautiful curly-headed babies and Jordan's mother, who I called 'Dr Ross' when we were teenagers. I don't know what to call her now as an adult.

'Chag Sameach,' Jordan says. He's tall, with the same droopy eyelids, although his sandy hair is now receding – the child I once knew, then the teenager, now rendered in an adult form. He grins at me and kisses my cheek. 'Whoever thought I'd be welcoming *you* at my seder table?' he says.

Seeing the inside of the house after fifteen years is like seeing the contents of an earlier life. In grade eleven we founded The Spaghetti Group, five of us meeting for intrigue at the home of whoever's parents were gone – which was almost always Jordan's. As I pass through the rooms, I catch glimpses of our teenage ghosts splayed out in front of the fireplace with bottles of wine. I have to be introduced to Jordan's grown siblings, even though I went to elementary school with them, too. I don't recognize them in their adult iterations. An aunt and uncle from Toronto arrive with a bag of wrapped boxes.

'Passover gifts?' I ask.

Jordan laughs. 'It's our daughter's birthday.'

'You have to be careful with us,' Degan says, 'or twenty years from now our kids will be getting presents on Pesach.'

Passover tells the story of the enslavement of the Hebrews, and Pharaoh's decision to kill the firstborn sons of Jewish slaves. Baby Moses is set adrift in a basket, discovered by Pharaoh's daughter and raised as a prince of Egypt. I am struck by this second tale of concealed identity: in Purim, Esther's Judaism is hidden from her husband, the king. In the Passover story, Moses is raised unaware that he's a Jew.

The Ross Seder is warm, and chaotic in a way that reminds me of *shul*: people coming and going, listening or not listening to the leader as they see fit. I feel a childlike thrill at seeing the seder plates adorned with egg and *maror*, the bitter herbs, just as we have learned. On my behalf, Degan gags down the gefilte fish, a traditional Ashkenazi dish of ground fish formed into balls. We follow along with the proceedings as best we can, and are gratified when the crowd bursts into a rousing rendition of 'Dayeinu', the song that we learned at our Passover workshop. After dinner, Jordan and Ilana walk Degan and me back home through the wide dusky streets. The smell of laundry drifts up from someone's vent: Jordan smiles at me and I know what he's thinking.

The next morning Degan and I sleep late at my parents' house and come upstairs to bacon and eggs. We excuse our way around the pork (not kosher) and the toast (leavened) and sit down with my parents to talk about the wedding. We have decided on a full weekend event at a retreat centre an hour from my hometown, so our friends can stay over and make a holiday out of it. We discuss logistics – who will staff the bar, how the older guests will navigate the path through the woods to the tent. I give my parents an update on what we are thinking with regard to a ceremony. They are relieved to hear we have abandoned the idea of a *chuppah*.

I look over at Mum: I can see there's something she wants to say. 'What?' I ask.

'Nothing,' she says, picking a stray crumb from an empty muffin tin on the counter. 'Just. Well. I was thinking that maybe I'd walk you down the aisle alongside your father.'

I look over at her stylish new haircut, the pearl studs in her ears. She is going elegantly grey. 'Really?' I can't keep the shock from my voice.

'Why not?' she asks, a little indignant.

I'm surprised that Mum, traditional in almost every way, would consider such a thing, and even more surprised at myself. I'm a feminist. I will not be – and wouldn't consider

– taking Degan's name. I know that 'giving away the bride' was a historical passing of property from one man to another. And yet, in the face of Mum's offer, I only want my dad. All my life I've dreamed that on my wedding day, I would walk down the aisle on his arm.

Degan packs up to go back to Toronto. He was able to take one night off work for Passover, but two would be pushing it. I kiss him goodbye and then sit down with Dad to do my taxes. 'I've only got an hour,' I tell him as he loads up the program on the computer. The screen flashes off and on, then off again.

'You're going to Peterborough?'

'To my friend Shayna's parents'. For the second night of Passover.'

'By yourself?'

'Degan has to work.'

'I could come with you, instead,' Dad offers.

I look over at his face, the deep lines on his forehead. First synagogue, now this. 'You'd be *welcome* to come,' I say. 'I love it that you want to come.'

The simple fact of his interest breaks my heart. It's really too last minute for him to join me this year, but my mind leaps immediately to next year. Where could I take him? Who would have enough space at their table not just for Degan and me but Dad, too? I feel lost trying to make him comfortable with something so unfamiliar, to give him a Jewish home I never had. And beneath the sadness is that bubbling anger: it was *his* job to give *me* that home.

When I arrive at Shayna's parents' place in Peterborough, a big suburban two-storey that backs onto the Otonabee

River, she runs out to meet me in a T-shirt and shorts, her face flushed. 'Hello, gorgeous,' she says, kissing me on both cheeks.

Her family has been at the park playing soccer.

'Chag Sameach?' I try.

She gives me the thumbs-up. Inside, she introduces me around. Her sister, even taller than Shayna, is at the kitchen sink washing parsley, which I deduce will be the *karpas*, the green vegetable to dip in saltwater representing tears, on the Seder plate. Shayna's mother is laying out dozens of Haggadot, the book that tells the Passover story, in the living room. Shayna riffles through them looking for one with transliterations, the cryptic Hebrew rendered into an approximation of English, so I can follow along.

It is tradition in her family to take a photo in the living room before the seder starts. I stand awkwardly at the edge of the group of family and friends, but Shayna wraps an arm around my shoulders, pulls me in. Then her parents go to their places at either end of the table. Her father welcomes us all. He has a bushy beard and a bald spot that is covered by his *kippah*. 'Twenty years ago,' he says, 'there would have been heated conversations about whether non-Jews would be welcome at the seder table. Now there are two of you, and we include you without even a thought.'

I look around discreetly, trying to locate my partner in crime.

The Marshak Seder is a little more cohesive than the Rosses' was – more fluent Hebrew speakers, more gusto with the songs – and the two littlest children chant the Four Questions with pride. Shayna's niece is about to become a Bat Mitzvah, and has been studying Torah with her bubbie, her grandmother, in the lead up. Now she tells the story of Moses and Miriam in such detail that I am rapt. She is chubby, with braces on her teeth, a strapless sundress, new breasts. On the cusp of womanhood. Her father is a convert.

I can see, as the rabbi preacher told us, that the whole Seder is enacted with the children in mind, and several times I have to squeeze my eyes shut against the intensity of my longing. My cells are tingling in recognition, something so long dormant sparking back to life with full force. This was what I imagined I wanted from Eli. A big table, beautiful and passionate, filled with Jews, both born and chosen. I belt out the words to 'Go Down, Moses', a tradition the Marshak's have added to their Seder, Shayna's voice soaring beside my own.

It is two in the morning by the time I arrive back in Kitchener. *I Was a Child of Holocaust Survivors* is lying on the desk among Dad's papers, and beside it, the *Globe and Mail* is open to a story about hidden Jews. 'I Swore to Never Tell', the headline exclaims. I turn away. I'm done with that story.

❧

During Passover, Jews don't eat anything leavened, including pasta, most processed foods and wheat, barley, spelt, oats and rye. Degan's version of 'Kosher for Passover' is no bread. Which is almost killing him. We stroll down Queen Street on his lunch break, looking for shoes to match his wedding suit. He tells me that at work he almost didn't order the fish because it was breaded. But the cafeteria worker told him there is no bread in breaded fish, only flour.

'Is flour okay?' he asks.

He is cramming a muffin into his mouth as he speaks.

My version of 'Kosher for Passover' is to eat everything I usually eat, plus matzah. And chocolate-covered matzah.

We stop at city hall to get our marriage licence. The man

behind the desk jokes with us about the couples he sees who fight so much he wonders why they are even bothering. Degan holds my hand in his lap, squeezes it.

The marriage licence form asks all kinds of questions: our mothers' maiden names, our dates of birth, our religions. We have to swear an oath that the information we give is true, so for religion I can't put 'Jewish'.

'Christian' feels like a lie.

I hesitate, and finally write 'None'.

Degan writes 'Spiritual'.

This will be there on the certificate forever.

We kiss goodbye and Degan heads back to work for the afternoon. On my ride home I see another biker, weaving wildly through heavy traffic, no hands, eating an apple, the fringes of his tzitzit flying out behind him.

SEVENTEEN

ON THE SPECTRUM OF MASCULINITY Degan is basically feminine – he gestures with his hands when he talks and is hopeless in the face of home repairs. So, not the sort of man to whom a bachelor party would normally appeal. But since we've decided to go all out with the wedding – white dress and everything – he thinks he may as well. On Saturday evening he heads off for beers with his friends and I drive to Kitchener for a wedding shower hosted by a friend of my mother's. The guests are women who refer to themselves as 'ladies', friends of my mother's I haven't seen for twenty years; they give me bedsheets and ask where we will live once we're married. Not a Jew in sight, of course. There is someone who is *married* to a Jew, though: Aunt Ruth is the wife of Dad's cousin Paul.

Paul was a small boy when war broke out in Czechoslovakia. He was sent away to boarding school in England and never saw his parents again.

Gumper, in his *Report from England*, recounted seeing Paul after the war. He was now a teenager. 'He doesn't speak Czech anymore,' Gumper wrote. 'He remembers me but can't remember his parents. He received the news of his mother's death without any signs of upset, and when I try to talk to him about it, he doesn't respond at all, and I don't know whether it means he doesn't want to talk about it, or whether it simply means nothing to him.

'He knows he is Jewish, of course,' Gumper also wrote. But Paul kept the secret religiously. When he got married, he did not tell his wife.

Back in Toronto, Shayna calls to ask me if I want her to perform some kind of ritual at our wedding ceremony.

'Yes!' I say right away. 'Like what?'

'Well,' she says, 'the Mi Adir, the traditional welcoming prayer, is always sung at a Jewish wedding.' She clears her throat. 'But if you want I can do something else. Whatever you think would be helpful.'

Where did I find her? I think, with gratitude. How on earth did I find her?

'The Mi Adir would be perfect,' I say to Shayna.

I eat a quiet dinner alone and then drive up Bathurst in the watery spring dusk for a rare evening therapy session. I discuss the wedding ceremony with Charlotte, the plan for Shayna to sing the Mi Adir, for Degan to break a glass underfoot as is Jewish custom. I wonder what effect this might have on my father's family. Perhaps, Charlotte suggests, allaying some of my fears, they might not even recognize these acts as Jewish.

I tell her my dream about a white dog racing toward me at full speed, teeth bared, only to stop short of me by an inch and nuzzle my palm. 'I don't know what the dog represents,' I say to Charlotte.

She seems to know but won't tell me. She only smiles, and rocks in her chair, and tells me what good work I have done. On the path to marriage I have been tested and tested again. And here I am, stepping into the power of it.

EIGHTEEN

I SPEND THE NIGHT BEFORE THE WEDDING with my family in Kitchener. We go out for ice cream, watch a silly movie. Although Degan has been around for years, there's something of a goodbye in the evening, as though our nuclear family of four has come to its happy conclusion. That night I dream I am in the billowing white wedding tent. It is filled with people, everyone I know and love. Then I see Dad, in the far back corner, alone, at a Sabbath table covered in white cloth. He is singing the blessing over the wine.

The next day we drive in convoy to the retreat centre where we'll be married, the cars loaded with tonic water, dried flowers, tripods, potted plants, ribbon, a guest book. Degan is sitting in front of the main building when we arrive, practising the knot on his tie. We kiss hello, then fall on the remaining logistics like wolves on bloody meat. 'The caterer just got here,' he says. 'She wants to know where we want the riser. And should they put flowers in the lounge in case of rain? And the DJ needs to know if we have extension cords.'

Degan's face is pinched, but I can see it's a happy kind of pinched.

'Oh,' he says. 'And one more thing. I spoke to Shayna. She doesn't want to sing the Mi Adir.'

I pause, and fiddle with Granny's wedding ring. 'Really?' I ask.

I suspect he has misunderstood. Shayna was so sincere in her offer to help in whatever way she could. I ask more. Degan reveals she was at school, surrounded by a bunch of five-year-olds when she called; it must have been hard for him to hear what she was saying.

The afternoon is sunny and beautiful. There are birds in the branches and the fragrant scent of lily of the valley along the trails. Wild mint in the cool spring mud. We rehearse the wedding ceremony outside in the field under the huge leafy oak.

My family is there, and Degan's sister from England, and our friends Michael and Christine, who will be singing in the ceremony in their rock star sunglasses and floppy hats and tight T-shirts. Their baby crawls around the field, sampling the dirt and grass like hors d'oeuvres. When the rehearsal is over, I take my dress in its thick plastic sheath to the hermitage, where I'll be sleeping alone. My last night of not being someone's wife.

Around five the guests start to arrive. We have planned a talent show for the first night. Sixty of our friends cram into the lounge, where we have made the hearth into an impromptu stage. Degan and I are the opening act: we perform a pantomime to music from *Chariots of Fire* about our long journey to marriage. It involves sweat, and red paint smeared on our faces, and beating off other admirers in the audience with a measuring stick. Mum's family has written a very long song to the tune of 'Daisy, Daisy': 'Aaaaalie, Deeeegan, tell me your answer do.' The verses are endless, and soon the audience is roaring with laughter as each new one begins. My cousin Lucy is representing the Picks, and she has chosen a poem to read. She introduces it by saying, 'Symborska is my favourite poet. Next to Alison, of course.'

After the talent show everyone mingles, and congratulates us. I drink a beer and try to say hello to as many people as possible. When I am finally ready to head off for bed, Shayna appears at my side and says she will walk me down to my hermitage.

The May night is chilly, with a fat moon that's almost full. We make our way along the dark path through the forest and find my cabin nestled in the trees. We sit on the porch and dangle our feet over the edge.

'So,' I say. 'We'd planned for you to sing the Mi Adir.' I pause. 'Right?'

She reaches for my hand; I feel her long, slim fingers in mine. 'I had a chance to really sit with it,' she says. 'To meditate. I feel so caught. In my desire to help, I wanted to offer anything. But I didn't listen. I assumed I *knew* what you'd want. There was arrogance in my assumption.'

I remove my hand from hers. I rub my temples with my thumbs, glad that the darkness masks the confusion on my face. 'It didn't seem arrogant,' I say. 'It seemed helpful.'

'I didn't think it through,' she says.

'You didn't think *what* through?'

There's a very long silence. 'I spoke with Rabbi Glickman,' she says finally.

I swallow, and remember the rabbi's words that it's better not to include 'Jewish elements' in the ceremony but to hold off and have a second Jewish wedding when and if we actually convert.

I keep making the same mistake, forgetting what a small world we're in, how everyone is implicated in everyone else's business. My hackles rise.

'What did she say?' I ask. 'That you'd compromise your professional integrity by singing an offical Jewish wedding song for non-Jews?'

Shayna looks surprised. 'No,' she says. 'It's not that. It's that she wants what's best for *you*.' She pauses. 'I want what's best for you, too.'

'And the mikvah?' I ask. The plan has been for Shayna to come down to the river in the morning with my sister and my closest girlfriends to say the blessings for immersion as is the custom before a Jewish woman gets married.

Shayna sighs deeply; I see where this is headed and am glad again for the cover of the darkness.

She finally speaks. 'My own first mikvah was with friends, in a river. At a place like this one.' She gestures around at the cabins, the trees, the knotted paths concealed in the darkness. 'My friend said, "We're doing mikvahs for Shabbat," just like that. So I did it and it was done.'

The implication is that this was a loss, like losing your virginity to an asshole.

Shayna continues. 'I'm not clear where your path is going. And if you do find some way to officially convert, I don't want to have taken the experience, your first time, away from you.'

Part of me, a rational part that nevertheless feels very far away, hears her words and her integrity. But another part, much closer to the surface, interprets what she says to mean that a mikvah when I am not *really* Jewish would somehow cheapen the ritual itself. I once again am not good enough; my participation will somehow sully the mikvah or demean it.

'Oh,' I say. 'Well –' I swallow hard '– the problem is that I don't know where the path is going, either. I don't know if the rabbis will accept me. So I might not ever have the opportunity . . .'

I swallow again, my throat thick with feeling. Under the sadness I feel a seething rage, not at Shayna but at Judaism in general; at the hand that has pushed me away not three times, as is customary, but what feels like hundreds of times. As many times as I've had the courage to approach.

'It's just that I want it so badly,' I say. 'That it's *already* who I am.'

Shayna is quiet, taking this in. She says, 'You are very brave.' I hear the sincerity in her voice. The genuine compassion.

'I really wanted to have some Hebrew in the ceremony tomorrow,' I say. 'It was what I was looking forward to most.'

She touches my arm. 'What if I sang something else?' She tugs on my sleeve, suddenly excited. 'It doesn't have to be the Mi Adir.'

I consider. 'That would probably be okay,' I say. I think of my evenings in bed with Degan practising Hebrew words. The truth is Shayna could sing 'Mary Had a Little Lamb' in Hebrew and we wouldn't know the difference.

'Try something,' I say.

'Okay,' she says. 'How about this? It's from the Song of Songs.'

I close my eyes and her voice takes me away. Her gift has never been clearer.

When she's done singing, she mistakes my silent awe for uncertainty. 'There are other options, too,' she says quickly, 'if you want me to sing some different pieces to both you and Degan, so you can decide together.'

'No,' I say. 'I'll make an executive decision. It's perfect.'

'And you understand about the mikvah?'

'I do.'

'I could come down to the water anyway and say a different Hebrew blessing . . .'

But her voice trails off and we decline together in mutual silence.

⌇

At six the next morning, I hear the hinges on the hermitage screen door squeak open.

I roll over, squinting in the half-light, and see them. My sister, Emily, who looks so much like me, like my Pick cousins, like Marianne. Lindsay, our cousin on the Martin side, who I grew up with. Emily Denton, a summer friend from North Hatley; and my best friend, Nicola, who knows everything about me there is to know. The ones I've chosen. I feel them gather around my bed and start singing, five women's voices weaving the harmonies of 'Down to the River to Pray'. I open my mouth to tell them that the ritual is off, that there won't be a mikvah. As I'm about to speak, though, I realize I *can* still go down to the river. That water is nondenominational; that the earth will have me regardless.

It is raining lightly as we leave my hermitage, the sound of the raindrops on the green spring leaves like a thousand little wedding bells ringing. We walk in silence, in single file, my friends in raincoats and umbrellas, and me in my bathrobe and running shoes. The gravel road gives way to forest, to a dirt path knotted with tree roots and a dense tangle of branches overhead. We step, one by one, over a trunk that has fallen across the path, and duck beneath a wall of cobweb, spangled with raindrops like jewels. My sister Emily has gone ahead earlier and scouted out a place, a clearing sheltered by a canopy of leaves, and a small pool in the fast-flowing river where the water is deep. We stand in a circle holding hands. Then they break into a line, my silent witnesses, and I let my robe fall away.

There is a blessing to recite concerning immersion, a blessing I have been working hard to memorize, but the first steps into the freezing water literally take my breath away and I forget the words immediately and completely. My ankles are numb, then my knees, my hips. Before I can change my mind, I draw a deep breath, close my eyes and lie down on my back. The icy river rushes over me, under me, through me, scouring me clean for what's to come. I break through the surface, gasping.

Back on the riverbank, my sister is holding my robe open; I slide my arms into it. My friends are still keeping the silence. We walk out of the woods, single file again, the raindrops beating harder now on the canopy of leaves overhead. When we get to the gravel road, I take Lindsay's hand on one side, Emily's on the other side. We make a chain, the five of us, walking toward the camp in the chilly early morning, singing our song again, which belongs to no one, to anyone: '"Oh, sisters, let's go down, down to the river to pray."'

The rest of the morning is a blur of hairdressers and nail files and stockings. The rain doesn't let up and we have to move the ceremony inside. Shayna and I have agreed that she will connect with Genevieve, the Unitarian chaplain who is marrying us, about how to introduce the Song of Songs into the ceremony, but I don't see either of them to confirm. I'm busy in the back room with eyeliner and curling irons. My mother has backed away from her request to walk me down the aisle, but she is there to help with my makeup, advising on mascara and blush. My heart pounds as Emily helps me into my long dress, clasps the pearls behind my neck. The photographer pokes his head in, snapping for posterity. There are ten minutes left. I can hear the crowd gathering in the living room, the collective voice of everyone who has come to send Degan and me off on our life together. The string quartet pauses. I make out the muffled sound of Genevieve's announcements: 'No photos, please turn off your cell phones.' Her voice falls silent and the music starts again. Time lifts her skirts. I turn and spot Dad, so handsome in his suit and tie. He smiles at me, reassuring, and takes my arm.

The first thing I see when I enter the room is the big wall of windows, and behind it, the deep green forest and the clear, steady-falling spring rain. Degan is standing against the backdrop of the trees; we look at each other, and I know everything is going to be fine.

Genevieve begins: 'Splendour is everywhere. Blessing is everywhere. May the one who provides this abundance bless this groom and bride.'

From somewhere in our crowd of friends, a baby cries out.

Degan's mother comes forward to light a candle in memory of his father, who passed away before I met Degan. My mother's reading is next. Then it's Shayna's turn. She steps forward in heels, adding another two inches to her willowy height, and a gorgeous orange dress. She pauses, looking at the crowd, from face to face, as though sharing the most wonderful secret with each of them. She takes a deep breath and places a hand on her abdomen. When she unleashes her voice, it is like nothing I've ever heard.

As the Hebrew words rise in the air above the crowd, I look out at the assembly. The faces are open, taking in the beauty of the music. Only Uncle Paul, seated in a prominent place in the front row, has his head bowed. I remember the words from Gumper's *Report from England*: 'He knows he is Jewish, of course.'

But it occurs to me that Uncle Paul has probably not heard Hebrew spoken in seventy years.

I can't tell if the look on his face is shame, or fear, or some more complex medley of emotions. I try to catch his eye, wanting somehow to reassure him, but he keeps his head bowed.

Our vows are from the Book of Ruth. When Ruth's husband died, she chose to remain with his Jewish family. She said to her mother-in-law, 'For where you go, I will go.'

The Book of Ruth is a conversion story. Ruth, a convert, eventually gave birth to King David.

Degan holds my eye as he recites his vows. ' "Your home will be my home," ' he tells me, ' "your people my people. And your God shall be my God." '

As he says this last part, his voice catches. We both know the God to whom he is referring.

When it comes time to sign the registry, I have a stab of deep regret that next to the place for religious denomination, I have written 'None'.

Despite the various oppositions to this, we have decided to include the Jewish custom of the groom breaking a glass to conclude the ceremony. The glass is concealed in a cloth bag. Degan raises his foot, stomps – and misses the bag. He stomps again, misses again. When the glass finally shatters, the crowd erupts in cheers. Nobody shouts '*Mazel tov!*' but everyone claps and hollers. Degan and I kiss. We are married.

In the receiving line, Uncle Paul won't look at me. I have to step forward dramatically and lean in to give him a kiss. My lips touch his cheek: he is barely there.

᪐

It pours rain throughout our wedding lunch. A friend of Degan's gives a blessing about showers of abundance; Dad speaks beautifully about wishing Degan's father were with us. Emily talks about the 'research' I am doing on our family history, calling it brave. She says she sees our late Granny Pick in me.

Heavy silver cutlery clinks against plates. After chocolate done three ways for dessert, there are photographs in the wet and cold with our families. We include Lucy, the only Pick cousin present, in the Martin portrait. I ask what she thought about the Jewish parts of the ceremony: the Hebrew song, breaking the glass. 'It was perfect,' she says, and I can hear that she means it.

'Oh,' she says, 'and I had a dream. There was a program, and on it, in big red letters, was a message from Granny: "Mrs Liska Pick very much regrets that she is unable to attend, and wishes Alison and Degan much happiness."'

NINETEEN

DEGAN AND I DRIVE TO KITCHENER to drop off some of the wedding paraphernalia. Dad comes out to the driveway to meet us. 'What a lovely ceremony,' he says, before we can even get out of the car. 'Your friend Shayna's voice is gorgeous!'

'I know. Isn't it?'

'If I were her age I'd ask her on a date.'

Degan and I exchange glances. What would that mean to Dad, to be young again, and dating a Jewish girl?

I remember our conversation at the photography exhibit: 'Did Gumper want you to marry a Jew?'

'Of course not.' It would have ruined all the effort that had been put into hiding.

There's a dull thud in my head from the previous night's festivities, which included dancing, followed by singing around the bonfire until the sun began to rise. Thankfully, we've planned the perfect honeymoon: a full week at the cabin with nothing to do but relax. I can't wait to get there and fall asleep in my new husband's arms. But Dad says, 'Come into the house. Just for a few minutes. My present to you is inside.'

In the living room, I find an old blue trunk in the centre of the rug. The kind of cumbersome, heavy case you'd see in a film about hoboes or orphans. 'Do you know what it is?' Dad asks.

'No.'

'It's the trunk that Granny and Gumper brought with them across the ocean to Canada.'

I pause, and look more closely. Frayed leather handles, stickers plastered to its sides. The initials *MB* are inscribed in black cursive on the top. 'Marianne Bauer?'

Now Dad looks closely. 'Oh, you must be right!'

Granny's mother's trunk. The trunk of a woman who went to the gas chamber.

Never have I experienced my great-grandmother so tangibly. She is no more than a ghost, but suddenly I can see the items she would have packed inside, the pale cashmere sweaters separated by tissue paper, the elastic and cotton of women's underthings. Dad has arranged for a glass top to be secured on the trunk so we can use it as a coffee table. It will be there, from now on, in our living room. The metaphor isn't lost on me: I'm being given her baggage. The grief of it, and also the gift.

Degan and I spend our honeymoon opening the incredible pile of presents we have received. We loll in bed throwing hundred-dollar bills in the air like a couple in a lottery commercial. We tear open boxes containing pots and pans, blankets and pillows. More cookbooks than we'll ever be able to use. Among them, from Shayna, is *The Essential Book of Jewish Festival Cooking*. The book is laid out holiday by holiday. Shavuot is up next, and now I'll know exactly what to cook.

The final gift we open is from Uncle Paul: a beautiful Bohemian crystal punch set. In my mind's eye I picture the wedding ceremony, Shayna's Hebrew song and Paul hanging his head. I feel chastened, like a very young child.

The second I am married my motherhood instinct kicks in. It has been simmering, just below the surface, for months, and the wedding is like a starting gun going off. Degan and I spend the first days of our honeymoon in bed. We get up around noon and make a breakfast of pancakes and mimosas. Then we go back to bed.

Later we go out and play tourist in a little tourist town on Georgian Bay. We stop for hot fudge sundaes; the ice cream parlour sells pottery imported from Tunisia. Degan sees a tiny blue and white dish that he likes. 'We can use it for *haroset* at Passover,' he says. *Haroset* is the goopy substance that represents mortar at the seder.

The drive back takes us along the edge of the Beaver Valley, fields and farmlands sprawled out below us, dappled with long evening light. We arrive home and stand in the tall grass at the side of the cabin. The river is fragrant with watercress growing in the muddy reeds. The light deepens; in the far trees the fireflies appear, one by one, like tiny lanterns.

'It's Friday,' Degan says. 'Shabbat.'

'Oh? Are you sure?' I've lost track of the days.

He takes me by the hand and leads me inside. The cabin is cool and dark. He lifts a bottle of wine off the shelf, then wrestles with the cork until it makes a resounding *pop*. We don't have challah, so I set out two pieces of pie, instead. I light the candles and we both cover our eyes. We've worked for several days at memorizing the Shabbat blessings, and it is a relief to be able, finally, to recite them by heart. Even if Degan never converts, even if I never do, we have turned a corner where ritual is concerned. I gather the light three times around my head. The wedding has given me courage. I can do what I want. I won't be stopped.

We take our plates out to the porch, the late-May dusk seeping in through the screens, the sound of crickets in the tall grass. We eat our meal. After, Degan retires to the couch, where he reclines like a prince and reads.

'I'm bagged,' I say. 'Off to bed.'

He says, in his pouty baby voice, 'Can you do something for me first?'

'Of course.' I think he's going to ask me to get him another piece of pie.

'Can you bring me my *haroset* dish so I can see if it matches with our Shabbat candlesticks?'

TWENTY

THE NEXT TIME WE GO to meet with Rabbi Klein, Degan wants to stop and look at the Judaica at the synagogue gift store to see if any of *it* matches his new dish. I finally have to take him by the arm and pull him to the rabbi's office.

'*Mazel tov!*' she says when she sees us. 'Can you just wait a minute while I go to the bathroom?'

The life of a rabbi: back-to-back meetings.

'How was the wedding?' she asks when she is again settled in her chair.

'Wonderful,' we both say at once.

I tell her how perfect the book of Ruth vows were, and how having Shayna sing in Hebrew felt like a kind of coming out.

'Shayna told me it was a beautiful ceremony.'

Aha. So they've talked. There's a long silence in the room. Outside, we hear cars, horns, the steady beat of a jackhammer.

Rachel peers at me. 'You seem so serious,' she says. 'What are you thinking?'

I'm thinking of my impromptu self-made mikvah; I'm feeling for the second time the freezing cold grip of the river as I lay on my back to let the water wash over me. How I gasped for breath as I broke through the surface, washed clean. 'About conversion,' I say. 'How right it feels.'

'That's wonderful,' she says brightly. 'I'm so glad.' She looks to Degan. 'And what about you?'

I can see he's biting his tongue. 'I'd rather talk about what we need to do for Alie to move forward,' he says.

Her face darkens – almost imperceptibly, but her frustration is clear. 'We're going to have to discuss your decision, too,' she says to Degan.

At her window, the tree so recently bare has grown a coat of bright leafy green. She focuses on him. 'Are you hoping to have kids?'

Degan and I turn to each other, almost shyly, and nod.

'Then let me offer this,' she says. 'It might not be clear to you now. But with a baby, it is *much* easier if everyone is on the same page.'

'How do you mean?'

'Well, for example, when a new baby is born, and the parents are both in synagogue for the baby naming, but the father isn't Jewish? I can *see* in his body language that he feels like an outsider.'

The rabbi twists her hair elastic around the bottom of her braid. 'Conversely,' she says, 'when the whole family is up on the bimah together, united in celebration . . .'

I well up, blinking to clear my eyes.

'Why are you sad?' Rachel asks, her voice rigid.

'Because I believe you,' I say. 'I know that you're right. But if it isn't what Degan wants, I don't want to force him.'

Degan breathes beside me.

'Can I ask you both something?' the rabbi says. 'Where do you feel joy in Judaism?' I open my mouth to answer, but she says, 'Because our meetings here are often fairly heavy.'

Degan reaches for my hand, squeezes it. I pause, choosing my words. 'You're right. Because the Holocaust is my access point, it's taking a while for me to learn the joy.' I blink rapidly. 'And in some ways I don't feel very welcome.'

The rabbi is silent.

Degan's instinct to smooth everything over kicks in. 'We're

thinking of going to Auschwitz,' he says, changing the subject. 'When we're in Europe in the summer.'

'I've never been,' Rachel says.

'To Europe?'

'To Auschwitz.'

'Really?' Degan says, genuinely surprised.

'I don't know what could make me go there.'

I get it. I know what she means. There's an appeal in that refusal, which is the same way Granny coped. Yet I have no choice but to try to face that darkness. It's my only hope of letting the light shine through.

⅌

My therapist Charlotte agrees with Rachel that Degan and I should make the same decision. But she takes the opposite tack about what the decision should be. 'Why do you need to actually convert? Why can't you embrace the multiplicity of your background? Nobody can stop you from enacting Judaism in your own home.'

'It just makes me angry. They're refusing me. It's so ironic.'

'Does that remind you of anything?'

Not this again.

'Of my father? That he's unpredictable too?'

She nods. 'And you feel the same desire for *his* acceptance and acknowledgment.'

But I disagree with her analysis. 'I don't think you understand,' I say. 'I just feel such urgency. To figure this out.'

'And the *urgency*,' she says, 'is our clue that something is amiss.'

I look at Charlotte, silent in her chair. She has dyed her hair from wheat blond to something slightly paler. It softens her expression, makes her face seem more relaxed.

'Oh,' I say. 'You mean the urgency indicates a projection?'

She holds her lower lip briefly between her teeth.

'What about your mother?' she asks. 'Where does she come into all this?'

And I retort, without pausing, 'What about her?'

I feel frustrated and unheard. 'I'm just not as compelled by that side of the family. No, "compelled" is the wrong word. I just relate to them differently.'

Haven't I already told her this?

She looks at me again. Outside her office, someone leans on a horn. 'You know,' says Charlotte, 'it's possible I might be wrong here.'

My ears perk up.

'It's possible I may be biased.'

She is deciding whether to say more. I use her own technique against her and remain attentively silent. It works, and she confesses, 'My husband is Jewish.'

'Okay.'

'And I am not.'

'Right.'

I wait her out some more.

'I, too, have considered conversion,' she says. 'And decided against it.'

Her husband! Jewish! The light bulbs are popping: Charlotte is a person! With a life beyond these doors, beyond me.

Charlotte has debated becoming Jewish.

'Thank you for telling me,' I say. 'I mean, that makes sense. I understand.'

She opens her mouth to speak. For a moment I think she is about to tell me something else personal, something else about herself, but my excitement at her revealing herself to me morphs quickly into dread. I don't want to know a thing. I need her to be anonymous. Yet she only says, 'We'd better wrap up. We're almost out of time.' And as soon as the chance is taken away, I am disappointed. I want to be her friend, her confidante. I want to know everything.

That night I watch another video of Vera – not the Shoah Project, but one filmed by Dad, who travelled to Newark, New Jersey, to interview her. In the Shoah Project interview, Vera seemed to identify strongly as a Jew, but in this conversation with my father, she tries to distance herself. Talking about the dirty Polish Jews from the *shtetl*. How they lived such a different life from her own. How there is only one other Jewish family in her building, and she doesn't have much to do with them.

She begins talking about 'bread that Jews eat' – but she can't think of the word.

Dad, who is interviewing her, keeps saying, 'Matzah?'

'Challah,' I say to the screen.

'Matzah?' Dad asks.

'Challah!' I shout.

But Vera never gets it.

Context is everything. Faced with the Shoah Foundation's interviewer, she was apologetic about her lack of Jewish education. She could not go to religious school since there wasn't one in her hometown, and her grandfather taught her only *some* of what she should know. 'Not enough, unfor-tunately,' she said, with genuine regret in her voice. Now, though, she wants none of it. Her voice is small and sad. She touches the bangles on her wrist. I wonder if they are the same bracelets her son sent me after her death, the ones that I accidentally left at a bar when we were living out east. I remember the panic I felt, arriving home drunk and tired and realizing my cold wrist was bare. I called; the barmaid said the lost-and-found box was empty. I went down the next morning, and she let me parse the green and amber bottles, dig among the containers of lemon wedges and maraschino cherries. My hand landed on two big copper hoops, and I couldn't believe it when they revealed themselves not as bracelets but as earrings, someone else's lost jewellery, looking so much like my own.

I never found those bracelets, and it still bothers me, still niggles at me late at night. A loss – unlike the other losses – that is bearable. Two copper bangles. A loss I can hold.

TWENTY-ONE

WATCHING VERA'S INTERVIEW confirms my desire to go to Auschwitz. I will be in Europe for a literary festival that will pay for my ticket, and Degan and I have scraped together enough for him to come along. It may be a once-in-a-lifetime chance.

Still, money is tight. I dig through the mail, looking for some notice of a grant, some kind of sign that I'll be able to finish writing my novel. My bank account is drying up, with no source of income on the horizon. I tear open a promising-looking envelope, but it is just one of Mum's famous newspaper clippings, an article from the *Globe and Mail* about Ashkenazai Jewish women being at a significantly higher risk for carrying the BRCA breast cancer gene than the rest of the population. One in forty-four versus one in four hundred, in fact.

Women's College Hospital is running a study, including testing for the gene.

Degan looks over my shoulder at the article. 'You should get the test.'

'Wouldn't it be awesome if I had it?'

He bugs out his eyes.

'Not the disease,' I clarify. 'Genetic proof that I'm a Jew.'

What have I been reduced to?

There is a phone number at the bottom of the article if you want to volunteer for the study. I dial it. A woman with an Australian accent answers, and I tell her why I'm calling.

'You're Jewish?' she asks.

'My father is.'

'That's fine.'

'My mother is *not*.'

'That's fine,' she says again.

She takes my info. They'll contact me. That is all.

❧

I'm closing in on the final draft of my novel *Far to Go*, editing obsessively, trying to make sure all the clues line up, all the threads resolve neatly, with subtlety and surprise. I'm at my desk working when the woman from the breast cancer study calls back the next morning. I recognize her accent right away. 'We've had an opening for this afternoon,' she says. She pauses, and I hear her reading from the schedule under her breath. 'Would one o'clock work for you?'

'Sure,' I say, surprised that the appointment has panned out so effortlessly.

'Remember to bring the history of cancer in your extended family.'

'Only my father is Jewish,' I tell her again, in case she did not understood the first time we talked.

'Great,' she says. 'Just remember the medical history.'

I hang up the phone feeling teary about being accepted, a kind of sadness that is mostly, I realize, hormonal. So, no baby again this month.

I close the document, save it, then save a second time for good measure. I go outside and unlock my bike. It's a short ride down to the hospital. I am shown into a windowless boardroom. Two heavily made-up women are talking about a nanny who drowned in a pool in Thornhill.

There are six packages of forms to fill out, pages and pages of questions about my health, my relatives' health, my family history. Do I have kids? Have I had cancer? Am I worried I'll get it? One question asks whether I want to be notified of my results. I tick yes.

I am asked to indicate whether both parents are Jewish or just one, but not *which* parent. Genetically, there is no difference.

My blood, the doctor tells me when eventually I am shown in, will be tested for mutations commonly found in the Ashkenazi Jewish population. I roll up my sleeve to the place, I think, where the numbered tattoo would have been. He brandishes a needle; I offer him my arm.

That night Degan and I go to dinner at a friend's apartment. A bunch of poets and novelists are there, and my editor Lynn. I give her a little update on the novel. Everyone drifts out onto the deck, where talk turns to television and to cats. We mix cocktails under summer's green canopy and watch the raccoons try to open the garbage containers. I only have one drink, plus an extra sip of Degan's, but when I wake up the next morning, I'm wrung out like a rag. I rarely miss a morning at my desk, but now I just want to stay in bed. I'm probably about to get my period; my breasts are awfully sore.

And then it occurs to me.

I leap out of bed, jump on my bike and race down to the drugstore to buy a pregnancy test. Back at the apartment, I peel back the foil, squat over the toilet and take aim. One line means the test is negative; two means it's positive. The first line appears, a turtle inching slowly toward the finish line. Then, five seconds later, like an arrow showing progress toward a fundraising goal, a second line inches up the screen.

I look away, count slowly to ten, look back. The second line is still there.

I pull my pants up halfway but forget to do the button: I race around the apartment looking for my phone, one hand holding my jeans up. 'I'm having a baby!' I shout to the air. I pull clothes out of drawers, empty all my purses onto the bed. Finally I find the phone in plain view on the top of my dresser and reach Degan right away. 'Hey!' I say, breathless. There are horns in the background, traffic.

'I'm on my bike,' he says.

'And talking on the phone at the same time?' The father of my unborn child is endangering his life. 'Pull over,' I order.

'I'm fine – it's a side street.'

'No, really. Pull over.'

There's the sound of some fumbling, gears changing.

'I have some news.'

'Okay?'

'I think I'm pregnant!'

'Because your boobs hurt?'

He doubts me. To his credit, he's heard this before. 'I took a test,' I say, smug.

Loud horns in the background.

'I thought you were on a *side* street.'

'You're serious?' he asks.

Degan begins to take slow, deep breaths, a kind of precautionary Lamaze. I check the second pink line to make sure it hasn't disappeared. 'Holy *shit*,' I say, over and over.

'Breathe with me,' Degan says. 'Breathe.'

❧

I pass the next half-hour, while I wait for him to get home, by looking at other people's babies on Facebook. I check out Diane and baby Tamara from our class. I am trying to imagine one of those fat, drooly creatures actually belonging to us. To *me*. I look online for midwives. The websites advise calling as early as possible because spaces are limited, but I can't muster the faith to actually pick up the phone. It's too surreal, too abstract. I count ahead to my due date, 'forty weeks from the first day of your last period': March 21.

Thirty-eight more weeks to finish my novel.

Degan arrives home and I lunge at him, holding the stick out in front of me like a crazy person. 'I'm crazy, aren't I.'

He peers at it. 'Yes. And pregnant.' He holds the stick up, squinting. We giggle at the absurdity.

'Let's buy a house,' I say suddenly. The market is abysmal, but we both agree instantly that we're willing to shoulder the debt. Our old lives slipping farther from view, like a small boat at the edge of the horizon.

'She'll be born in March,' I say. 'It's perfect. We'll spend the summer outside.'

'She?'

'It's a girl,' I say, and Degan grins. His confidence in me complete.

He looks at the ceiling, cursing softly and with pleasure. Then all at once he starts rummaging madly through his bag. 'I just remembered,' he says. 'I have something for you.'

He holds out an envelope; I open it tentatively. Inside is a CD of *Don Giovanni* and tickets for the Prague State Opera House.

'Oh,' I say. 'I kind of forgot about our trip.'

'Let's listen to it!'

'To what?'

'The CD,' Degan says.

'I wonder if I'm allowed to travel.'

'I love *Don Giovanni*,' Degan says.

I can see he's in shock, but I'm *pregnant*. Opera is the last thing on my mind.

'Hey,' I say, trying to distract him. 'I think I saw a blessing in one of our textbooks for finding out about conception.'

'And that would apply to us how?'

More giggling. But the truth is slowly becoming real.

I pull down the stack of heavy books from the top of the piano. The Contents page in *On the Doorposts of Your Home*, which has a swirly New Age pink-and-purple cover, lists a prayer called On Learning of a Pregnancy. We thumb through the pages.

'Here it is,' I say.

'Should we?' he asks.

I laugh.

'Let's do it,' Degan says.

We stand shoulder to shoulder and recite the first part together: ' "We stand humbled before the Power of Creation with joy and fear . . ." '

(With fear! With fear!)

I read the lines assigned to the WOMAN: ' "Deep inside me a seed is growing. I am at once afraid and filled with ecstasy . . ." '

Afraid! Yes!

Also embarrassed. The prayer feels silly, like we are auditioning for a child's school pageant or a commercial for natural deodorant.

Degan reads for the MAN: ' "I stand with you in awe before the wonder of existence . . ." '

I can see from his face, though, that he's still thinking about his opera tickets. There's a long paragraph in transliterated Hebrew: I wonder what it means.

On the opposite page is a blessing to say upon a miscarriage, but I am not worried about my baby's viability. That night I dream about a filament, buzzing brightly in the centre of a bulb.

ᐸᐳ

I visit my doctor, Dr Singh. Her hair is pulled into the high bouncy ponytail of a cheerleader. She tests my urine, confirms the double line's augury.

'We're going to Europe,' I tell her.

'When?'

'On Friday!'

Surely this isn't allowed. 'Am I okay to travel? To fly?' I ask.

'So long as you feel up for it.'

I feel up for it, I tell her. I feel *fantastic*.

There are things I have wanted in my life, things I have longed for. To have a book published. To meet a partner. But this particular longing to be a mother is different. Only in its consummation do I realize its extent, like a vast continent whose hinterlands I've purposefully ignored. I've spent the past decade bracing against pregnancy, trying not to capitulate to its allure. Only now that I am pregnant and therefore undeniably fertile can I acknowledge how I long for a child. There is nothing I want more in the world's farthest reaches.

ᐸᐳ

We spend the next couple of days getting ready for our trip. Degan cleans the kitchen and I tidy the bedroom for our subletters. I fight my impulse to hide the Sabbath candlesticks, the *tzedakah* box emblazoned with the Star of David, the books by Martin Gilbert. Most people are good, I reassure myself. I'm safe.

Degan reads aloud to me from the guidebook about the Jewish Quarter in Vienna: it was a hotbed for antisemitism, yes, but also an epicentre for Jewish culture before the war.

Vienna, I've always thought, would make a nice name for a girl. And the *V* would go well with Degan's last name, Davis.

TWENTY-TWO

I'M MYSELF, AN AVERAGE WOMAN boarding a plane, and then all at once, I'm someone else. Somewhere high over the Atlantic a transformation occurs, sudden and complete, an eclipse of the moon, a slap across the face. 'It's just jet lag,' I tell Degan when we land in Austria. I gesture to some cracked plastic chairs at the back of the arrivals lounge. 'Can we just stop here for a quick rest?'

I'm so tired he has to drag me out of the airport by my arm. I fall asleep the second the taxi starts moving, so I see nothing of where we are, where we're going. The taxi drops us off in the middle of a concrete square. It's five in the morning; everything is closed. I lie like a dishrag in the front lobby of a tanning salon while Degan figures out the directions to our hotel.

When we get there, I sleep for fifteen hours. When I wake, Degan is dressed and shaved. He hands me a coffee – I flinch and push it away, acutely nauseous.

His eyes widen. Never in the decade he's known me have I refused coffee.

We visit the rooms where Sigmund Freud saw patients, and the bustling Naschmarkt. Degan tours Schubert's apartment while I sleep in the stairwell outside. When he emerges, he mistakes me, briefly, for a vagrant. At dinner I scarf down three-quarters of a roast chicken and a huge plate of spaghetti. Six weeks pregnant. The hunger is for the new person I'm growing inside me, and the new self, the mother I'll become.

In the evening I am too exhausted for Don Giovanni and Degan goes alone. The next day is Friday and we take the bus down to the Jewish Quarter in the late afternoon, looking for a place to make Shabbat. We have to stop and ask directions. In our single day here, Degan has learned enough German to be mistaken for a native speaker. The man he stops gives long directions, pointing and gesticulating. Degan nods and smiles, although he doesn't understand a word.

The synagogue, when we finally find it, is flush with a row of office buildings. It is distinguished only by two guards outside the door.

Where are we from? the larger bald one asks. Are we part of the Jewish community in Toronto? Can he see our passports? How are we related?

'We're married,' I say.

He's looking back and forth between the passports, his brow furrowed.

'Oh!' I say. 'We just got married a few months ago.'

'*Mazel tov*,' the guard says, but he isn't done with the interrogation.

Have we ever been to Israel? Do we celebrate Shabbos and the High Holidays?

He turns to whisper something to the other guard; I see he has a bug in his ear.

Several metres away is a third guard, a machine gun slung over his shoulder. I clench with indignation and then I remember the terrorist attack described in the guidebook, in which thirty people were wounded and two killed while they were attending a bar mitzvah service here in 1981.

Finally we're granted access. As we enter, we hear the woman behind us in line pleading with the guard. 'I'm a *Jew*,' she cries. 'I just want to pray.'

Inside the synagogue, I climb a stairway to the balcony, where the women are segregated. Four teenage girls in long skirts are looking down into the synagogue proper, where there are maybe forty men, most with black hats and beards. These men are wandering up the aisles toward the bimah, draping their arms over the backs of pews, chatting with their neighbours. I locate the top of Degan's head and watch him find a seat. It's hard to tell whether the service has started or not. Eventually the rabbi rallies the troops, turning to his Torah and calling out page numbers in Hebrew. He bobs back and forth at the waist as he chants, pumping his fist in the air like a teenager at a rock concert. The bimah is crawling with little boys with long ringlets beside their ears. They cling to the tassels of the rabbi's tallit, then try to crawl completely beneath the prayer shawl.

It dawns on me that the rabbi is their father. They are here with him at work.

The service is, mercifully, in English, to accommodate an unusually large number of visitors to the city. Still, I feel irrelevant, segregated in the rafters. The rabbi looks up at the women once during the service, and once he addresses us directly, making sure we all have siddurs. Otherwise, he speaks to the men. He talks about Tisha B'Av, the annual fast day that is approaching. It commemorates the destruction of both the First and Second Temples, tragedies that occurred on the same Hebrew date but 655 years apart. How could the bereft Jews possibly mark such events? Three suggestions were put forward, but it was the third suggestion that took, that at Jewish weddings a glass be broken. 'At almost *every* Jewish wedding a glass is broken,' the rabbi says. 'Why?'

He answers his own question.

'Because it is a time of such great, overflowing joy. We can remember our persecution and move ahead, as well.'

I catch Degan's eye below me; we share a smile.

At the end of the service the rabbi alludes to the number of Jews killed in Vienna before the war, to the antisemitism that characterized the city. I remember Degan reading to me from the guidebook, about Jews after the Anchluss being forced to scrub toilets with their prayer shawls. 'You might think of this place as relatively evil,' the rabbi says. 'And I am not denying that horrible things happened here.' He pauses. 'But things are changing. It's different from before.'

As though to celebrate this, the dance that Jews seem to love erupts, the dancers linking arms in a large adult version of Ring around the Rosie; it always reminds me of a Newfoundland folk dance. The balcony obscures half the circle: I have an aerial view of the bobbing black hats, and the edge of the circle as it turns, heads coming in and out of view like the portion of a wheel visible beneath the fender.

That night, I wake in the darkness from a dream in which Degan has to retrieve something from a toilet. The feeling in the dream, which Charlotte always says is the most important part, is not shame but joy. There is a document in those fetid waters, something from the past, and Degan is the one to fish it out.

Our next stop is Prague. Because of an article I've been commissioned to write, we are put up in the Czech Republic's most resplendent hotel. Our bags are whisked to an opulent suite where chocolates and champagne await. The smell when Degan uncorks the bottle makes me run for the bathroom. I spend the whole day curled on the bed in the fetal position. The lavish buffet is lost on me. I emerge at dinner to eat off the 'beige menu': dry toast, bananas.

'I can't even enjoy good food!' I wail.

'Be gentle with yourself,' Degan says. 'It's a lot. *All* of this.' He gestures around at our fancy hotel room, but I know he's referring to much more, as well.

Since I'm here, I've decided to take advantage of the chance to delve into my family history. I leave Degan at the hotel, bundle up and head down into the street, looking for some scrap of Granny's life *before*. Thinking of Gumper's *Report from England*: 'There is no trace of the Bauers and we must assume they are no longer alive.'

It's mid-afternoon by the time I make it down to the Jewish Quarter. The place is crawling with school groups, teenage boys elbowing each other, laughing about the mandatory *kippahs* they have to wear to gain access to the various synagogues. I hesitate in front of a display of Judaica. The vendor tries to explain, in halting English, that the six points on a silk tallit represent the points on the Star of David.

'I know,' I tell her. 'I already know.'

I head down to the Pinkas Synagogue, a monument to the Czech Jews killed in the Holocaust. The names of the murdered are written on the walls. Granny visited this synagogue in the 1980s with my cousins. She wasn't interested in hanging around inside for too long, so they went outside and sat on a wall and she smoked a cigarette. She told them that she imagined her mother, Marianne, had looked after the chickens in Theresienstadt. Unlikely, yes. But the confidence with which Granny said it made it seem true.

Later, when they were getting into bed, Granny said she felt that if she began to cry about everything that had happened, she would never be able to stop and might go mad.

I brace myself and enter the building. I, too, have been here before, but in the intervening decade the monument has been completed, and now every square inch of wall space is covered with names. Each last name is written only once, in bold letters, followed by all the first names in smaller writing. My stomach flutters as I scan the dense script. I find the name Bauer, Granny's maiden name, and gasp to see just how many of them were murdered. A whole band of different Bauers, with their own families, their own stories. It takes me ages to find Granny's parents. I run my eyes along the long list and land on the names with an odd mixture of gladness and grief:

Oskar 29 xi 1880 – 20 1 1943;
Mariana 8 viii 1894 – 20 1 1943

The memorial does its work and my eyes film over. I touch my belly, both to share the act of remembering with my unborn child and to protect her from it. I take a few deep breaths and try to absorb the moment but am jostled from behind by a group of laughing teenagers; I lose my footing, and when I regain it, Oskar and Marianne have disappeared back into the mass of writing on the wall.

I catch the scent of someone's body odour and my stomach rebels. I push through the crowds and stand outside, gulping the fresh air. I want to do something else; I want some other, better way to honour them. I approach the beleaguered woman in the ticket booth. 'Is there somewhere to go to an actual service?' I ask.

She launches into a rickety English explanation of the various synagogues my ticket gives me access to.

'No,' I say. 'A service.'

'Now?'

'For Shabbos. Tomorrow.'
'Oh,' she says. She doesn't know.

Degan and I decide to get up early on Saturday regardless. The Charles Bridge, flanked by its famous statues of saints, shimmers in the pink light of sunrise. St John the Baptist, St Francis of Assisi, the lesser known saints Norbert of Xanten, and Sigismund. We sit outside the locked Pinkas Synagogue, rubbing our arms against the chill. I want to show Degan what I've seen, the names of Granny's parents. Why is nobody here? When I pull out the guidebook, I see that the synagogue is closed for the Sabbath.

'I fumbled it again,' I say.

Degan hugs me. 'I'll visit it when you're in Plzen,' he says. 'Okay?'

I sniffle. I am set to head off to research my article for the travel magazine. 'You'll stay here?'

'I'll meet up with you on Monday.'

I sniffle again and nod.

'Let's read the Kaddish,' he suggests. We've practised the prayer for the dead in the preceding weeks, going over and over the unfamiliar syllables. Degan pulls out the folded sheet. We read it in halting Hebrew, all the way through. I'm thinking about Lucy's dream: 'Mrs Liska Pick very much regrets that she is unable to attend.'

The next morning I board the train to Plzen, home to the most famous Czech brewery. The article I've been commissioned to write, irony of ironies, is about beer. I am to tour the country's world-renowned microbreweries, sampling the wares. 'Alcohol is prohibited!' my daily pregnancy email warns cheerfully. As if I had a choice. I turn away glass after glass, bile rising hot in my throat.

The tours of the breweries cover hectares of hallways. I race after my guide, through a pea-soup fog of malt and hops. I gag and sweat. It is as though I'm being trained for a marathon, maybe, or for some more ancient relay involving armour, a crossbow and a unicorn.

I keep my hand pressed against my stomach and picture the cells multiplying. I make up a silly song and sing it under my breath: '"My little baby. Oh! My little baby."' It's a lullaby, and a hymn, and a mantra.

❧

Degan takes the last train from Prague and meets me at the hotel. We lie on the bed and have a huggle. 'How were your last few days?' I ask.

He tells me about his own trip to the Pinkas Synagogue. As he talks, I recall how the names covering every square inch of the walls are written in tiny cursive script barely legible to the naked eye. But Degan entered the room, raised his face, and the names jumped out at him, as though Oskar and Marianne themselves were waving hello.

'Wow,' I say.

'I know.'

'I also saw an Irma Pick. That was your Gumper's sister, right?'

'Really? I didn't see her!'

Alone in the hush of the room, Degan recited the Kaddish. Whereas when I was there, the place was full of tourists.

We brush our teeth – the toothpaste makes me gag, the feel

of the bristles against my back molars, and flossing is out of the question – and collapse into bed. I sleep for thirteen hours, unmoving, like a corpse. The following day we take the train to Auschwitz.

TWENTY-THREE

SEEING THINGS THROUGH THE LENSE of cinema is a cliché of North American culture, but all I can think about as we board the train to the death camp is who should score the soundtrack and who the starring actress should be. It's late afternoon, and a violently bloody sunset streaks the sky. The set designers add a last layer of red. The trip takes several hours, the train left over from the Cold War era: metal, utilitarian, and almost empty. The slow rocking of the carriage makes me gag. The closer we get to our destination, the slower we move. The laboured clacking of the wheels over the tracks is audible: *ca-lunk, ca-lunk, ca-lunk.* At the penultimate stop, a bald tattooed man in tall lace-up neo-Nazi boots boards. He sits in the seat across from us, eyes forward. As the train starts to move again, I look out the window and see an abandoned gravel lot, and standing at its border, three gaunt children in tattered overalls, holding up their cameras to take our picture.

❧

It is, of course, impossible to travel on a train to Auschwitz and not think of others who did so in different circumstances. It is summer now, and warm, but in her video interview, Vera says that she and her family were sent on December 17. I try to imagine the cold, but my mind trips and falls. They didn't sit for three days. Her children clung to her. They were jammed into a freight car, with one bucket to use for a toilet for a hundred people. People were sick. People died.

It was night when they arrived. There were SS men, dogs, people in striped pyjamas, Nazis yelling, 'Raus! Raus!' 'It was a scene from a madhouse,' Vera said. 'Yelling. Beating. You didn't know where you were.'

The men and the women were separated on the platform. I imagine little Eva, gripping the edge of her mother's dress. What is a five-year-old like? She needs help cutting her meat. A story before bed, the sheets tucked up around her chin. She is bright enough, smart enough to understand the adult world around her. You can see the first signs of the person she'll grow into, but she still has the smell of a baby about her.

Eva had curls and big cheeks. She was born in the unlucky year of 1938. She held her mother's hand as they were loaded into the back of a truck. They were beside a woman Vera knew who had been a prisoner for some time. The woman said, 'You're in Auschwitz. We're all going up that chimney.'

Vera says to the interviewer, 'We didn't understand.'

The next morning they were sent to the showers. Those little spiked nozzles on the ceiling, so portentous. But it was water that rained briefly down on them. Naked, in December, tiny Eva shivering. I picture her thin arms, the way her small shoulder blades would have jutted from her back like wings. The prisoners had been forced to leave their clothes on a peg outside; at the end of the shower, their belongings were gone. There was only a huge pile of other people's clothes. They scavenged to find something to wear. Vera tears up. 'I was glad I found clothes for little Eva. I was so worried she would catch cold.'

Later they stood in line to get tattooed. Vera pulls up her sleeve as proof, to the interviewer, to the part of herself that still refuses to believe.

'Was it painful?'

Vera doesn't answer. 'Eva was very smart,' she says, instead. 'Some of the children were crying terribly, but she didn't cry.' Her daughter understood not to make a fuss, in case compliance could help them.

Vera's number was 71251.

Her little daughter Eva's was 71252.

I try to imagine, as though I am there, Eva pulling up her sleeve. The fabric getting caught, bunching up. Maybe Vera had to help her, holding her daughter's arm steady under the pain. Little Eva clenching her milk teeth while the hot needle burned into her skin.

A five-year-old still likes to hold hands.

Tears roll freely down Vera's cheeks as she remembers. Mid-winter, in Auschwitz, a friend of Vera's brought Eva a gift. It was a tiny stuffed toy, sewn from a scrap of old cloth. A little mouse.

Vera's tears are for the smallness of this pleasure, and for its enormity. For the generosity of her friend in the face of the unthinkable. Tears remembering her daughter's real delight. That her daughter *could* be delighted in such circumstances. That she will never be delighted again.

⁂

When the train stops at Auschwitz, Degan and I are the only ones who dismount. The station is abandoned. We walk around aimlessly, looking for a taxi; the driver we eventually find doesn't speak a word of English. Only through a crudely acted pantomime of execution, a finger slit across the neck, are we able to tell him where he should take us. Our hotel is located directly opposite the camp gates. We can see the infamous wrought-iron slogan, ARBEIT MACHT FREI –

'work sets you free' – from the lobby. The man who greets us at reception has one arm.

Like college roommates, Degan and I fall into the twin beds and a deep, unconscious slumber, and wake to a world where anything could happen. 'Maybe we should just forget it,' I say. 'Relax in the hotel and watch TV.'

A joke: there's no TV. And Degan is already putting on his nicest shirt and tie: he wants to dress up to honour my family.

It's a grey, rainy morning at the world's most infamous death camp. Tourists of all ethnicities mill about. We join a four-hour English walking tour and are herded around, a mass of humanity, which I can't help but find ironic. A large man in sweatpants drops an empty nachos bag casually on the floor of one of the barracks. Our guide shows us all manner of gas and execution chambers, piles of shoes, piles of human hair, Zyklon B crystals, graphic photographs demonstrating the results of Dr Mengele's 'medical experiments'. Eighty per cent of the people getting off the train, we are told, were sent directly to the gas chambers.

Oskar and Marianne were among them.

Vera and her children were not.

Auschwitz, I remember Rabbi Klein telling us, is sometimes seen as the inverse of Mount Sinai. Receiving the Ten Commandments was the time we were closest to God. And here at Auschwitz – I look around at the size of it – when we were the farthest.

I keep the button on my jeans undone out of necessity, periodically touching my belly. 'My little baby. Oh!' I hum to our daughter. Degan bends down and whispers, 'Hello, little blastocyst.' The movie-set quality of the tour recedes only once, in the face of a display case of baby clothes. Two or three cloth diapers, a moth-eaten sweater and a pair of tiny booties, their owner long flown to heaven's angels.

I search for Eva's tiny stuffed mouse, believing I might actually find it there.

At Birkenau we walk beneath the famous guard tower, then down the railway tracks to the gas chambers. This is where the real killing took place.

Eva.

Jan.

Oskar.

Marianne.

We sit against the base of one of the chimneys and, for the second time, recite the Kaddish: "May His great Name grow exalted and sanctified,' I stumble, 'in the world that He created as He willed.'

PART THREE

The truth is the thing I invented so I could live.
– Nicole Krauss

ONE

AUGUST IS ON THE VERGE of expiring by the time we arrive back in Toronto. Degan will be busy preparing for the new semester, so I fly on alone to Quebec, where my grandparents lived and where my parents still spend their summers, to tell them the news. 'Why are you smiling?' Dad asks when we see each other at the baggage carousel.

'No reason.'

I touch my stomach unconsciously.

I've decided to wait until we get back to the house in North Hatley – a two-hour drive from the airport – so I can tell him and Mum together, but as soon as my suitcase is in the trunk of the car and Dad starts easing out of the parking garage, I blurt it out: 'I'm pregnant!'

Dad slams on the brake.

'That'll be twenty-five dollars, sir,' says the man in the booth.

Dad says, 'But you just got married!'

'Three *months* ago.'

'Sir?' the man in the booth says. 'There are other cars behind you.'

Dad pays, forgetting his change, and we move out into the turning lane, his face strained with some emotion I can't read.

'Aren't you happy?' I ask.

'I *am* happy,' he says, and like magic, the smile on his face grows. 'I'm delighted! But I wasn't expecting it yet. I guess it makes me feel old.'

'Me, too. I'm an adult.'

Dad laughs. 'When's the baby due?'

'March,' I tell him.

'I'll cancel my Taos ski trip,' he says, now really excited, on board and eager to do whatever he can to help.

I fall asleep almost as soon as we hit the highway and wake up, two hours later, in North Hatley. I've been coming here my whole life, but the beauty surprises me every time. The fields and farmland, the picturesque red barns giving way to the enormous summer houses nestled in the woods around the water. The lake spills its shimmer of blue below the rolling hills. We pull up the long gravel driveway to the house Granny and Gumper built all those years ago. Mum comes out to meet us in her bathing suit cover-up, with her sunglasses pushed back on her head. I give her a hard hug. 'Alison has some news,' Dad says.

She looks at me expectantly, her eyebrows raised, her skin tanned and sun-flecked from hours on the tennis court.

'I'm pregnant!'

Her eyes widen. 'You just got married!'

From inside the house the dog starts to bark.

'Three months ago,' I say.

Mum's face is blank, registering her shock.

'Aren't you happy?

'I *am*.' Et cetera.

Those two are meant for each other.

When the routine is completed for the second time, I need to lie down. I climb the stairs to the blue room with twin beds that was my father's as a teenager. Granny and Gumper built this house in 1966 and it is full of their belongings from the Old Country. The framed maps of Bohemia, the enormous dark wood armoire. Granny's parents didn't escape themselves, but managed to send a large amount of furniture out of occupied Czechoslovakia. It spent the war in two containers in Antwerp. When the furniture arrived and was unpacked, the empty containers were so big that Gumper gave them to friends, one to be used for a hunting camp and the other for a garage.

Delaying my nap, I go into Gumper's old study and look at the six-pronged menorah pushed to the very back of the shelf.

The carpet, I notice for the first time ever, is covered in a pattern that resembles Stars of David.

I point this out to Dad. He scoffs. I'm seeing things where there's nothing to see. Why am I so interested in Judaism when it was so 'unimportant' to Granny and Gumper?

Over dinner, I drag myself through a long song and dance about how the Judaism I'm studying is different from that of our ancestors, how I'm drawn to it of its own accord.

Very drawn to it.

Dad dips a piece of pork chop into his applesauce. 'There's something I want to ask you about,' he says.

I wait.

'It's about my portfolio,' he says. 'My financial portfolio.'

He launches into a diatribe about his fear that we will mismanage his estate, not out of intent but out of ignorance, and how everything he's worked for, and everything Gumper worked for, will be lost.

I try not to be discouraged. But clearly I need a new approach to the topic of Judaism.

I stay in North Hatley for a week. My mother cooks me heaping plates of spaghetti bolognese, and I get out of bed only to float in the emerald swimming pool, with the view of the lake below. I wave at the farmhand haying our field;

he has been taking care of the property for decades. In the evenings I watch the satellite TV: Wimbledon, the Summer Olympics. On my last night, Dad joins me for a movie. At the climax, when the children are taken away from their parents, he starts to make sounds. Loud wincing. I look over at him; his hands are balled up, his eyes squinty. 'Ouch,' he says. 'Ouch, ouch.'

This naming of his emotional pain as a physical symptom is familiar; he did the same thing at church in the difficult year after Gumper's death. His forehead on the pew, tears leaking from his eyes. Dad is forever leaving movies, walking out of the theatre because, in his own words, he can't distinguish the real from the made-up, the truth from a story. His *own* truth from the story.

A friend once asked me, 'Who in the world are you most afraid to lose? Don't censor!'

'My father,' I said.

I will not be able to exist without him in the world.

'Ouch, ouch.' Dad winces, doubled over.

'We can turn it off,' I say.

He sighs with relief.

We sit in the high-backed, leather-covered European armchairs.

'I had the most amazing religious talk of my life,' he tells me. 'Just the other day. With Father Gagnon, the Catholic priest.'

'What did he say?'

Dad summarizes: That all religions are the same. That religion is a tool to greater spiritual knowing.

This is his line, the one he learned from his beloved grandmother Ruzenka, that the *particular* religion doesn't matter so much as the practice of religion itself. Any religion will do.

Later, after Dad has gone to bed, I watch a rerun of the old

TV show *Six Feet Under*. Brenda, the New Age girlfriend, says to the main character, Nate, 'You channel other people's pain.'

Nate teases her. 'Dad always said it was my talent.'

Brenda's face grows serious. 'It is,' she says. 'It's a gift.'

⚬

There are babies everywhere: in the small North Hatley post office, on the plane on my way back to Toronto, in the airport. I ogle their plump arms, unable to peel my eyes away. I'm nine weeks pregnant. So nauseous I could weep.

Dr Singh calls to schedule a checkup. 'How was your trip?' she asks brightly when I see her.

'I feel a little . . . sick.'

She smiles brightly again. 'That's normal!'

It means, she reminds me, that the pregnancy is progressing.

⚬

Music Night is scheduled for the first Saturday I'm back. The leafy back porch is crammed with writers. A novelist friend says, 'You're not pregnant, are you?' She eyes my apple juice.

I shake my head emphatically: *No*.

As though the baby has heard my remonstrance, when I excuse myself to go to the bathroom, I find blood in my underwear. I gape at it in the same way that I gaped at the pink line on the pregnancy test: something of intimate, immediate consequence that at the same time feels as remote as a star. I look away, look back. It's still there. Not the blood of a menstrual period – not quite – but any blood is reason for consternation.

I bleed steadily for a week, unable to think of anything else. I meet Dr Singh's reassurance that spotting is 'normal' with flat-out disbelief. I have, by this point, also procured myself a midwife and I call her, too, hoping she'll be more sympathetic. Finally, in face of my relentless wheedling and cajoling, she agrees to send me for an ultrasound. The technician squirts jelly on my stomach, brandishes her magic wand. 'Let's see if we can hear your baby's heartbeat,' she says.

Wait.

What?

My *baby?*

My baby's *heartbeat?*

On the screen is a blizzard, fierce wind and snow. And then, a tiny flashing blip, a flicker, like some kind of beacon.

'There it is!' The technician beams, as though she's never seen this before.

It is stunning in a way I could never have imagined. All this sickness, this exhaustion, has had a purpose. There's something – *someone* – inside me. *My little baby. Oh! My little baby.*

Tears roll down my face, into my ears.

I am sent home with a photo of our dreamer, a whisper of an image as ethereal as the minute being herself. When Degan gets in from work, I tell him what I've heard.

'Seriously?' he asks. I can see he only half believes me. He squints at the picture, trying to arrange the grey flecks into something resembling a baby. We lie down on the bed. He presses his face to my tummy. 'Hi there, little one,' he murmurs. 'I hear your heart is pretty strong. I have to be honest: I don't know what I'm doing. But I can hardly wait for you to arrive.'

September 8 is my thirty-third birthday. My bleeding eases up. I'm still nauseous, but nothing like before. I'm out of the gates, out of the first trimester, thirteen weeks pregnant to the day. Everyone says now I can relax, which means, I guess, that I can stop worrying about a miscarriage. Only, I haven't been worrying at all, since I'm not going to have one.

Degan suggests it's time to share our news more widely. I send an email, and am floored by the many answers that flood back. All at once it's true: I'm going to be a mother. We're going to have a *child*.

TWO

THE FOLLOWING EVENING is our first JIC class back after the summer. It is held at Toronto's Holocaust Centre. Degan and I drive up Bathurst Street, which goes on forever, to the part of town I've heard referred to as the Gaza Strip. There is an intercom at the parking lot gate, where we have to state our purpose, and a security guard at the front desk. We are issued hot-pink name tags, which we are instructed to wear in full view; a burly man with a mullet asks us to write down our exact time of arrival. The class begins to congregate in a hallway upstairs; people are smiling and waving. Diane approaches with Tamara on her chest. 'Oh! She got so big!' I say.

Diane grins proudly. 'Hi, Tamara,' I say, playing with her toes. 'Hi! Hi, Tamara!' One hand on my stomach, as though linking our 'little blastocyst' to the healthy, thriving infant in front of me.

Harriet appears in her lavender UGGs, surveying us like an unpleasant reminder, like something distasteful she has almost managed to forget over the two months away. She gathers us in front of a huge set of double doors that are like something out of Harry Potter or Narnia, carved with the Hebrew letter *shin*. 'What words start with the letter *shin*?' she asks.

'Shoah,' says Diane.

'Shalom,' says Tom.

'Shabbat!' Debra shouts.

I catch her eye and smile, and mouth, 'Hey!'

She mouths in return, 'Welcome back.'

Several more *shin* words are suggested. It's as though the doors will swing open to Sesame Street if we stumble across the magic word.

Harriet talks for a very long time about how the Shoah must never happen again. I try to connect her words to Vera, to Oskar and Marianne, but cannot. The whole class shifts uncomfortably. It is hot; there is nowhere to sit down. Finally Harriet pushes a small, well-concealed button on one of the door handles and the huge mechanized doors creak open. We file past a montage of famous European Jews (Modigliani, Einstein, the Rothschilds) and settle onto chairs arranged in a semicircle in front of a large screen. We are shown a half-hour movie called *Into the Deep*, replete with sinister organ music and black arrows depicting the Nazis moving across the continent. There are stock shots of men in *tallitot*, dangling from the gallows; piles of spectacles and wristwatches; the row of blank-faced murderers at the Nuremberg Trials. The same items Degan and I have just recently seen behind glass at Auschwitz itself. The mountain of baby shoes brings a lump to my throat, but I swallow and focus, instead, on the back of Diane's head and on the smaller head of Tamara, asleep on her stomach. I cannot go back into that blackness now. I make a little wall of light around myself and shut everything else out.

Unfortunately, though, it is hard to tune out the survivor whose speech is the final item on the evening's agenda. It is clear from the way Hilda mounts the podium, like a prizefighter entering the ring, that she has given this talk many times. She has props: laminated photos of her relatives who were murdered, an armband with a Star of David – not the original, she tells us, but one she sewed herself for these presentations. Hilda was a girl of fourteen when the war broke out. She spent five years in the forests, starving and running and hiding, surviving against all odds to arrive here in prosperous Thornhill to talk to us tonight. She tells us bluntly of the horrors she endured: Washing in her own urine to keep the boils away. Letting a friend who was labouring in childbirth bite her arm. Why? So the Nazis, directly above the cellar where they were hiding, wouldn't hear.

'The baby had to be strangled the moment it was born,' she says, looking at us one by one, nonchalant, daring us to react. 'If it had the chance to cry, we'd all be discovered.'

Diane pulls Tamara closer into her chest.

'Besides,' Hilda says, 'we were partisans, starving in the woods. What would we do with a baby?'

Hilda jumps, in her thick accent, from anecdote to anecdote. I see the psychology of the survivor, which I've been reading about. Hilda has never left the forest. Each time she talks of it, she goes back. She has a desperate hunger to process the experience, which she attempts to do by recounting it over and over. But no amount of talk can fill the void. I picture Granny in the centre of a crowd at a cocktail party, her cigarette aloft in her manicured fingers, as she holds court over the assembly. I think about the inadequacy of language in the face of experience, and about the fact that in twenty years, the survivors will be gone. I am living in the tiny window of time in which we can hear the testimony from the source. Yet if Vera's story was hard to imagine, Hilda's feels completely abstract. My own months of psychic turmoil battle against hers, erecting a defensive barrier. I conjure up the image I've seen on the ultrasound screen, our little blinking heartbeat, and focus on it instead of what she is saying.

Hilda has obviously been told she goes on too long, because at several points she asks, 'You are tired? You are wanting me to stop?'

But either the rest of the class feels differently or they are better at feigning attention, because they murmur collectively, 'No, please continue,' and Hilda launches back into the stream of words from which I fear we will never emerge.

From directly behind me comes a low snort, a snuffle. I turn around in my seat: our instructor, Harriet, is asleep.

After, we congregate in a boardroom upstairs to debrief the session. 'We'll talk about what you've just seen in a moment,' Harriet says. 'But first, did anyone have a really remarkable summer?'

I put my hand on my belly and whisper to Degan, 'Should we tell them?'

He clears his throat. 'Well, on the topic of tonight's class, we visited Auschwitz.'

I wince at his misunderstanding. The last thing I want to do is talk more about the gas chambers. Soon, though, I will be glad he hasn't shared the real news.

THREE

WEDNESDAY MORNING my nausea reappears, a stomach sickness more barbed than the one I've grown accustomed to. Degan finds me on the bathroom floor with my cheek pressed against the cool tiles. He leads me to bed, tucks me in. 'Rest,' he says. 'I'll call you from work. And try to get out for some fresh air.'

I mumble something unintelligible.

'Promise?' he asks.

I nod weakly.

I sleep for three hours, and wake with the intent to do what I've been told. My bike has a flat tire, but filling it seems like a manageable goal. Out on the front porch the late-summer air is dense, the edges of everything hazy. I heave my bike down the cement steps to the sidewalk. It feels inordinately heavy. Almost as soon as I start pushing it, I am shaking and perspiring with the effort.

I reach the intersection I've been heading for, and realize my destination is still another block away.

I eventually get to the garage, and crouch in front of the counter, hanging on to my stomach, sweat pouring off me. I hobble to the bathroom, where I throw up violently and am granted a few moments of relief. A kind stranger fills my tire with air. Back outside, the day is bright and boiling hot. And then, just as quickly, freezing cold. The hill facing me on the way home looms like a ghoulish apparition. Although I now have two full tires, the hill is way too steep to ride, so I'm again resigned to the Sisyphean task of pushing. My breath is shallow and shaky. I cross with the light. When I at last reach the apartment, I'm confronted by the steep concrete stairs. I have no idea how I manage to get my bike up them. Finally I'm crashed out on the bed. I call Degan and tell him I feel bad. *Really* bad.

In the week after, he will replay my messages and cry.

Degan arrives home early. He tucks me in and phones our midwife, Hedrey. She tells us to come in to her office the next morning. We'll see if we can still hear the baby's heartbeat.

That night I have a fever, low at first but rising. I toss in my sweat-soaked sheets, holding my cramping stomach. I get up to pee and am not surprised to see I have started to bleed again. I fall back into a fitful sleep and wake up just twenty minutes before we're due at the midwife's. 'Why did you let me sleep so late?' I snap, but I see from Degan's face it was because he is worried about me; he wanted to let me rest as much as possible.

At the clinic, brimming with toddlers and breastfeeding pillows and women in overalls, Degan checks a book on morning sickness out of the lending library. It has a single, sad-looking soda cracker on the cover.

Maybe I just have really bad morning sickness.

Hedrey greets us with a sombre smile. I lie down in her examining room, decorated to resemble a bedroom with brightly patterned curtains and photos of newborn babies on the walls, so animal in their pink hairless helplessness. Sun slants hotly through the windows. I lift my shirt; Hedrey places her Doppler on my belly.

I wait for the sound of the heartbeat, but there's nothing.

Only the eerie *whoosh* of my own blood through my veins.

Hedrey averts her eyes, concentrating. She moves the instrument lower, just above my pubic bone, where my stomach, in the last week, has started to protrude. I can now actually feel the knot of a human there, inside me.

Still nothing from the Doppler. I crumple the edges of my skirt in my wet palms.

Then, suddenly, there it is. The galloping hoofbeats, fast and steady. *Da-dun, da-dun, da-dun.*

Hedrey beams. 'Hello, baby!' And then: 'The baby is fine!'

We're all silent, listening to the heartbeat, relief washing over us. I look over at Degan, his blue eyes wide, full of tears.

❧

The baby is fine. The baby is fine. I repeat this to myself as Degan drives up Bathurst Street. *The baby is fine.* But such a high fever isn't good for her. We need to try to bring my temperature down. Hedrey has instructed me to go see Dr Singh.

Degan stops at a red light, and I call Mum on my cell and give her the update: 'The baby is fine!'

But I'm still feeling awful.

I hang up the phone and a paroxysm of pain overwhelms me: jagged little claws grabbing at me from the inside. I hunch over in the passenger seat, my knees tucked up to my chest. A sound escapes my lips, a sound I don't at first recognize as coming from my own mouth. Degan reaches for me, holds my shoulder awkwardly with one arm while turning the car onto Eglinton with the other. The jabs are sharpening, converging. I cry out again and pull my knees in closer.

In the elevator on the way up to the doctor's office, I double over involuntarily. The elevator door dings open and I run down the hall to the bathroom, my whole body clenching and squeezing. I throw myself into a stall and slam the door behind me.

When I pull down my pants, my underwear is soaked with blood. In the crotch, a cylinder of thick red jelly.

I crouch over the toilet. The cramps tear me apart. Not cramps. *Contractions.* My insides are falling out, big chunks of red splashing beneath me. I bend over with my head between my knees, sweat pouring off me, my body finishing its task of its own accord. I finally manage to stand, minutes or hours later, rising on wobbly legs as though I've just been born. The toilet bowl is full of blood, and feces, and something else, which my eyes flinch away from. From beneath me there's a roar: the automatic toilet flushing.

My little baby. Oh! My little baby.

Every bit of her gone, swallowed away.

FOUR

A GURNEY HAS APPEARED, magically, in the hall outside the bathroom, accompanied by two ambulance attendants. All I've ever wanted is to lie down. The attendants insert an IV. I am wheeled into the elevator, then out onto the street, where I blink in the bright sun. Passersby turn their heads as I'm lifted into the ambulance. From somewhere far away, I hear Degan saying he'll drive the car and meet me at the hospital. A siren starts up, announcing our procession. I'm a queen being carried through the streets on horseback. Traffic parts around us.

For the second time in a week, my ears are wet, filling up with tears.

☙

At the hospital, morphine. Oxygen tubes in my nose. A male nurse with a ring through his eyebrow says, 'You've lost a lot of blood. Your blood pressure is still very low. Without that IV you would have needed a transfusion.'

'What IV?'

I look down at the line into my arm.

Through a thin curtain, a man's gravelly voice: 'I normally drink three bottles of wine a day. But I went cold turkey on Monday.'

His doctor asks, 'Do you ever hear voices? On the TV, say, talking to you?'

A woman chimes in: 'He's paranoid about his bosses at work.'

To my right, another woman, who took all her husband's heart medication. She keeps repeating, 'It's okay. It's fine. You don't need to help me. I don't want to live.'

I'm moved to a different room. The nurse with the eyebrow ring appears again, asks, 'How are you feeling?' I roll onto my side, wipe the tears from my cheeks.

'We need to know your blood type,' he says. 'But your father gave us the rest of the info.'

'The info?'

'Your address and birthday. Those things.'

Should I correct him? 'I think you mean my husband,' I say.

'No, I mean your father. He's in the waiting room.'

'That's my husband.'

'It's your father,' he says.

'My father lives in another city.'

The nurse shrugs.

'How much morphine did you give me?' I ask.

❧

The man in the waiting room is in fact my father. He came into Toronto for an errand earlier in the day. But bad news travels like dominoes falling, and now he's here with me. Not an angel, not exactly. But close.

Dad smoothes the hair back from my forehead. 'Hi, sweetie,' he says. I have a sudden visceral memory of the lily of the valley he would bring to my bedside when I was a girl, a small vase on my dresser. The lush, heady fragrance announcing itself in the long spring evenings: *Beauty survives.*

Later – hours, or days: time has gone elastic – Degan appears with a wheelchair. He pushes me down into the basement of the hospital. We are shown into a dark room where an ultrasound technician is tutoring his trainee. He mumbles something; there's a long silence, and I realize he's talking to me.

'Pardon me?'

'Get on the table,' the technician says.

Degan corrects him under his breath: 'Get on the table, *please.*'

He helps me up tenderly, as a mother might help her child. I arrange my hospital gown over my legs, but the technician yanks it back up. He squirts a glob of jelly on my stomach and moves the wand across my flesh. The screen appears grey, an undifferentiated stretch of snow. This time there is no blinking beacon.

I flush with the ignominy of what my body has done.

Degan's eyebrows are up, though, and he's smiling. 'I think I *see* something,' he says.

I can hardly stand his hope. He has been waiting for this moment, for *his* first glimpse of our child, and now his heart imagines what his mind knows isn't there. Because, of course, this is not the ultrasound he's been looking forward to. This is something different altogether.

A doctor arrives with the results. The fetus, the egg sac, all the 'products of the pregnancy' are gone. We gather up my blood-soaked clothes in a plastic bag. I am given a skirt from the hospital's lost-and-found, and a new shirt: some other woman's clothes. Degan drives us home. Along Spadina, night has fallen swiftly. Street lights and pizza joints. Two of us, where this morning there were three.

∾

I sleep the whole next day. When Degan gets home from work, he tidies the bedroom while I cook rice and cut vegetables. There is a mushroom that has a smaller mushroom fused into its side. I chop the mother and baby apart without mercy.

Friday morning we make raspberry smoothies, and French toast with last week's leftover challah. I move around the kitchen, my head in and out of the fridge, with no nausea whatsoever. After having sworn I would never again – *never again* – drink coffee, I brew a pot and guzzle it with relish. The pregnancy hormones are draining out of me like liquid through a sieve, my body giving up the task it has been performing so diligently for the past thirteen weeks.

I go into the bathroom and find Degan staring at himself in the mirror.

'What are you thinking?' I ask.

'Nothing.'

'No, really.'

'Can I see the ultrasound photo?'

I go into the bedroom and pull it out of its thin envelope. Degan cradles it, slight as a moth's wing, in his palm. We peer at the charcoal smudge against the field of darker grey. Who was she? Who would she have become? Someone. A person. We'll never know.

In the evening we bring candles into the bedroom and lie together in the low flicker. When it's time to go to sleep, Degan wants to blow them out. He's nothing if not aware of a fire hazard. But I see him linger a little longer over the third light, for our lost child, before snuffing it out.

He eventually falls asleep, but I'm awake and alert, a hole in my chest the wind is whistling through.

I understand for the first time – really understand – the thin membrane between death and life. Everyone will die. *Everyone* I love. It's banal, and obvious, and earth-shattering.

I push back the covers and pad through the dark apartment. A sliver of moon just visible through the kitchen window. The quiet hum of the dishwasher finishing its work. In my study, I reach for the ultrasound picture; it is not on the table where we left it. I look beneath papers, between pages of books. When I still can't find it, I panic, ripping through drawers and turning out pockets. If I can't see the photo, I will die.

It's there, all at once, in full view on my desk. I cry with relief and despair. The little grey blur. The inkling. All I'll ever know of my daughter.

On Saturday morning Shayna picks me up early, takes me to a Shabbat service held in someone's home. There are maybe twenty others, mostly strangers to me. We chant single lines of liturgy, weaving them through the morning like strands of golden thread. The last chant is from the Song of Songs: *zeh dodi v'zeh rayee* – 'this is my beloved; this is my friend.' As we sing, we circle around each other, looking each other in the eye. Seeing, being seen. Such raw power.

After, the leader asks, 'Does anyone need to say Kaddish?' Kaddish is recited when someone has died, and therefore, by The Mourner's definition, been alive. So my baby doesn't count.

The circle is quiet. Shayna reaches for my hand; I hold tight to her thin fingers. The leader looks around at us all, his eyes falling for a long moment on me. 'I'll say it for us all,' he decides. And he begins: 'Glorified and sanctified be God's great name . . .'

FIVE

ROSH HASHANAH ARRIVES without fanfare. It's Jewish custom to dunk apples in honey and make wishes for the New Year. Degan and I wish for world peace, for Obama to win.

'I wish to have our baby back,' I say.

Degan squeezes my hands. 'I wish, God,' he says, 'for you to accompany our baby wherever it will be.'

But where *will* it be? Who will take care of it after the warmth of my womb? I think of my little dreamer with the big fish eyes. If there is a heaven – which I don't think there is – but *if* there is one, my baby is in the same place as Vera's lost daughter, little Eva. With Gumper, and Granny's parents. With Granny herself.

Maybe my great-grandmother Marianne is taking care of our child. Draping a wing over her little shoulder.

My heart hurts as I look at the little bowl of honey I've set out, the apple pieces slowly going brown. I picture small hands dipping and young voices laughing, the silly wishes a young child would make. I picture Eva, with her halo of wild curls.

༄

I'm grateful, though, that we have somewhere to go for the first night of the holiday. Last year at this time I did not know the meaning of Rosh Hashanah, let alone have anyone to celebrate with. This year, Aaron and Sylvie's invitation was so warm that in a fit of boldness, I have asked whether my parents could join us, as well.

'Do we dress up?' Mum emails to ask.

I don't really know.

'I'll wear a jacket,' Dad says.

'I guess it's like Christmas dinner,' I say.

Mum nods. This she understands.

I head over early to help Sylvie set up. The hall walls are covered with photos of her father, a famous opera singer, in *Tosca*, *Madama Butterfly*, *Don Giovanni*. I think of Degan's opera tickets, produced at the same time as the news of the pregnancy, and squeeze my eyes shut against the tide of feeling. The Filipina maid mistakes me for more hired help, tapping me on the shoulder and directing me briskly to where the silverware is kept. When she realizes her mistake, she flushes. 'I'm sorry,' she says. 'Welcome.'

In the dining room the second life-sized maid, the one made out of papier mâché, has been removed.

An hour later the doorbell rings. It's the Hamburger King and his son who dated Monica Lewinsky. We smile, say hello. The bell rings once more and I hear my parents' voices in the front hall. 'Good to see you again,' Aaron says to Dad. 'The last time was at your father's *yahrzeit*.' Stating this for the benefit of the other guests. I want to run and bury my face in Dad's chest, to curl up in his arms like a little girl.

Mum, absent at the *yahrzeit*, is introduced around. She hands Sylvie a bouquet of irises, a bottle of red wine. 'Hi, sweetie,' she says casually as she hugs me hello.

I can see they have no idea how symbolic the evening feels from my perspective, or how emotionally exhausting the anticipation has been. But she knows, of course, about the miscarriage, and her touch is especially gentle.

'Well,' Dad says loudly, to the growing gathering, 'this is one of the most stressful days of my life.'

Everyone stops talking; people shift their eyes nervously.

'Because it's your first Rosh Hashanah?' I ask tentatively.

'Haven't you seen the papers? Congress didn't approve the bailout plan. The economy is tanking. As we speak. Now! And now! And now!'

There are murmurs of agreement.

'You would not believe how much money I've lost today,' he says, his forehead in his hands. Then he looks up at the room full of strangers. 'We need a fiscally prudent budget,' he booms. 'And for that we need a majority government.'

The election is coming up, and Dad wants everyone to vote for our current prime minister, Stephen Harper, who he believes is our only economic hope.

I wince at how this might be received, since his politics are so different from my own and so different, I am certain, from everyone else's in the room, but the moment passes and the chatting guests shift positions. We move to the table, set with cut crystal and white linen tablecloths. There are the usual blessings, the bread and the wine, and a blessing over the honey and apples. And the *Shehechiyanu*, which is the blessing for firsts, because it's the New Year. We dig into the meal: the same clear chicken broth in glass bowls, this time with a matzah ball floating in the centre. I watch my father divide his in half with his spoon. He starts telling the Hamburger King about his background. 'I was one of those Jews whose parents didn't tell the kids they were Jewish,' he says.

'After the war?' the Hamburger King asks.

Dad nods yes. 'We've never been to Israel.'

The King raises his eyebrows. 'How would you identify yourself?'

'Religiously?'

A nod.

Dad pauses. 'Well,' he says. 'I was raised Christian. All my religious experience is with Christianity. But truly? In my heart, I know I'm a Jew.'

It is as though someone has struck a gong from his corner of the table. My eyes widen. His comment rings in my ears throughout the rest of the meal, so I can barely hear what anyone else is saying. When Degan and I get up to clear the plates, he whispers to me in the kitchen, 'Your father is *Jewish*.'

'I *know*,' I say. '*Weird*.'

Over dessert, Sylvie confirms again that very few Jews were able to get into Canada in 1941.

Dad says, 'How many? Fifty?'

Sylvie says, 'I'd put it lower.'

The Lady Boat that brought Granny and Gumper to Canada was torpedoed on its way back to Europe. I am here, in this world, by luck alone.

⁊

Degan and I have a big fight when we get home. I'm sad about the baby and wrung out from the visceral stress of the evening. I ask why he hasn't returned the emails from the real estate agent. 'Can't you see how hard I'm trying here?' he says, his voice tight.

'It's just one tiny email. It would take you two minutes.'

'I'm doing my best,' he shouts. 'This is hard for me, too.'

'*What's* hard for you?'

He glares at me.

'Do you think the baby was just yours? That I'm not sad, too?'

He's right, but his yelling scares me. I close myself in the bathroom and sit on the toilet with my head between my knees, thinking of our lost baby, or lost history and rituals. The night was so momentous. My father celebrated Rosh Hashanah and labelled himself Jewish. It seems something more is called for now, some acknowledgement or marking, but I'm lost. I slink upstairs to sleep alone, but Degan follows me. 'Don't be like that,' he says.

He holds me, and I cry.

Later, although it's forbidden due to the *chag* – 'holiday' – I turn on the computer. My cousin Lucy has written 'L'Shana Tova' on my Facebook wall. Her message is there for everyone to see. I feel the old terror of being revealed for who I am, or worse, for who I hope to become.

Dad, for his part, seems unfazed. He has sent an email thanking us for including him in the holiday. 'I enjoyed it very much. The people were very warm. There's just one thing I wish had been different.' A beat. 'I wish there had been more reading from the holy texts.'

SIX

THE NEXT MORNING, Dad calls to say that his cousin, my uncle Paul, is dead.

Last August Paul had a heart aneurism. He was open on the operating table for six hours, but the surgeon could not get the sleeve into his artery. When he woke up and they told him, he cried.

Now his heart has given up entirely.

I gather the pieces I know about Uncle Paul's life like so many blue marbles in the palm of my hand. I think about him as a small boy, sent away to boarding school in England during the war. About his household, where nobody spoke of Judaism. I think of Paul putting his Jewish stepmother into an old-age home. And of my wedding, when Shayna sang in Hebrew and his face crumpled and his chin fell to his chest. I assumed it was shame. Could it have been something sadder? He wouldn't hug me in the receiving line. Now he is gone from this earth. He is the small boy in the novel I'm finishing, put on a train and sent away forever.

I sit at my desk to do some more reading. My research has led me to an article on trauma and memory. Knowing and not knowing, remembering and forgetting, and the psyche's brilliant dance between the polarities. The article details case studies: a woman who escaped before the war, assimilated, and did not even recognize her own husband and children when they came for her after surviving the camps.

Her family. She didn't know who they were.

I think of Gumper's *Report from England* about his nephew Paul: 'He knows he is Jewish, of course.' But maybe Uncle Paul had truly forgotten who he was, where he came from.

The article suggests that in art engaged with trauma 'there often is a "lie", a distortion, covering over the as yet unworked through and unknown aspect of trauma.' My novel deals with themes of secrecy and denial. It tells a story very different from my own family's, a story that depicts characters dying, rather than escaping in the nick of time as my grandparents did. Still, I have chosen to use many of my relatives' names, spreading them among the fictionalized ones so the two might appear indistinguishable.

What are the unknown aspects of our family's trauma? I can see their outlines, but they won't speak, won't reveal themselves.

Degan finally contacts the real estate agent and we make an appointment to see some houses. There's nothing remotely within our price range, and I resign myself to spending the rest of my life in an apartment. There are worse things.

Besides, since losing the baby my nesting instinct has leaked away, too. Back home, we order takeout Thai for our Sabbath meal. The blessings are becoming routine. We make love, and read aloud from the Heschel book *The Sabbath*. The prose is as rich and dense as honey cake. In the morning we sleep in, read the newspaper in bed. I have a pregnancy test in the medicine cabinet; it flickers at the edge of my awareness. I don't want to wait for my period to come – or not – to tell me if I'm pregnant. 'Just going to the bathroom,' I say to Degan casually.

I peel back the silver foil. When I pee on the stick, though, only one pink line spreads across the window.

No baby for another month.

I crawl back into bed, into Degan's arms. 'Sing to me,' I say. And he makes up a beautiful song about our lost little one on her way to eternity.

Later, we sit on the couch and talk more about conversion. What would it actually *mean* to be a Jew?

We practise asking each other, 'What church do you go to?'

'I'm Jewish,' I say.

A smile plays across my mouth.

'And what church do *you* go to?' I ask in turn, but now I start to giggle.

'I'm Jewish,' Degan says, laughing.

'Merry Christmas,' we say to each other. And practise answering, 'Thank you. But I'm Jewish!'

More laughing. We roll around holding our stomachs.

Finally I say, 'I'm tired. Let's have a nap.'

'A Shabbatnap?'

We crawl into bed laughing. 'Good one,' I say.

Degan tickles me.

'Stop,' I say. 'You're ruining the Shabbatmosphere.'

The following morning, though, I wake up feeling low. Later today, I will go to Uncle Paul's funeral. The days are getting dark again. I was supposed to spend this winter plump and pregnant, knitting booties in a rocking chair beside a fire, like a woman in an insurance commercial. But my baby is gone and the new test has come back negative. I'm suddenly terrified of another winter like the last, immobilized beneath the SunBox, the bad blood pinning me to my seat. I drag myself to contact improv but barely have the energy to roll around, and flinch when anyone tries to touch me.

Michael sidles up. 'What's up, lollipop?'

I ask if he will fast for Yom Kippur, which is coming up shortly.

'I've got a big day at the theatre ahead of me. So no.'

Ariel pirouettes past us, leaps wildly through the air. I wave at him, and he wheels toward me and bows deeply. 'Yes, m'lady?'

'Are *you* fasting for Yom Kippur?'

He snorts. 'Um. No? I'm secular.' And he flounces away.

I leave before the closing circle, unable to face the goodwill and sharing, and drive to Brampton for the funeral. Uncle Paul's brother speaks, and his son. They mention his sense of humour, his kindness, his financial success. Nobody says anything about his religious background; nobody speaks of his background at all. But in the front hall of the opulent country club where the reception is being held there's a pile of photo albums of his earlier lives. Paul as a chubby baby in a bonnet, in the arms of his uncle, my Gumper. Paul as a little boy in pre-war Czechoslovakia, with buckle shoes and short pants and a rascally gleam in his eye. Paul with his mother, Mary, Gumper's sister who didn't survive the war.

He received the news of his mother's death without any upset, and when I try to talk to him about it, he doesn't respond at all, and I don't know whether it means he doesn't want to talk about it, or whether it simply means nothing to him.

Do people really change? Is it possible to start life anew?

SEVEN

I ASK CHARLOTTE MY QUESTIONS ABOUT CHANGE. Her answer is a resounding no. People can't change their essential selves. But what they *can* change how they relate to themselves. And that makes all the difference.

It's early on a weekday morning, mothers walking their kids to school along the leafy residential street outside Charlotte's office. She looks fresh, her hair still damp from the shower. 'I can't stop thinking about evil,' I say.

I tell her about little Eva on that cold morning in Auschwitz. Five years old. Pulling up her sleeve, clenching her milk teeth against the pain of the tattoo. Trying not to cry. This is the detail that has lodged itself in my mind, the detail I cannot forget. 'Is evil archetypal?' I ask Charlotte. 'That kind of evil?'

I expect she will say yes – Jung's framework is her framework – but instead she is silent. 'It's not useful to try and understand it,' she says.

'So what can I do?'

It is perhaps the most honest question I have ever asked of anyone. I am entirely childlike in my desire to know. How can I make sense of a world where this could happen?

'You could try to imagine what they would want,' Charlotte says.

'What who would want?'

'Your dead relatives. The people who were killed.' She coughs. 'Your great-grandmother Marianne.'

I look at her blankly. 'But what is evil? Is it an impulse in all of us?'

I think of my university courses in social psychology, the famous studies where subjects, *many* subjects, could be goaded into delivering larger and larger shocks to a victim until the shocks were purportedly big enough to kill.

'The Holocaust must have been imagined by sociopaths and then executed by unthinking followers,' I say. 'And the depressed economy, people hungry and willing . . .'

Charlotte is silent.

'It makes my own suffering seem ridiculous,' I say. 'Like, like . . .' I am searching for an apt comparison, for something without the cliché of 'a grain of sand' or 'a speck of dust'.

'Your suffering is also valid,' Charlotte says. 'Talking yourself out of it only gives it more power.'

I think that my suffering is a shard of their suffering. Again the clichés.

'There's one thing I know,' Charlotte says. '*They* would not want you to suffer.'

'Who?' I ask.

'Well, Marianne, for example. Little Eva.'

But I resist. If I don't suffer, Eva will be forgotten. The small girl with her stuffed mouse in the freezing cold barracks in Auschwitz. My suffering is, I realize, a perverse kind of tribute.

'Think of it in reverse,' Charlotte says. 'Would you want her to suffer for you?'

'Of course not!'

'Well?'

It occurs to me then – comes over me in a wave of feeling – that there *is* a light that shines on all things. That shines and can never be extinguished.

On the evening of Yom Kippur, I take the bus up Bathurst Street in the rain. I am meeting Degan for Kol Nidre, a prayer that annuls the previous year's vows for the upcoming year. It is the most misunderstood of Jewish prayers, the one most used by antisemites as evidence that Jews aren't to be trusted.

On the bus I sit beside a middle-aged woman in a black dress with a bright pink umbrella. 'You're on your way to synagogue,' she states matter-of-factly.

I nod. How did she know?

In the parking lot, Degan is just arriving, the hood of his yellow raincoat pulled up. A security guard comes out of the building. 'You can't leave your bike there.'

Degan bristles but does as he is told, moving it out of sight of the BMWs and Audis, locking it to the rack behind the building. We're a half-hour early for the service, but inside the place is packed. The men are all wearing dark suits and prayer shawls, and the women Prada and Gucci. The custom of eschewing leather shoes in favour of sneakers, which I know is practised at other synagogues in the city, has not taken root here.

The only seats left are in the nosebleed section, where we have a perfect view of the top of the lead rabbi's *kippah*.

The service is like a collective confession, but whereas in Christianity the emphasis would be on the sins themselves, here the emphasis is on redemption. The idea that we are forgiven, actually *forgiven*, is hard for me to take in.

The cantor's voice pierces me, pulls a taut stitch through my heart: 'When the wrongs and injustices of others wound us, may our hearts not despair of human good. May no trial, however severe, embitter our souls and destroy our trust.'

Words are cheap, but the sentiment monumental. *No* trial. *However* severe.

The sermon is about Jerusalem, the city of peace. The rabbi speaks about the three great religions that all lay claim to it. His talk is beautiful and generous but followed up by a pitch for money. If we buy Israel Bonds and donate them to the synagogue, it counts as a mitzvah, we are reminded.

After, Degan leaves his bike and we take the bus back down Bathurst Street in a rain that has turned into a downpour. My feet hurt in my black patent heels. At home, I change into a track suit and wool socks. The fast, which lasts for twenty-five hours, has technically begun, but I remind myself that pregnant women are exempt, and to fast would remind me that I am not among them.

I have started to bleed, which could be my period, or could, as apparently often happens, be my uterus expelling a second round of tissue.

'What are you doing?' Degan asks as he watches me peel a pineapple.

'My fast includes fruit.'

'Just fruit?'

'And vegetables.' I run the tap and fill a glass. Degan raises his eyes. Water is forbidden. You're not even supposed to brush your teeth.

'What about protein?' he asks.

'Right! And almonds.'

'I fasted today for four hours,' he says. 'Between meals.'

I giggle. 'We're wimping out.'

'Speak for yourself,' Degan answers. 'I'm just gearing up.'

On the morning of Yom Kippur, I get up and go to my desk. The prohibition against 'work', which includes the use of a pen, not to mention a computer, feels harder than the prohibition against food. Still, I eat a bowl of blueberries and put the kettle on for coffee.

Degan fasts.

We arrive at the synagogue and join a service for people in their twenties and thirties, the same crowd from Shayna's Shabbat Nation Fridays. I am compelled by the beautiful liturgy, by the sombre and reverent atmosphere. We read aloud together:

> *Each of us is a shattered urn,*
> *Grass that must wither,*
> *A flower that will fade,*
> *A shadow moving on,*
> *A cloud passing by,*
> *A particle of dust floating on the wind,*
> *A dream soon forgotten.*

Reciting this ancient poem gives me shivers up my arms, up the back of my neck. I have started off on the wrong foot but vow now to fast for the rest of the day.

On Yom Kippur decisions become final: 'How many shall pass on, how many shall come to be.' I feel again the pulse of my body convulsing against my will, pushing our baby out of my womb, out of the world entirely. I think of Vera's Eva, born at the wrong time, in 1938. Lining up for the showers at Auschwitz. Vera afraid that her daughter's clothes had been removed and now she would catch a cold.

I realize that Leonard Cohen's song 'Who by Fire?' is taken from the Yom Kippur liturgy. The ways we might die, the places and time our life will end. In the final line of the song, when Cohen asks who shall he say is calling, there is a challenge, an anger. It is as though Cohen is asking who has the *right* to decide such a thing. The way someone will die. The length of their last breaths.

The day proceeds with hours of intense prayer. It is rigorous, a spiritual scouring. I'm amazed by how quickly a bit of hunger pushes me up against my mortality. Marianne on that first morning when they could not leave the house to buy bread. Vera faced with her children's rumbling stomachs. Did little Eva ask for cereal? Did she beg? We sit and stand, sit and stand, stumble along with the Hebrew. After six hours, Degan whispers to me, 'I'm done. I want to leave.'

We slink out of the synagogue and head home to sleep, trying to ward off our hunger. It's late afternoon when we wake. The rain has subsided, the sidewalks giving off little breaths of steam. From our bedroom window I see red and orange crimping the edges of the maple leaves. The last of the sun disappears behind the high school in the field behind our apartment. 'That's our cue,' Degan says. 'It was a good fast.'

I agree.

We tuck into a meal of bread, spinach salad and lentil soup as though it were a race to the bottom of our bowls. Pacing ourselves is physically impossible. I think of Marianne's empty stomach, her cold body banging up against the other cold bodies in the cattle car. What she would have given – what they all would have given – for a simple bowl of soup.

At the end of our meal, we lean back and fold our hands

over our bellies. Degan has a little smile on his face. 'What are you thinking?' I ask him.

'The New Year has started,' he says.

And I believe it is so.

EIGHT

THE HARBOURFRONT FESTIVAL rolls around again. I get an email from the organizer asking if I'd like to introduce the Czech writer Josef Skvorecky. I do a bit of research, and learn that he lived in the same town as Gumper before the war. I email Mr Skvorecky and introduce myself. Yes, he says, he remembers my grandfather. They used to drink coffee together at the famous café in the town square.

I met Eli at the Harbourfront Festival exactly a year ago. A nice guy. Whatever.

On Friday evening Degan and I head up to the synagogue. 'Just going to the bathroom,' he says when we get there. When he returns he tells me he was in front of the bathroom mirror, trying unsuccessfully to pin his *kippah* to the centre of his head. In a fit of frustration he said to his reflection, 'It's fucking hard being a Jew.'

When he came out of the bathroom, there was a woman waiting her turn, grinning at him.

The service brims over with goodwill, and singing, and the Newfoundland folk dance I have learned is called the *hora*. After, Shayna gestures us over to her table and we eat with the Shabbat Nation band, like roadies. She slings an arm around me, a chunk of challah in her hand, and leans across to Degan sitting on the other side of me: 'I'm in love with your wife.' She leans her head on my shoulder; I can smell the faint citrus scent of her shampoo.

'That's okay,' Degan says.

'Just a little bit.'

He grins.

'We can share,' she says.

Degan sings a wistful line from a song we both know, Leonard Cohen's 'The Gypsy's Wife'.

'I love Leonard Cohen too,' Shayna says. 'The name "Cohen" is Hebrew, meaning a member of a special tribe of priests.'

'Oh?'

'The line is patrilineal, actually,' she says, pivoting to look at me. 'If your *father* is a *cohen* – a direct descendant of Aaron – then you're a *cohen*, too.'

***

The rest of our Sabbath is quiet and lovely. In the morning I lie in bed reading an anthology of essays about childbirth that my friend Christine Pountney, who also sang at our wedding, has lent me. Christine's piece is breathtaking, the kind of writing that makes me want to give up altogether because I will never be that good. I skip from her essay to one by the Israeli-Canadian writer Edeet Ravel, in which she talks about how she wanted a girl so desperately because of 'the circumcision problem.' Her partner was not circumcised 'in case the Nazis came again.' And she did not want to inflict any more suffering on a tiny infant.

This gives me pause.

In the end, she gives birth to a girl.

Degan sleeps in; when he wakes up, we make love. The window in our bedroom is open a crack and I can smell the crisp leaves, the first intimations of frost. The hint that things are on the cusp of change. I think of Degan calling himself a Jew to his own face in the mirror. I say, stating the obvious,

'You're warm to Judaism these days.'

He shrugs. 'I feel closer to being Jewish than I do Christian,' he says. 'And I like supporting you. But I don't—'

'I know,' I say, rushing in to reassure him.

He pauses. 'I should probably tell Rabbi Klein I don't want to convert. Remind her. To make sure she knows, too.'

In the afternoon we go for a long walk in the Don Valley; in the ravine below the bridge, the city is wild, leaves and vines creeping over the concrete. Back home we print out the words to 'L'cha Dodi' and practise. We go outside and look for the first three stars in the sky, signifying that the Sabbath has ended. Havdalah is the ceremony marking the change between Shabbat and the rest of the week; we light a braided candle, say the blessing, then extinguish the candle in a goblet of wine in a hiss of smoke and steam. The ceremony typically ends with the song 'Eliyahu Hanavi'; we listen to a Klezmer band's rendition on YouTube, shouting out our coarse interpretation of the words and slapping our thighs.

Degan harmonizes.

Harriet has been right about one thing: there is sadness when the day is over. I'm glad to remember Shabbat will come again next week.

Reluctantly we turn our phones back on, our computers. There is an email that my cousin Heather has given birth to a son. Heather is Mum's brother's daughter, which is to say she's as wasp as they get. Her husband is Chinese. The baby will be called Cohen.

NINE

WE'RE SUPPOSED TO MEET with Rabbi Klein every six weeks, but it's hard for me and Degan to coordinate our schedules, and months pass before we find a time. When we finally do, Rachel moves to hug me in the waiting room outside her office, but I back away. 'I've got an awful cold,' I say. Degan says, 'And I'm all sweaty from biking uptown.'

It's already dark at five thirty, bruised clouds billowing above the city, but the rabbi's office is snug and warm. It has the faint smell of ink and of postage stamps, of books on shelves gathering dust and books whose spines have been cracked again and again. We sink into the red armchairs.

'So,' she says, and smiles. 'Catch me up.'

We tell her about the High Holidays, about my dad coming to synagogue and about Uncle Paul dying.

'I'm so sorry,' she says. 'May his memory be for a blessing.'

I can see, by her soft face, she means it.

There's a silence, in which we hear the first smatter of rain at the window. 'And we want to talk about conversion,' Degan says. 'We wanted, or rather *I* wanted—'

But she jumps in before he can finish. 'The process is different for everyone,' she says. 'Your final exam must be coming up?'

I nod.

She continues. 'Some people convert right away after finishing the class. Some people wait years. Some have one or two things they want to brush up on.'

The rain picks up, small hands tapping at the glass. The rabbi crosses the room, digs around in her filing cabinet. She passes us a sheet of paper, a list of ten questions to determine whether you're ready for conversion.

'I think the answer to these is supposed to be yes!' she jokes.

We look over the questions silently. I'd answer yes to maybe half.

Beside me, I hear Degan shift in his seat, crossing and uncrossing his legs.

'You look so serious!' she says. 'Don't be. You'll know when you're ready. I promise.'

I swallow, open my mouth. 'What if,' I start to say, and then stop, regrouping, trying to find the right words. 'I want this so much. I do know the policy, but what if *I'm* ready and Degan wants to wait?'

Her smile slips a little. She turns to face Degan, raising her eyebrows to ask if what I've said is right. He nods his confirmation.

'Degan,' she says solemnly, as though bestowing a blessing upon him. 'You're a thoughtful and introspective person. You're really wrestling with conversion. You don't want to make such a big decision without considering all the angles.'

'That's right.' He nods.

'But there's another perspective,' she says. 'Which is that you don't have to wait for a thunderbolt. In my experience, that doesn't happen. Or happens rarely. You *don't* have to wait until you're the perfect Jew. None of us is the perfect Jew.'

I look at Rabbi Klein closely. The warmth in her eyes. 'There are lots of situations in a relationship where one of you waits for the other,' she continues. 'You take care of each other that way. There's nothing I can do to change the situation. But I *do* want to acknowledge that I understand it's difficult.'

Beside me, I feel Degan's shoulders fall, his muscles soften.

'Thank you,' he says. He rubs a palm over the stubble on his chin. 'I know the tradition is for rabbis to push potential converts away with the right hand while welcoming them with the left . . .' He trails off.

'You need a little more left hand,' Rachel says.

'I would need *some* left hand. If I was going to consider it.'

I sit up straighter.

Rachel says, 'You need a *double* dose of left hand, since neither of you grew up Jewish, so you don't have a family to welcome you.'

But I know this does not mean she'll relent.

From the parking lot we hear a woman's voice: 'Samuel, I said *give* it to your *sister.*'

I try to steer the conversation back on course.

'Can I go ahead?' I ask. 'If Degan doesn't want to?'

I should know by now to leave the negotiating, the subtle communication, to Degan. At my blunt question, the rabbi's jaw tightens. Now it's her turn to find the right words. 'I advise that you wait until you're both ready,' she says finally. Her gaze is steady, but she worries the elastic that holds her dark braid, turning it around and around. 'We don't want to make Judaism a wedge in a relationship,' she says. The now-familiar line.

I'm quiet, blinking. The silence stretches out like the bleak hours of dawn.

'What are you thinking?' she asks.

'How hard this is,' I say. 'For us, the opposite is true. It puts pressure on our relationship to have to both make the same decision.'

Rabbi Klein takes this in. 'We had a meeting recently,' she says, 'with the Board of Rabbis. We were talking about this exact problem.'

I hope for a moment that she is about to say they agreed

that something has to change, but instead she reiterates the existing point of view. 'There was a rabbi who converted just one member of a couple,' she says, 'and the marriage fell apart. And he never forgave himself.'

Degan clenches and unclenches his hand in his lap.

'And what are *you* thinking?' The rabbi turns to ask him.

'That I'm angry,' he says. The words hang in the air for a second or two before he adds, 'Not with you. But the policy is painful. I see what Alie's going through. To me, she's already Jewish. That she should be held back because *I'm* not ready—'

He falters, but his opinion is clear.

There's more strained silence, the rain thickening to sleet at the window, announcing that winter is coming again, and soon. Finally Rabbi Klein says, 'I don't want this to be a stumbling block. Let's park it for a while. Keep doing what we're doing. What *you're* doing. There's still time left before you finish the class.'

This won't solve anything, but I'm glad for the cue to stand up and gather my things. At least it's all out in the open. She knows where we stand. We know where *she* stands. The conversation shifts to Degan's thoughts on a book that Rachel has lent him. He is taken with the idea of an intangible, unseeable God preparing the Jews for a life of abstraction in thinking. There is no Christ equivalent, no messiah we can picture. Are Jews drawn to the world of the intellect because they must use their minds to see God?

❧

The pile of typed pages that is *Far to Go* grows. I've planned to go away to the cabin for a final push before giving it to my agent, but there is a mix-up and the family we share the cabin with already has it booked. Shayna emails to say I am welcome to join her in Prince Edward County, where she is going for the week, to the home of an old friend.

I write back, 'So long as there is a desk. I need to work.'

It's settled. We'll head off early Tuesday afternoon.

When the day comes, though, we stay in the city for several extra hours, each of us in our respective homes, glued to the radio coverage of the American election. A few polls are already closing, with Obama in the lead. We eventually load up the car and start driving, listening along the busy 401, then down the dark country highway, the announcer's voice crackling in and out of range. We arrive to the trees, and the silence of the lake, and race inside to turn on the radio and listen there, as well.

John McCain's concession speech is surprisingly genuine. He calls Barack Obama 'his president'. Obama himself takes no time to revel in victory. There's a hard road ahead. The economy is the worst it's been for over a century. But a black man is the President of the United States of America. People are cheering in the squares in Chicago, on the streets of New York City. Raising their fists, foisting signs. The TV shows an elderly black woman, down on her knees, sobbing. She never thought she would see the day. It is the start of a new era. The world is rejoicing.

The only country that isn't happy is Israel.

The Sabbath sun has already set on Friday by the time I get back to the city. Degan comes to the door in torn jeans and my Amnesty International T-shirt advertising a concert that happened twenty years ago. 'Should we say the blessings?' I ask. 'Light the candles?'

He shrugs. 'I don't want to.'

I look at him slantwise but decide not to push. 'Okay,' I say. 'How about pizza?' We walk along St Clair to our favourite Italian joint, talking about our weeks. Degan says he cried when Obama won.

The following day we loaf around the apartment, reading the newspaper. In the afternoon we lie down for a Shabbatnap. We fall deeply asleep, the kind of sleep where you wake up with drool on your pillow and it takes you a minute to remember where you are. We're supposed to go over to a friend's house to play Mafia, but at the last minute we decide to stay home and rent a movie. I'm in a rom-com kind of mood, but Degan wants Charlton Heston's *Ten Commandments*. 'I'm upset about our talk with Rabbi Klein,' he says. 'I want to watch something that will make me feel connected to Judaism.'

The movie is an epic saga that begins with Moses abandoned in the bulrushes and ends with him leading the Hebrews out of Egypt. In other words, the story of Passover. It was filmed in the fifties – I imagine that the scene where God parts the Red Sea must have been very high-tech at the time.

On Sunday morning I go down to the contact jam. I lie on my back and listen to the sounds of physical release all around me, dancers stretching their hamstrings and calves, cracking their necks, the little grunts and moans. A few flakes of snow drift lazily past the studio window. I dance with Ariel, with Shayna, with Michael. The Jews. After the closing circle, Michael invites me to the Ontario jam, which I gather to be an even bigger rendezvous of rolling and hugging hippies.

'It's around Easter, right?' I ask him.

'I guess.'

'I mean Passover.'

He smiles. 'Easter is adjusted for Passover, though.'

I look at him blankly.

'Also,' he says, 'there are eight days between Christmas and

New Year's. Between Christ's birth and the New Year. Why do you think there are eight days between a birth and a *bris*?'

'A *bris*?'

'A circumcision.'

I give him a bland half smile and wander away to retrieve my water bottle. I have no idea if he's kidding or if he's serious.

TEN

I'M EXPECTING MY PERIOD ON SUNDAY, but it doesn't come. I still don't have it by the JIC class on Tuesday, which is about Hanukkah. Again! Already! I make a note to buy jelly doughnuts: two years in a row makes a tradition.

On Wednesday I print out a final draft of my novel. The pages have a heft to them, a thrilling, weighty presence. I touch the pile softly with my fingers and then, checking that no one is watching through the window, with my lips. I fire off an email to my agent, telling her I'm finished. In celebration, I eat six Mr Christie Pirate cookies. I'm craving carbs.

By Friday at noon my period still hasn't arrived. When Degan calls from work, I feel brave enough to say I might be pregnant. *Might* be. But he is still doubled over with a week of hard clients and a cold – he wants to wait until the morning to take the test.

On Saturday, Degan sleeps late. When he finally wakes, he calls up to me at my desk. 'Did you take it?'

'I was waiting for you,' I call back down.

We go into the bathroom together. I unwrap the foil on the pregnancy test and pee on the stick. A line creeps across the screen, a single line. The familiar punch to the gut: I will never get pregnant again.

'It's negative,' I say.

And then we both see a second line emerging, perpendicular to the first, forming a plus sign. Plus, for positive.

We peer at the plus sign like senior citizens peering at the small print of a crossword puzzle. 'I can't really believe it,' I say.

We whoop and hug, but there's a hollowness to the celebrations. Degan wants to make love, but I curl my body away. He crawls over the bed toward me, puts his stubbly face next to my belly. 'Hello, little one.'

He looks up at me, his blue eyes wide. 'Oh! I just remembered! I had a dream last night that we had a little boy. He couldn't speak, and then all at once he came out with a full sentence.'

I smile. 'A boy.'

'Not a boy *yet*.'

'No,' I agree. 'Just a little blastocyst.'

But 'blastocyst' is what we called the first baby, and we both fall silent, remembering.

We rest in the afternoon, and cook paneer and chickpea curry. Then we go out for ice cream. 'My tummy hurts,' I say on the drive home.

'I'm feeling sick, too. My cold.'

Degan sniffs, pulls out his hanky.

'Should we make Havdalah when we get home?'

'I don't feel like it.'

His face is hard, and I recognize the look he gets when he's triggered, when difficult things from his childhood have been, as Charlotte would say, 're-stimulated'.

'I keep thinking about our talk with Rabbi Klein,' Degan says suddenly. 'I feel bullied into making a decision. Especially now.'

'I don't think she was trying to—'

But Degan interrupts. 'If there was ever a thought of me converting, it's gone.'

'Do we have to talk about this right now?'

'Last week, when you were away, Harriet got me in trouble – like a child – for being ten minutes late to class.'

'I know,' I say. 'I just think this isn't a great time to get into it.'

But getting into it is exactly what Degan wants to do. He veers out into the passing lane. I flinch as a station wagon barrels past us.

'I can *drive*,' he says.

'I know. I'm sorry. It's just with the baby . . .'

'Don't you trust me?'

'To drive?'

'To do anything.'

I'm silent. I know he's lashing out because I'm here.

Later, we sit on the couch, studying for the final exam for the JIC. Half the things on the checklist we received, things we are supposed to have learned over the year, have never even been mentioned by Harriet in class. We flip through our books, looking for the answers to fill-in-the-blanks, multiple choice. 'This is bullshit,' Degan says.

'You seem pretty down about Judaism,' I say, thinking how quickly he has swung from one extreme to the other.

He grunts.

I say, 'I'm worried you won't want to celebrate Hanukkah.'

He agrees. He might not want to.

For the first time it occurs to me that Rabbi Klein might be right. That it's better to have both people committed.

A single tear rolls down my cheek. Degan softens, holds my hand. He says, 'I'm angry at everything right now. It's hard for me to speak at all from this place.'

I nod.

He says, 'I want to go through the Jewish calendar systematically and learn about every holiday.'

I refrain from saying that this is what we were supposed to be doing during the class.

Rubbing my eyes, I push myself up off the couch and close the textbook. In the bathroom, I splash my face with water. When I sit on the toilet, my underwear is full of bright red blood.

The sack of cells has heard our fighting. It thinks it isn't welcome.

Come back, little plus. Please come back.

⟨ℯ⟩

I bleed all day in a numb kind of stupor. Degan sits beside me in bed, an arm around my shoulder. 'I'm sorry,' he keeps repeating. 'I'll be better.'

He, too, thinks our fighting has scared the baby away.

Shabbat is waning, but we don't make Havdalah. We don't say the *Shehechiyanu*, the prayer for firsts; we don't get the textbook back out to read the prayer for conception, or the one for losing a child. I'm in between, in an awful place of limbo. Part of me wishes to wake up soaked through with blood. If this is what is happening, I'd rather get it over with.

Instead, the pale dawn brings more of the same. The blood in my underwear is still fresh and red – which the Internet unilaterally declares to be a bad sign – but still only splattered delicately across the cotton. The crimson drops are oddly beautiful, like a fresh kill on crisp white snow. Out on the street there's the sound of a car door slamming, then a man's muffled yelling. I make decaf coffee, take a few notes at my desk. Eat a breakfast of oat bran and organic yogourt. Bargaining for what I've already lost. Degan will be gone at work all day; I'll be here alone, losing our second child.

⟨ℯ⟩

I sit down to answer emails but find myself unable to concentrate. The spotting continues. Mid-morning I get up from my desk and speed-walk over to the drop-in clinic on Dufferin as though possessed. In the waiting room, I flip through greying fashion magazines and read the doctor's framed degrees on the wall. One is in Hebrew; Sokol is a Jewish name.

When I finally see the doctor, a balding man with wiry eyebrows that peak above his horn-rimmed glasses, he is preoccupied and brief. He says that an ultrasound won't show anything at this point, but he will check my beta levels. Then we can see if they rise over the next several days.

Back in the apartment, I change my pad, which looks like the second day of my period. More blood, still bright red. Degan comes home from work and runs me a bath, makes me a cup of hazelnut tea. Later, we drive up to the synagogue for our last class with the JIC.

When we get there, another student stands at the front of the room. 'Harriet has been a wonderful teacher,' she says.

The rest of us sneak sideways looks at each other. Beside me, Debra snickers.

'I'd like to present her with a gift.'

Harriet flushes, and undoes the paper. The gift is a framed copy of Eshet Chayil – 'a woman of valour' – the hymn sung in the home on Shabbat in which a man thanks his wife for all she has done over the week. A woman of valour is energetic, righteous, capable.

'You guys are so sweet!' Harriet says sheepishly. But she looks like she cannot believe anyone would think her worthy of being called valorous.

As promised, the exam questions are exactly as they appeared in the study guide. We whip through the multiple choice, short answer and fill-in-the-blanks. People start handing in their tests fifteen minutes after they've been distributed. A half-hour later, everyone is outside in the hall, saying goodbye, keep in touch, Chag Sameach.

'Merry Christmas!' Debra shouts.

Gales of laughter. The laughter of pent-up release.

And then we leave, in groups of twos and threes. The class is over, just like that. We float out into the snowy darkness, into our different stories, our various versions of what-happens-next.

ELEVEN

ON TUESDAY MORNING the clinic waiting room is full, but Dr Sokol calls me up to the front of the line. There's a big pile of files on his desk, and one of those happy-face squeeze balls to help relieve stress. 'Can I ask why you've come here, instead of going to your family doctor?'

'We just live a few streets over. It's easier to get here.'

I don't have the heart to tell him that Dr Singh reminds me of the last baby we lost.

Dr Sokol flips through his papers and pulls out my results. 'Good news or bad news?' he asks.

My stomach falls. 'Good?'

'Your beta levels are stable.'

I exhale, but not too far. 'What's the bad news?'

'They're not rising the way I'd like them to. They're just sort of sitting there.' He wrinkles his forehead and pushes his thumbs into his temples. 'It'd be nice to know where this is going,' he says. 'Are you pregnant or not. We'll take some more blood today.'

'Okay,' I say, my voice flat.

'There's nothing else. Unless you have any questions.'

'No.'

I turn to leave, then turn back toward him. 'Chag Sameach,' I say.

He looks at me properly for the first time, his eyebrows protruding above his glasses.

'To you, too,' he says. 'I'll call you when I know.'

❧

We spend the evening curled up with Thai takeout watching Woody Allen's film *Annie Hall*. Annie, the Gentile, brings her Jewish boyfriend home for dinner. There is a parody of her family in the dining room: polite restraint, long silences interspersed with comments about other people's illnesses. It might as well be my parents' table.

There is a shot of Annie's mother looking slantwise at Woody Allen and seeing, in his place, an Orthodox man with a black hat and sideburns.

After, we lie in bed; Degan puts his head under the covers and presses his mouth to my belly. 'Hi, you,' he says to the baby. 'How's it going? I've got some things to tell you.'

He lowers his voice; I can't hear what he's saying. The whispering goes on for a long time. When he's satisfied, he raises his voice again so I can hear. 'Okay,' he says. He wraps up the conversation with, 'Sweet dreams. *Laila tov.*'

He relaxes his head against my stomach; I stroke his hair. The pregnancy is so precarious. And with such a good father waiting in the wings.

❧

Degan leaves for work the next morning and I prop myself up in bed with the laptop on my legs. I still haven't watched the second half of Vera's Shoah Project interview. I haven't been able to bring myself to, but suddenly – who knows why – I have the courage.

I begin at the place in the interview where Vera describes the living conditions in Auschwitz. She tells the camera about the daily food ration: 'coffee' (black water), a tiny crust, very rarely margarine. The so-called soup had all manner of debris in it.

They were slowly starving. Once, she says, they were allowed to write and mail two cards each, saying, 'I am healthy and fine,' in exchange for bread.

The dreaded 'selections' were made by several Nazis, including Dr Mengele, the Angel of Death. Mengele, of the mice inserted into mouths and vaginas. Mengele, who would make a mother hold her newborn while the child starved. 'They were the *meanest* men,' Vera says to the camera. But here her voice trails off, unable to find more words. Because, indeed, *mean* is not even close to adequate.

Eventually, in March of 1944, Vera's mother, Ella Kafka, was selected for 'work'.

'I asked the Nazis to take me, instead,' Vera says. 'My mother was old.' Here she smiles ruefully, telling the camera, 'She was fifty-six. Her body wouldn't withstand it.'

Of course, it was not 'work' that Ella was being chosen for.

Vera doesn't say explicitly what happened to her mother but returns, instead, to that chasm in the psyche between knowing and not knowing, consciousness and willed ignorance. She says, 'An engineer we knew said it was impossible. They couldn't destroy five thousand people at a time.' She gazes at the viewer. 'So naive we were.'

In June of 1944, the Germans needed manpower. They were losing the war. There would be a selection of men for bona fide work. Knowing it could save him, Vera tried to sneak her son, Jan, onto the work transport. She managed to get Jan behind the main gate, but a quarter of an hour later he was back. The chance lost.

I pull my laptop in closer to my chest, as though I could somehow hold Vera, give her comfort.

Vera soldiers on in the face of the questions. Her face betrays a heartbreaking eagerness to please, a gratitude that finally someone is listening, and a young, foolish hope that maybe now something can be done. She tells the camera that on July 3 there was another selection. The Germans were getting desperate; now even *women* would be used in the war effort; even *Jewish* women. Those who were chosen had to stand five to a line. Vera heard the commander shout, 'I am missing one!'

A beat.

He pointed to her. 'You go!'

A second beat. A skip in time.

'I can't,' she said. 'I have children.'

'I said go!'

Vera looks intently, piercingly, into the camera. 'He slapped me. He beat me,' she says, her eyes wide. 'I wanted to run, but there were SS, dogs. What could I do?'

She asks this of the viewer not rhetorically but genuinely, *desperately*, as though she could go back and act differently if she could finally figure out the answer. 'Tell me, what could I do?'

A long silence.

'It was the worst time of my life,' Vera says. 'You are half-crazy in a situation like that.'

'Where were your children?' the interviewer asks.

Vera looks into the lens as if to say, *Have you not understood what I have been telling you?*

'In the barracks without me,' she answers.

'Her thought process dwindled, ceased,' writes William Styron in *Sophie's Choice*.

She could not believe any of this. She could not believe she was now kneeling on the hurtful, abrading concrete, drawing her children toward her so smotheringly tight that she felt their

flesh might be engrafted to hers even through layers of clothes.
Her disbelief was total, deranged.

There was nothing Vera could do. She was taken from her children.

She doesn't bother to tell the camera what happened to a child in Auschwitz who had no protection from a parent.

❦

The rest of Vera's story feels somehow irrelevant. The worst thing has already happened.

Her children are killed, but Vera survives against all odds. She is moved to a labour camp near Danzig and is brutally beaten. In January she is evacuated because the Russians are approaching. She walks in the snow for two months, wearing clogs. One night it's snowing so hard that she and some other women are able to hide in a ditch. The march continues on without them. They stumble through the storm to a barn. The heat in the pig stalls is heaven. They are so hungry they eat straw.

The Russians, their eventual liberators, cannot distinguish the victims from the perpetrators and treat everyone the same. 'They were like animals,' Vera says, several times, and her emphasis somehow implies sexual degradation, rape, but she leaves the particulars to the listener's imagination.

There are more months of struggle. Vera finds her way back to Czechoslovakia. There's a man in a truck is driving around looking for a Vera Lowenbach.

'It's me,' she tells him.

The man doesn't believe her: she looks too old.

The same thing happens when she meets the mother of an old school friend. 'I'm Vera Bondy,' she says, using her maiden name.

'You must be *Ruzenka* Bondy,' the woman replies, referring to Vera's aunt, to Gumper's mother. A woman fifty years older than Vera.

At the end of the tape, the disembodied voice of the interviewer wants to know if Vera has anything else to say.

'Pardon?'

'Do you think about the Holocaust often?'

'Yes. You can never forget it. Mostly I just socialize with people who were there.'

'Is there anything else you want to say?'

Her pause is imbued with futility, both desperate and resigned.

What is left to say? What could she possibly say?

'I just really hope that nobody should experience something like this again,' she answers finally.

TWELVE

DEGAN AND I SPEND AN UNEVENTFUL New Year's at the cabin. The smell of the wood stove makes my stomach lurch, as does Degan's aftershave and the mere sight of a single dirty dish in the sink. Nausea. A good sign.

I read trashy magazines on the sofa, popping Diclectin, the drug prescribed for morning sickness, like candy. Degan sits on the armchair opposite me with Martin Gilbert's biography of Winston Churchill on his lap. He reads to me about Churchill's friendship with the Jews, and how he sought to support them during the war. Vera's brother Friedl was one of them. He fled mainland Europe and worked with the Royal Air Force. The Nazis found out, and as payback, his father, Hermann – Vera's father, too – was beaten and tortured.

The diabetic father whose insulin was taken away.

Daddy.

Meanwhile, in today's news, Israel has begun an attack on Gaza. Bombs, a ground invasion. The Palestinians can't get across the border. Their diesel supply is cut off, their drinking water compromised. The Israeli defence minister says it won't be a short operation.

We drive back to the city. Degan spends the first week of January with his eyes glued to the TV. 'Unbelievable,' he curses. 'Sickening.'

I'm pulling on pyjamas for bed when my phone rings.

Dr Sokol's voice is bright. My HCG level has gone from 14,108 last Wednesday to 43,980 this Monday.

'HCG . . . ?'

'Human chorionic gonadotropin.'

'So my beta levels?'

He laughs. 'It's good news.'

Later, I check my email. Harriet has written Rabbi Klein, copying us. '*Mazel tov!* Degan and Alison have completed all the requirements for the JIC. It was a pleasure to work with them.'

We're done.

THIRTEEN

THE MOST CONFUSING PART of my thwarted desire to become Jewish is the mounting evidence that I already am. In January, out of the blue, my father is awarded money from a claims tribunal that returns assets stolen from victims of the Holocaust. Dad emails me, appending the formal deed, and then writes to my sister, Emily, and me that he wants the two of us to share this award, as we are the furthest away in generations and age from the victim. The deed pertains specifically to the accounts of Friedrich Bondy. I battle against my psychic inertia over the names of dead relatives and pull down the family tree Dad gave me for Christmas. No wonder I'm confused: there were *two* Friedls, Vera's brother, who worked for the RAF, and Vera and Gumper's uncle. The claim pertains to the latter. He lived in Vienna from 1914 until March of 1938, when he fled to Zurich, then London, then finally New York. We have pictures of Uncle Friedl, grey-haired and lolling on the beach, and my cousin Lucy has an old dressing gown that belonged to him. He used to visit his sister, Ruzenka, at the Wylie cottage in North Hatley. Even though Uncle Friedl was almost deaf, Granny remembers him sitting on the porch reading symphony scores.

'A true gentleman,' Dad says. 'Who do you know today who can read a symphony score?'

I smile.

Dad: 'Other than Degan.'

Friedl was married briefly to a woman named Auguste Furth, otherwise known as Gusti, about whom Vera, his niece, had a little rhyme: *Gusti je tlousty.*

Dad translates this variously as 'Gusty is tubby', 'Gusti is roly-poly' and, finally, 'Gusti has a fat ass'.

'Keep this memory alive,' Dad writes. 'Love, Dad.'

∾

I burn through Friedl's money quickly, and pretty soon I'm scraping around in the dregs of my bank account. Then, in early March, an envelope from the Canada Council for the Arts arrives with the results of my grant application. I know from years of experience that if the envelope is thin, it contains a single page rejecting the application. If, on the other hand, the envelope is thick, it contains acceptance forms to be signed and returned.

The envelope is thick.

I walk downtown in the late-winter sunshine, floating a half-inch above the pavement. *Far to Go* will be my fourth book, so I've qualified for the heftier sum afforded to 'mid-career writers'. The grant, the equivalent of about half a year's salary for a social worker, *maybe*, is enough for me to live on for *years*. I could live off it for the rest of my life if I had to.

The windows along Bloor Street are shiny in the bright afternoon and I consider the goods I might buy. I think of fancy groceries: marinated artichoke hearts, creamy French cheeses I am not allowed to eat while pregnant. I am ogling a wedge of Camembert when my cell vibrates in my pocket.

My agent's number pops up. 'Hello?'

She says something I can't make out.

'Just a sec,' I say. I duck into the front hall of Brunswick House; the smell of spilled beer and, beneath that, vomit, radiates off the stained carpeted stairs. It's dark, and my eyes need a moment to adjust. I sit on the bottom stair. 'Okay,' I say, 'go ahead.'

'We've had an offer on your book!'

'Oh?' I am cautious, bracing myself, but Anne is excited. She tells me the number. I have to ask her to repeat it to be sure I've heard her correctly.

'That's good, right?'

'In this climate? It's *amazing*.'

I touch my belly, round with our son. I have suddenly 'popped', my stomach going from paunchy to visibly pregnant between days. There's a solid lump of something inside me, a solid mass of person.

Walking home, I can't stop grinning.

That night I dream I am naked, and huge, my pregnant belly dripping fat drops of water as I rise from the mikvah.

℮〜

At twenty weeks, Degan and I go downtown for the big ultrasound, the one that reveals the health of the baby and, if we want, its sex. Degan is asked to stay in the waiting room; he'll be called in at the end. I undress and lie on my back, then I shift and wince, the baby falling back against my spine.

The technician has dyed blond hair and a thick Slavic accent. She brandishes her wand and globs my stomach with jelly. I cannot help but think of the last ultrasound: 'the fetus and the egg sac entirely absent'.

'Baby look good!' the technician says right away, but she seems to be moving the wand across my belly for an awfully long time.

'Is everything okay?' I finally ask.

'Baby flopped over,' she says, bending at the waist and touching her toes to demonstrate. I can see the dark roots at her scalp. She straightens. 'Baby make me work to get the pictures.' She laughs, oblivious to my anxiety.

I nod.

She pauses, a sly little smile cresting her face.

'You want to know the sex?'

'Yes,' I say.

'Okay. We wait until your husband is here. But already have I seen something.'

Something. A penis.

I take a deep breath and instinctively put a palm flat on my heart. The baby is a boy. I've known it from the start. Still, my chest contracts. I don't buy the argument that circumcision isn't painful. I don't want to inflict trauma on my newborn child. And now my conversion – *if* I convert – may only last one generation. This boy, if he marries a Gentile, will have children who are back where I started. Whereas with a girl, those children would be taken care of.

The technician is happily chatting away to the baby. 'You straighten out for me, baby. Otherwise Daddy will to be angry when he come in!'

She sighs, both exasperated and pleased, as though the baby is demonstrating his precociousness already. 'Only I see one in twenty babies in this position,' she says, folding in half at her waist to demonstrate a second time.

At last she gets the pictures she needs. Word goes out to Degan; he sprints into the room and sits down, his elbows on his knees and his chin in his palms. He is bent toward the screen, staring as though at some marvellous sporting event. The technician moves the wand around my belly, showing us first the walls of the uterus, then the placenta. Our little swimmer twists his head toward us. Degan swears under his breath, in awe. He wipes his sleeve over his eyes. 'Look at that sweet little lentil.'

As though to show off, the baby starts moving his lips, making perfect little nursing motions around a nipple he is already dreaming.

We gasp with pleasure. 'Did you *see* that?' Degan asks.

I nod.

The technician turns to Degan. 'You want to know the sex?'

I've already said yes, but in her world, Daddy gets the final word.

Degan affirms. She points to the screen. 'You see here?'

He squints. 'A penis?'

She laughs. 'A little coffee bean.'

Degan clears his throat. 'We're pregnant with a coffee bean?'

I squint, too, but I can't make anything out.

'A vulva,' the technician finally says. 'You no see?' She points again, and the fuzzy image swims into focus. Neither of us moves. We are glued to the screen, helpless in its glow, in the image of our future that it offers.

'Okay,' the technician says. 'We get good pictures. All finish.'

We continue to stare, our eyes wide.

'All done!' She claps her hands.

Finally she angles behind us, a hand on each of our backs. She gently pushes me off the table and nudges Degan up to standing.

We get as far as the foyer of the office building before we have to sit back down on a plastic bench, trying to absorb the news. Degan is beaming. 'I'm so happy,' he keeps saying. His relationship with his father was difficult; he thinks his love for a daughter will be cleaner, clearer. But I feel grief for our little boy. I'm saying goodbye to a son I've only imagined – which doesn't make the goodbye much easier. Still, I realize that I, too, am getting what I wanted; it's suddenly clear that expecting a boy was defensive, a way of steeling myself against disappointment. I want a girl. I've always wanted a girl. The baby turns her somersaults, so everything inside me is moving all at once. I think of the life I want to give her. Of my dream of climbing out of the mikvah, my belly leading the way. If I can convert now, she, too, will be Jewish, and her children will be Jewish. Now is our time.

FOURTEEN

THE NEXT DAY I go down to my publisher's to sign the contract for my new novel. My editor Lynn hugs me hard in the hallway. 'I love the book,' she says. 'I'm so thrilled for you. And for us.'

She takes me by the arm and leads me through the office, introducing me to the publicity people, the marketing people, the interns. She gives me a pile of free books and says she'll have the substantive edits to me by the end of the month. When I get home, there is a message waiting from Shayna. She's been thinking of me all day. She has something she wants to talk about.

I call her back and tell her all the news: the book is sold; the baby is healthy. A girl!

'Oh,' she says. 'That's amazing. I'm so happy for you.'

My phone beeps; another call, which I ignore.

'And the conversion stuff?' she asks. 'Any news?'

'Nothing new,' I say. 'I can't see a way around the policy.'

There's silence over the phone line and then another click, the other caller leaving a message. 'That's what I wanted to talk to you about,' Shayna says.

'Oh?'

'I was having a conversation with my rabbi in Peterborough,' she says. 'I was telling him I felt sad about you and your situation. That I wanted to help you.'

'Thanks,' I say. 'I appreciate it.'

There's a pause. It sounds like Shayna is trying to decide whether to say more. She clears her throat, then finally says, 'He said the policy was changed.'

'Which policy?' I ask.

'On just one spouse converting.'

I swallow. 'Changed how?'

'Changed to give the sponsoring rabbi more leeway. Leeway to assess each case individually. So Rachel could potentially convert you.'

I pause. '*Really?*'

'I didn't want to meddle. And I wanted to be sure, too, so I called the head of the board. He had the paper in front of him, the new draft resolution. He confirmed that the sponsoring rabbi has the final say.'

'Wow.'

'I know.'

I pick at a hangnail, trying to absorb this information. 'So the end of the story is *not* that I'm denied.'

Shayna laughs, a bright peal of bells. 'I'm not a writer. But even I can see that's the wrong ending!'

'So I just have to be patient?'

She says, 'You and Degan are at the forefront of a change. You're the ones helping *us* learn.'

⸎

At our next synagogue meeting, we plunk ourselves down in the red armchairs. 'So,' Rachel says, 'catch me up.'

'I'm pregnant,' I say.

She laughs. 'I gathered!'

I look down at my belly. 'I guess you can tell.'

'I was waiting for you to announce it.'

I tell her about the miscarriage, how it made me wary. How

I didn't want to tell anyone about the new baby until I was sure.

'That's wonderful,' she says. *'B'sha'a tova.'*

'Why not *mazel tov?*'

'The Talmud states babies are born at either seven or nine months, so we hope the baby will come at its own right time. *May it be at a good time.'*

I nod. We chat briefly about morning sickness, about the marvels of Diclectin, with which she seems familiar. 'And what else?' she asks, turning to Degan.

'We finished the class.'

'I heard,' she says. *'Mazel tov.'* She smiles. 'In this case it applies.'

'So now is when people convert,' I say. 'Tom and Diane, for example.' Rachel is sponsoring them, too, so she knows they're proceeding, but her face remains noncommittal. She is a consummate professional.

'I'd like to go ahead, too,' I say. 'Especially now that . . .' I put a hand on my belly.

The rabbi's face falls, not in disappointment or disapproval but inner conflict. She sighs heavily. 'And you?' she asks Degan. 'How are you feeling about proceeding?'

Degan is quiet. And Rachel's expression shows she already knows the answer. 'I'm sorry,' she says, looking at my palm resting on my stomach. 'But now more than ever it's important you be on the same page.'

I am struck by this unfairness: first my partner and now my child will be used against me. I know this is not what Rachel intends, but it's how it feels to me. I try not to cry; I don't want to cry.

Rachel passes me the Kleenex box from her desk. 'I was clear about the policy from the beginning,' she says.

I sniff, take a breath. 'About the policy,' I say.

She looks up.

'I heard something. And I wanted to ask if it's true.'

She holds her body still. Her beautiful eyes wide.

'I heard that the policy has changed,' I say. 'For situations like ours. For cases where just one spouse wants to convert.'

Her jaw tightens. 'Where did you hear that?'

I'm silent. I can't divulge my source.

She sighs. 'No,' she says finally. 'Not changed. Just *revisited*. So that rabbis who feel they have an exception can bring that particular case before the *beit din*.'

It is clear from her voice that she doesn't think we count as such an exception.

Now I start to cry in earnest, tears rolling down my cheeks faster than I can wipe them away. I give in, and put my face in my hands and sob. I'm overcome with helplessness and despair. I think of Gumper's words: 'Not if I were the last Jew on earth.' And of Lucy's dream: 'Mrs Liska Pick regrets that she is unable to attend.' Of Marianne's bare legs in the cattle car. Maybe it's I who am wrong to want to go back there. I could push Degan more, help him wrestle with his doubts. The truth is he would probably do it for me if I asked him. But I don't have the energy; I don't have the comfort or the confidence. I am *different* from the other Jews, who have something concrete, a roof and walls, to invite their new spouse into. My Jewish home is built of straw and grass, of the flimsy cobwebs of dreams.

I look up and blow my nose. Degan holds out a hand for me and puts my snotty tissue in the wastepaper basket. 'So you won't take our case to the Board,' I say to Rachel flatly.

She looks me in the eye and then her gaze moves for a second time down to my belly, straining the waist of my new maternity jeans. I see her face change, a series of emotions moving across it like weather. She sighs and squeezes her eyes shut. When she opens them, her eyes are soft. 'I will,' she says. 'If you want me to.'

I sniff, and nod, surprised. 'Really?'

'I will.'

She sees my skepticism. 'It might be hard for you to believe,' she says, 'but I really do want what's best for you.'

I remember our first meeting: *What a happy story.*

I nod again, wipe my nose.

'Trust me,' she says. 'I'll represent you well.'

FIFTEEN

AS MY PREGNANCY PROGRESSES, my hunger to learn more about my ancestors grows. I find myself wondering about Granny's parents: her mother, Marianne; her father, Oskar. They, like Vera, lived a life of privilege. In the fall of '38 and the winter of '39, they would have met the same string of restrictions Vera described, with the same disbelief: no servants, no radios, a curfew.

In her video interview with Lucy and Dad, Granny doesn't speak much about her parents – nothing about what they liked, what they were like as people. To evoke them would have led her into a darkness she couldn't bear. My own depression has retreated in recent months, and I think I understand Granny's desire to keep it at bay. She does so by sticking to the realm of anecdote in the video, talking about her childhood friend Nena, whose grandfather was ambassador to Argentina. Granny recounts going to Nena's house during the occupation and seeing something sticking out from under the sofa.

'I said, "What's that, Mr Proskowitz?" And he said, "That's the Nazi flag. I'm supposed to put it out. There's nobody will make me do that."'

'Like in *The Sound of Music*!' I hear Lucy laugh, invisible to the camera.

Granny continues. 'The other thing about Nena was that she had a very heavy—' Granny points to the camera and mock-whispers, 'Is that thing on?'

'No,' I can hear my father reassure her, both of them in on the joke.

'She had a very heavy *bust*. When I came back from my honeymoon, I went to see her, and she opened the door and she was naked. She said, "Look!" She'd had the first breast reduction I'd ever heard of.'

Granny is less forthcoming about her own story. It emerges slowly. Her father, Oskar, had a business colleague who was a Nazi, and Oskar used this connection to procure paperwork permitting the family to leave. There was also a Viennese lawyer involved. This lawyer was ennobled two days before the Hapsburg Empire fell and was president of the largest bank in Austria. 'He had a beautiful Belgian wife,' Granny says. And then, as an afterthought: 'He was a little bit after me.'

On April 24, 1939, with Gumper already out of the country, Granny flew from Prague to Zurich. She had my uncle Michael with her, still in diapers. From Zurich she travelled to Paris, where Gumper met her and then brought her to England. In 1941, they travelled by boat to Canada. Granny expected her parents would meet her there. They never arrived.

Granny says to the camera, 'They didn't believe and they refused to go until *I* was gone. And then I was gone and they procrastinated. They had visas to Cuba. I was sure they were in Cuba when we arrived in Canada. Only, they weren't. By that time . . .' She trails off.

'They procrastinated,' she says again. 'They just wouldn't go. I remember my father saying, "What do you expect me to do? Sit in a lobby of a hotel for the rest of my life?"'

On October 12, 1941, Oskar and Marianne were transported from Prague to Theresienstadt.

When I try to imagine them there, my mind skitters away from the horrible things I know. Instead, I see another story, the one Granny told my cousins, the one she must have used herself, late at night, thinking of Marianne: her beloved mother, dirty but healthy, her head wrapped in a paisley kerchief, looking after the chickens.

Then on January 20, 1943, Oskar and Marianne were transported from Theresienstadt to Auschwitz.

Here it becomes harder to find another story.

Joseph Mengele did not arrive in Auschwitz until April of that year, so it was not 'the Angel of Death' who met them on the platform but some other monster.

Our family lore has it that they went 'straight to the gas'.

I strain and strain for an image of Marianne. I can see her laughter, her face tipped up to her male companion: *Stuckerl* – 'piece of work'. I picture her arm thrown around Granny's shoulder. That she was a woman, like my own sister, my cousins, like *me*, full of failure, full of feeling, does not make her easier to imagine.

It occurs to me that as Marianne went to her death, she would have assumed her own children were safe – her son in the United States, Granny in Canada – and in that there's a small shred of mercy.

SIXTEEN

THE SPRING PASSES QUICKLY, like the pages of a calendar in a silent movie blowing away in the wind. I edit my novel, and feel pleased with my progress. The baby goes through a phase of vigorous hiccuping, the sensation inside me like the quick drawing of breath – only, in my womb instead of my lungs.

Degan and I begin our childbirth classes, where we plunge our hands into buckets of ice and count how many seconds we can tolerate the pain. I have the hazy suspicion that this is a poor approximation of a contraction but don't bother to articulate this to him. Rachel is set to plead our case in late May, but I am distracted by my sore hips and strange dreams, by the child taking up more of my body and more of my thoughts. Two days after the date passes, I realize I haven't heard from Rachel.

I email her to ask the verdict.

She writes back right away: 'I have good news for you.'

My heart dips and leaps. I'm going to be a Jew.

❧

Degan and I bike up to the synagogue to talk with Rachel in person. She is calm and relaxed again, as though, having navigated through this point of contention, she can now return to the generosity that is so obviously her nature. It's possible I have never loved anyone more. 'You'll have to decide on a Hebrew name,' she says. 'Have you thought about that at all?'

I have. A Hebrew name. For *me*.

'My great-grandmother Ruzenka's last name was Bondy,' I say. 'Which came from *bon dia* in Catalan. Meaning "good day". Or in Hebrew, *yom tov*.'

She nods.

I pause, suddenly nervous. I take a deep breath. 'I thought about taking the *tov*, and being called Tova.'

A smile breaks out on the rabbi's face. 'A beautiful Israeli name. That sounds just about perfect.'

The next task will be a Hebrew name for Dad so I can, as Rachel says, 'secure his line'.

Normally a Jewish name references both mother and father. Jordan's Hebrew name is Shimon ben Michael Anshel V'Tzivia – meaning Michael Anshel is his father and Tzivia is his mother. Shayna's full Hebrew name is Shayna Gila bat Tziyon Lev V'Chana Rivka. In my case, the name will just reference Dad. I will be Tova, daughter of Thomas. But in place of Thomas we need something Hebrew.

After a handful of emails back and forth, Dad settles on the simple Thom. He seems both pleased and abashed, like a child bestowed an unexpected gift.

For his imminent role as a grandfather, he decides on the Hebrew word *saba*. I have suggested *zaide* – the Yiddish word I remember Jordan calling his grandpa when we were growing up – but Dad asks his Jewish dermatologist, who tells him *zaide* would be 'going overboard'.

But Dad isn't ashamed.

Better: He's happy.

On the morning of the *beit din*, I open this email from Dad.

Dear Alison:

Good luck today in your new life as a Jew. I am proud of you, and admire the courage that you have shown in pursuing this venture. Your ancestors up in heaven are applauding!!

Mum joins me in wishing you much happiness and health as well. Love Dad.

P.S. You might want to bring the poem you wrote that refers to Auschwitz and the smoke and ashes etc. I think the Rabbis would be impressed with the depth of your feeling, and also the fact that it was published in Israel.

P.P.S. I've just finished a 500 page history of Israel, written by Martin Gilbert. What courage these people showed, and show today, in building their oasis in the sand, against almost universal lack of caring.

P.P.P.S. Remember to bring your poem.

Before the *beit din*, I go get my nails painted red. Then I pick Degan up at work and he quizzes me as we drive north. Rabbi Klein has assured me the questions will be easy, but part of me expects to be asked about the history of the Temple between 529 and 502 BCE.

'What church do you go to?' Degan asks.

I laugh. 'Trick question.'

Moving north on Bathurst, we pass bagel shops, stores where you can buy *tallitot* (prayer shawls) and *neirot* (candlesticks), Orthodox men talking on their cell phones. The Canadian Council of Reform Judaism is housed in a brick building, square and red, unassuming. Inside, we find another couple, also here for the *beit din*, camped outside the third-floor office. The woman pulls on the handle. The door remains closed.

'Is it locked?' I ask.

'They must *really* not want us,' she says.

We laugh, united in our nervousness.

Finally, someone inside the office answers our knock. I've been told to expect an assembly line, that today is the big day for all the prospective converts in the city, and true to promise, the tiny waiting room is crammed with people. I notice a woman with red hair who has a lap full of sippy cups and board books and stuffed animals, her daughter plunked on top of the pile like a cherry. I hold my pregnant belly with both hands as I squeeze my way past.

Several people offer me their seat, but I want to stand. Degan leafs through a magazine. My palms are sweaty, and I swallow repeatedly, unable to clear the lump from my throat. I feel someone tap my shoulder and I turn around. It's Debra. She has just emerged from the boardroom. 'They took me!' she says.

'Congrats!' I say. 'I mean, *Mazel tov!*'

She smiles.

'What was like it?' I whisper.

'Easy,' she whispers back, and leans in to tell me the questions, but from across the room I hear my name being called. It's my turn.

I hug Debra, kiss Degan goodbye and follow the secretary through an office jammed with photocopiers and fax machines. There's the *whiz – thunk! Whiz – thunk!* of copies falling into a tray. I enter the boardroom and see three women, the rabbis assigned to my case. Two of them are around my age, one also very pregnant. We exchange conspiring smiles. I exhale. She motions for me to sit down.

The third rabbi is much older, and wearing wire-rimmed

glasses in the fashion of a schoolmarm. 'What brings you here today?' she asks.

I launch into my family history, beginning with my great-grandparents, Oskar and Marianne. The rabbis shift, clear their throats. The pregnant one heaves herself into a different position. It is clear from their collective body language that they want the abridged version. I sense interest from them, and authenticity, but more overpowering is the feeling that we're pressed for time.

Their minds are made up already. I'm just not sure in which direction.

'What do you love about Judaism?' the second young rabbi asks.

'Shabbat,' I say right away. I explain, in as few words as possible, about '24 Hours Unplugged'. There's a collective gasp. I'm encouraged.

'That really sealed the deal for me. Although,' I add hastily, 'it's been clear all along. Like recognizing something that was always mine but got lost along the way, along the generations. Of course there have been challenges, but—'

The rabbi with the wire-rimmed glasses interrupts me. 'Tell us about one of those challenges.'

I pause, thinking carefully. 'I grew up not knowing very much about Judaism,' I say. 'Not knowing *anything*. When I learned my Dad was Jewish, I assumed I could be, too, if I wanted.' I take a wheezy breath, the baby suddenly pressed into my lungs. 'Then when I first met Rabbi Klein and she told me that I might not be able to convert, given that my fiancé wasn't Jewish, I experienced it as . . .' I pause. 'As a kind of rejection.'

The stern rabbi's face softens and she nods. 'It was hard not to take it personally?'

'Yes.'

'I can understand that,' she says, speaking more to the other rabbis than to me.

I look to see if I should say more, but they want to move on.

'Speaking of your marriage, how do you think you'd feel if Degan –' she looks to me to see if she has his name right and I nod '– if Degan changed his mind?'

'Changed his mind about what?'

'About eventually converting.'

I'm worried there's been a misunderstanding, so I clarify. 'He doesn't think he *will* convert.'

They nod. I'm confused and decide to use the opportunity to tell them about Degan's support. His intellectual curiosity. The pieces of Judaism that resonate deeply for him.

'Can you give us an example?' the pregnant rabbi asks.

From outside the closed door the photocopier takes up its humming again, followed by a series of loud beeps.

'*Tzedakah*,' I say. '"Righteous giving". He grew up in a family of activists. So, on Shabbat, it's always Degan who says, "Don't forget the *tzedakah* box," or "Let's talk about where the *tzedakah* will go."'

I am about to elaborate, but the rabbis' faces show that they are satisfied. I wait for the next question. We've not spoken about Israel, about the commitment to synagogue, about my father's response to all of the above. But the stern one looks to her younger colleagues, who both nod. Outside the window a siren screams by.

'That's great,' the pregnant one says. 'Is your husband here with you?'

'Yes.'

'Then step into the waiting room and we'll call you both in a minute.'

I find Degan reading a magazine article about Obama and

the auto workers union. I tap his shoulder and he looks up, expectant. 'So?'

'They're going to call us in.'

A frown crosses his face. 'Both of us? Are they going to ask me questions?'

'I think they just want you there.'

But he closes his eyes to prepare himself, just in case.

The deliberations last *maybe* five minutes. When we enter the boardroom again, the pregnant rabbi speaks. 'There's good news,' she says.

I brace myself for the logical conclusion to the phrase: *And bad news.* She sees my concern and laughs. 'There's only good news. Welcome to the tribe!'

I start crying right away. The relief is so strong. It is all the months of waiting, not knowing, the ambivalence, the uncertainty. The weight of the past on my back. I reach for Degan's hand, and feel the cool lip of his wedding band against his warm fingers. Marianne in the cattle car. *Stuckerl* – 'piece of work'. Granny's silk handkerchief embroidered with an *A*. Gumper, who was not, it turns out, the very last Jew on earth.

My girl jabs a foot into my heart: I'm here.

The pregnant rabbi clears her throat. 'Rachel brought your case to the board,' she says. 'I'll be honest, there was some hesitation. There were rabbis who chose not to sit on your *beit din* today.'

Rabbi Glickman's face appears before me, her features tight and pinched.

'They didn't want to be part of making an intermarriage, which is, in effect, what we are doing.' The young rabbi pauses; we both touch our pregnant bellies. 'But we're convinced you will have a Jewish family, and we want to welcome both of you.' She looks at Degan and then at my belly: 'All of you.'

My tears fall, unhindered. Degan hugs me hard. I can see

the older, sterner rabbi eyeing us, pleased with their decision. A good day's work.

She signs the papers, passes them to me, and it's official.

On the way out I ask the pregnant rabbi when her baby is due. 'In two weeks!' She stands up. 'So you'll understand that I need to leave and pee.'

I laugh, wiping away my tears. 'Absolutely.'

Debra has left me a present with the secretary. I open it in the car on the way home. It's a beautiful coffee table book about Jewish mothers, from all different backgrounds, with all different stories. For a moment I think, But why has she given it to *me*? And then the gladness rushes through me again and I understand.

SEVENTEEN

BACK AT THE APARTMENT, a letter waits for me on the hall table. It's from Women's College Hospital. I rip it open. It announces unceremoniously that I have tested negative for the BRCA breast cancer gene.

That's that. A wave of relief.

That evening Degan and I get ready for the Griffin poetry gala, the place where I first met Rabbi Klein two years ago. I try on a series of identical black maternity dresses to see which makes me look less enormous. Degan stands in front of the bathroom mirror, tying and re-tying his tie. At the last minute, he walks up to St Clair to get me takeout. I can't wait the two hours until dinner.

The party this year is Mexican-themed; the warehouse is decorated with sombreros and piñatas and colourful crepe paper streamers. We sit with fellow writers and poets, one of whom has a four-month-old baby girl sleeping beside her in a basinet. I look, look away, then look back again. The only thing able to distract me is the piece of rare steak a waiter sets down in front of me, my appetite for red meat verging on ferocious. Mark Blume, who first introduced me to Sol Jalon, who introduced me to his wife, Rachel, is on the jury this year. The prizes are awarded; the band strikes up and the music begins. Everyone who is now part of my Toronto world is here. Throughout the evening people want to touch my stomach. They ask me when I'm due and if they can get me a glass of . . .

water. They tell me that pregnancy suits me, and although I know they are lying, it is good to be in my element, with my people.

Including Rachel, who is here again with Sol. At the end of the night, after champagne and dancing, I notice her packing up to go home. There's a kind of reassurance in seeing her out of context, or rather, in her role as a person, not a rabbi.

I cross the glitter-speckled dance floor toward her.

'I heard it went well today!' she says.

I grin. 'It was *fast*.'

'I primed them. They knew you were a good candidate.'

'They had to get through lots of people.'

'Maybe,' she says. 'But also, I told them you were good.'

'I realized it's been two years since I met you. To the *day*.'

She smiles.

'*Bashert*,' I say. 'Fate.' And then: 'I guess you don't need me to translate.'

The rabbi reaches out and gives my shoulder a squeeze. She picks a piece of pink confetti from my hair, and I smile at the intimacy. 'So you're happy? About the *beit din*?' she asks.

'I'm happy,' I say.

She nods. 'The only thing left is to get in the bath.'

EIGHTEEN

THE NEXT MORNING a call from our real estate agent. The market is so crazy that we've given up looking, but there's a small three-bedroom in the Annex he thinks we should take a peek at. It has exposed brick in the kitchen, and lovely hardwood floors, and a park with a playground directly across the street. We don't need long to decide. In three short weeks we pack up the apartment; I work for five minutes, rest for ten, work for five, rest for fifteen. I'm so fogged up with hormones I can barely remember my name. It's a beautiful feeling, though, hazy around the edges. Despite being more bound by my body than ever, I feel an accompanying sense of absolution, as if the tethers of the material world have momentarily slipped me free.

⁓

My mikvah is set for a clear spring day in June. I wake early and lie quietly for a few minutes, breathing in the fresh air from the open window, luxuriating in the sense of unhurried imminence. The future is coming for me; I don't have to chase after it. I think of the long months of darkness behind me, and how they have transformed into the light pushing in through the screen. I feel lightness inside me, too, spreading through my limbs, my face, the tips of my eyelids. I know my depression isn't over for good, isn't somehow solved like a puzzle, but I am grateful for the respite.

Degan rolls over on the other side of the bed. I heave myself over to hug him.

'Take that, Phil,' he says.

Phil is the name we've given to the long maternity pillow I sleep with my belly propped up against.

Degan leaves for work, but I linger in bed, listening to the robins outside our window and the sputtering cough of a motorcycle someone is trying to start. I eventually get up and send a few emails as the baby throws her punches and jabs inside me. I go out for groceries, fill the car with gas, review the blessings I will have to recite later this afternoon. I struggle to remove my toenail polish, my stomach almost too big for me to reach my feet. But the rules are clear: for immersion in the mikvah, the body must be unadorned.

Later I meet Degan at the mikvah. We have to sign in at the front desk; there is a hundred-dollar fee. Downstairs, he kisses me goodbye and goes to wait in the small room adjacent to the mikvah. Rabbi Klein greets me, shows me into the change room. With effort, I reach behind me for my zipper and slowly step out of my dress. The enormity of my naked body, a world unto itself. My big breasts and my belly. The child huge inside me.

I look in the mirror and think of Granny: *If I start crying, I will never stop.* Of Gumper: *Not if I was the last Jew on earth.* Of his mother, Ruzenka, fasting quietly, secretly on Yom Kippur.

I think of what Judaism has come to mean to *me.* Of Shabbat, of *tzedakah,* of the shivers down my spine when I hear the prayer for the dead. There's a knock on the change-room door. 'Ready when you are,' Rabbi Klein says.

I look around for a robe and realize I've forgotten to bring one. I improvise and wrap my blue flowered maternity dress around me like a toga. Rachel laughs when she sees me. 'Full points for creativity.' Then she says, in a serious voice, 'I'll turn my back. You can enter the pool.'

I have been picturing a beautiful green stone pool, but the mikvah looks more like something from a health club or a physiotherapist's clinic. Cream plastic with an armrail on the stairs. I let my dress fall and take my first steps in. The water is lovely and warm. It rises up over me: ankles, knees, hips. The huge bulb of my daughter, ready to burst. Once I am standing up to my shoulders, Rachel turns to face me. She shows me a pipe I haven't yet noticed, shunting rainwater gathered according to Jewish law into this holiest of baths. 'Flowing water is fitting for this particular day. For *you*,' she begins.

I swallow.

'A river symbolizes continuity,' she says. 'Today we are thinking of your family. Your father, his parents and grand-parents behind you. The life within your belly, flowing forward to the future.

'In the Torah we learn that the mikvah waters are called *living* waters. Living waters come from one source and are propelled to another, stopping along the way at many junctures. You are standing in the mikvah, at the juncture to official conversion. This is not a beginning or an end in itself, but rather, a beginning out of something that has existed, and that will continue to exist in the future.'

She reads a beautiful passage from the Torah, and then it is time for the dunks. She tells me to spread my fingers and toes so the water will touch every part of me. I have read so many things about immersion having to be kosher, not a strand of hair allowed to graze the surface, about dunks being annulled because a toe bumped the floor of the pool, but Rachel is very casual. 'Make sure you're immersed, but don't stay under too long. Ha ha!'

But once I am under I never want to come up. I churn my arms to stay beneath the surface. The water holds me; my water holds my child. Finally I need to breathe. When I break the surface, Rabbi Klein says the blessing concerning immersion. I repeat it.

Then it is time for the third and final dunk.

When I come out of the water, I will be a Jew.

As a writer, I believe in the power of words, but there are things words cannot speak to, worlds that language cannot name. The mikvah, for me, is one of them. In the long year of classes, of learning Hebrew and making Shabbat, it has not occurred to me that the bath would be more than a rite, that I might truly be transformed. But when I emerge, I am different. My skin shines, as though every inch of me – inside and out – has been purified. I think of Shayna's wisdom at my wedding, how she preserved the ritual so I could appreciate it fully at the proper moment. She was right. I turn to Degan now with the face of his wife, and with another woman's face altogether.

Outside, the June day is blustery and bright. I blink in the sunshine. There is a playground beside the school, and beyond it a small grove of trees. We linger on our backs, looking up at the sky. The clouds make a canoe, a mother duck followed by a trail of ducklings. I twirl a thick blade of grass between my thumb and forefinger and lazily brush an ant off my calf. Basking in the warmth, the sense of completion. Degan rolls onto his side, props his head up with his elbow. He pushes a gift-wrapped bag toward me. Inside are two small packages. I unwrap them carefully: a Magen David, or Star of David, to wear on a chain around my neck, and a beautiful mezuzah for our new home. I touch each object, my fingers taking them in, learning what they mean about who I now am.

Eventually we get in the car to drive home. On our way, we stop at the downtown synagogue where we will be picking up our organic vegetable share every Tuesday throughout the summer. I look around at the families choosing peppers and pears, children up on their fathers' shoulders, a small boy in an even smaller *kippah*. After my long exile, these are my people. There is no uncertainty, nothing halfway about it. All at once, I belong.

At home, I fall into bed in utter exhaustion. I sleep on my side, my belly out in front of me like a huge crystal ball. An oracle. I feel our daughter's foot, the curved world of her head, and dream the colour orange and the smell of baking cardamom. I wake to a phone message from Shayna. She tells me *mazel tov*, and to check outside my front door. I find blueberries, kosher cookies, a huge bouquet of lilies.

I turn on the computer. An email from Rabbi Klein is waiting: 'You've worked hard for this, Alie. Fighting history isn't easy.'

And one from Jordan, who twenty years earlier on the playground saw me for what I really was. 'So it's come to this, has it?' he writes. 'You are officially Jewish. Well, welcome. Is it strange?'

Eli and I have been in touch a bit over the past weeks, and his response to my news is a single word: 'Hooray!'

The last email comes from Dad. He is in Europe – in Prague, as fate would have it. He writes to tell me he went to synagogue on Shabbos morning. When he arrived, the rabbi asked about his background. Ten Jewish males make up a *minyan*, the minimum required for the public aspects of prayer.

At the synagogue in Prague there were rarely enough. Today, there were nine. Until Dad arrived. The rabbi questioned him at length about his background and finally declared him a full Jew. My father's presence made for great celebration. Because he was there, they could bring out the Torah.

NINETEEN

NEWS OF MY CONVERSION reaches my extended family slowly, one by one. They give me strange looks, not unkind, but looks of befuddled curiosity, as though I have converted to Islam or announced that I will henceforth be referred to as the king of Siam. In their minds, there is no precedent for what I've done, and no reason for it. The logical underpinning has been thoroughly erased. 'Call me Brunhilda!' I have declared. Or, 'I only have one foot!' They are, though, excited about the baby. A new life is something everyone understands.

I practise the *Shehechiyanu* for months. The prayer for firsts. The first fruit of the New Year. The first Passover Seder. The birth of a child.

My false labour starts and stops several times, over several weeks, always on Shabbat. Two nights before our daughter's birth there is a late-summer windstorm. The sky billows purple and howls down the narrow city avenues. A tree blows down in front of our house. Degan collects a branch and waves it over my stomach. When I finally go into labour in earnest, thirteen days past my due date, he says his magic did it.

We have set up a plastic birthing pool in the living room of our new home, a pool smaller than the mikvah but equally symbolic of change. As the contractions deepen, I square my shoulders to face a kind of pain I could never have fathomed. It stalks me silently, huge paws, low snout, and when it finally pounces, I'm torn open into screams. It rips through my insides until it has had its fill, then just as quickly retreats. It hides itself entirely for stretches of time, stretches of time that increase rather than decrease. The relief is incredible, but I deduce from my midwife Hedrey's frown that it is also a problem. My labour is slowing. By eleven on Saturday evening, my contractions are back down to one every five minutes. I say, 'I guess she won't be a Shabbat baby,' and check Hedrey's response shyly, like a new bride.

When our daughter is born in the hospital eight hours later, she is laid on my stomach. There is a commotion between my legs – only half the placenta has emerged. There are repeated and urgent requests for me to push to avoid internal bleeding, which I heed half-heartedly. My daughter is in my arms. There is nothing else in the world. I do not think to look at her but to learn her through feel alone. My first words I tell her are the Jewish prayer of newness, whispered into the tiny whorl of her ear.

Someone in another place tries to show me how to breast-feed. There are stances, apparently, strategic holds. I bat the person away.

I am busy falling in love in a way I have never known. With every cell of my being. To say this is my 'purpose' would be to miss the point. It is not a purpose but a self I am meeting, not a new self but a *real* self that has been lying in wait every second of my life up until now. This is not something I decide, or a moral argument in favour of reproduction; it is an irrefutable truth, like a coin falling heavily into a slot.

Her name is already waiting. Ayla.

Her middle names. Emily. Ruzenka.

And her Hebrew name. Ayala.

We drive her home in the Sunday-morning light, a little scoop of a person in the bottom of her car seat, her limbs loose like a handful of noodles. Every particle of the known world rearranging itself around her presence. We eat bean salad and mango juice and a dense dark chocolate birthday cake. I sleep on the couch for four hours while Degan holds the baby. He lays her length across his forearm, her head in his palm, the whole world cupped there in his hand.

In the same way I did not worry about a miscarriage I have not seriously entertained postpartum depression. It has not been explained to me. Or: It's been explained, but I have not understood. I think it is something that happens to women who do not want their babies, women who don't have adequate support. I realize with a start that I have never observed new motherhood up close, have never been in a newborn's presence for longer than a few hours.

In the slew of congratulatory emails comes one from Jordan, whose wife is a midwife: 'I hope you feel wonderful! And if for some reason you feel like you've fallen down a rabbit hole, that's normal too.'

Interesting.

Around the seventh day of Ayla's life darkness starts creeping in, a blur of black at the edge of my eyes. It is August, but I shiver. I force myself to leave the house to go out for a walk, but the sun blinds my eyes. I blink and blink, trying to clear my vision. Several times, the lights dimmed in the living room to help the baby sleep, I see mice that don't exist scuttle across the hardwood floor.

I am shocked to discover that I will now spend the rest of my life breastfeeding on the sofa, a complex arrangement of cushions strapped to my waist, and my chest exposed for anyone who wanders into the house to see. How have I not known? I have managed to get through an entire pregnancy without anyone once mentioning this.

My breasts burn and sting. I develop blocked milk ducts, mysterious mammary ailments with flowery names like mastitis and candidiasis. My nipples tear and bleed. I take Advil before feeding the baby. There are trips to the hospital in the middle of the night with fevers. Potato poultices. Antibiotics. Appointments at every clinic in the city.

The nursing problems exacerbate my new depression, a darkness that feels different from the usual bad blood. I am not heavy and draggy so much as blown open, the blinders I usually rely on to get through the day blasted off entirely. I am unshielded, without protection. I pace the kitchen with my girl bound to my chest like a bomb about to go off. I can't help myself – I think of the war. Of Vera being taken away from her children. Only now do I really understand what this means.

She was taken from her children. Her *children* were taken away.

In what is supposed to be the time of ultimate joy, my mind drifts to families living in hiding, behind walls, and to the mothers who smothered their own infants so they did not cry and give away the family's location. I pace and bounce, trying to lull Ayla to sleep.

Mengele, 'the Angel of Death', who forced that new mother to hold her daughter without feeding her. Six days of unimaginable suffering.

I hear Hilda's words: 'We were partisans, starving in the woods. What would we do with a baby?'

My daughter has colic. She does not *technically* have colic, but she cries all evening as though enraged about being born. As though the human condition is intolerable to her, entirely unacceptable. I wrap her to my body, tying her against me with the sling. She finally falls asleep on my chest, our sweaty skin sticking us together as though we were again one single animal. Her diaper is redolent with sickly sweet-smelling excrement. I pace and pace with her, reading to pass the time. The father and child in my book are bound together in misery and love. When the father dies, his boy stays by his body for three days, repeating his name over and over. *Daddy. Daddy.* I hold the book up in front of my face like a shield.

Narrative begs an ending. The desire to wrap up loose ends, to make meaning, is human, and ancient. But things do not end. There is only progression, shape-shifting, the flow of a current that crashes and tumbles, diminishes, almost dries up, only to give birth to itself again a little farther downstream.

The baby changes my experience of depression in the same way that the conversion does. She alters it, knocks it askew. I am not fixed or healed, but I am different, as though a part of me that had always existed as an outline has now been fully coloured in. I am a mother, and a Jew, which is to say the *me* who has suffered in the past is now a new me entirely.

I know now, too, that the darkness heralds healing: that with each bout I am invited to a deeper place within myself and, paradoxically, to a deeper release. If I give myself over to depression, engage with it rather than resist it, it will take me places I never would have imagined.

For example: when *Far to Go* is published the following year, it is awarded the Canadian Jewish Book Award for Fiction. The organizer writes me to tell me the news. The subject heading of her email is 'The Beatrice and Martin Fischer Award'.

Why does that name sound so familiar?

I email Dad: 'Do you know a Martin Fischer?'

He writes back right away: '*Dr* Martin Fischer? He was my

therapist when I was in my twenties. The one I've told you about.'

Of course he was. I've been given an award in the name of the man Dad thought was *good*, the man whose funeral occasioned my father's first-ever visit to a synagogue. In a way, he was my first therapist, too: Dad brought me along to see him when I was an infant, fast asleep in my car seat, my hands curled up tight beside my head.

Ayla's colic improves, and thankfully so does my postpartum depression. It diminishes slowly, a balloon in the corner of a playroom, losing air until, one day, it is just a scrap of bright plastic amid the toys. Ayla thrives. Our feeding issues resolve and she grows plump with my milk, her pale skin doubling over so she looks like nothing more than a doughy Czech dumpling.

When Ayla is several months old, Degan approaches me in the nursery. The shades are drawn and the small lantern lit. Ayla is nursing, her little hands balled up at her chest and her knees tucked in. I inhale the sweet and slightly sour smell of baby – her scalp, milk, old skin collected in the creases between fat.

'I have some news,' Degan says.

'Pass me that pillow?'

I tuck it in beneath Ayla, adjusting her position, supporting her delicate skull in the crook of my hand. I motion and he passes me a second pillow.

'What's the news?' I ask.

'I'm going to convert.'

I pause, and feel the steady sucking right at the heart of me, our daughter growing bigger by the minute. *Really?*

Degan smiles.

'What made you change your mind?' I ask.

He sits down on the big green yoga ball across from me, bouncing subtly, out of habit, even though there's no baby in his arms. 'I kept thinking about what Rachel said.'

'Rachel said a lot of things.'

'True. I mean, what she said about not needing to wait for a thunderbolt.'

I nod. I take a minute to switch Ayla to the other breast, clipping up the right side of my bra and unclipping the left. She latches back on and the tugging resumes.

Degan says, 'I've decided the things that I love about Judaism are enough. The absence of original sin. The spirit of inquiry and debate.'

I move the baby to my shoulder and begin the long ritual of burping, starting at her low back and moving slowly up to her tiny wings.

'So?' Degan asks. 'What do you think? Are you happy?'

I pause. The onslaught of new motherhood has absorbed me completely, removing me from myself in a way that is both pleasurable and immensely disconcerting. I have to take a moment to dig around inside myself and sort out the complexity of what I'm feeling.

I remember the pregnant rabbi's question at my *beit din*, the one I didn't understand: 'How would you feel if your husband changed his mind?'

I realize it only as I say it. 'I guess that part of me – just a little part? – was glad you weren't going to yield. So our old lives would still be represented.'

Degan grins and runs a hand across his stubble. 'Sorry, babe.'

'We're locked in?'

'We're locked *in*.'

'Merry Christmas!'

'Thank you. But I'm Jewish.'

I laugh.

Ayla pulls off my breast and looks in the direction of her dad's voice. 'What do you think?' I ask her.

She makes a little cry. But it's a cry of happiness, I'm sure.

TWENTY

IT'S BEEN MONTHS since I've seen Charlotte; I am surprised by the comfortable familiarity of her room, with its sand table and rocking chair, like returning after a long time to the house of my childhood. Everything smaller than I'd remembered, and comfortingly worn. She smiles when she sees me. 'There's a lot less of you than when you were last here.'

I look down at my diminished belly. 'And a lot more.'

She nods knowingly.

We chat in a catching-up kind of way, like old friends who haven't seen each other in some time. I tell her about *Far to Go*, about the mikvah, about Degan's recent decision. She rocks, and asks her usual thoughtful questions, but there's a neutrality of tone to our conversation. The urgency has gone out of it.

'Well?' she asks, seeing the look on my face.

'I was just realizing that I don't feel the same –' I pause, searching for the word '– I don't feel the same *pressure* as I used to feel here.'

I hesitate, afraid of hurting her feelings, but she nods to show she understands. 'I used to feel that there was so much to *deal* with, to do something about. But now I have the urge to –' I falter, and she nods again. 'To just let it be.'

Charlotte crosses her legs and rocks. She absently touches the earth in the small potted aloe plant beside her, then nods, satisfied it has enough water. She says, 'There are times to contemplate life, and then there are times to just live it. Maybe this is one of those times.'

She checks my reaction. I see she does not want me to feel pushed away, wants me to know this isn't a rejection but an option, an invitation.

'Is the work over?' I ask.

She laughs; in all our time together I've never heard her laugh and I am surprised at the brightness of it, like sunlight sparkling on a lake.

'To be continued,' she says.

'Okay.'

'Go live your life,' she says.

She sends me away with the instruction, of course, to pay attention to my dreams. That night, I find myself in a café with Marianne. It is Prague, before the war. An aproned waiter pours coffee from a tall silver pot. The cups are bone china. Marianne wears a blue hat with a veil of sheer netting over her face. I have the sinking feeling that I know something she doesn't, that I alone can see what is coming. She sighs, and stirs a cube of sugar in her coffee. The delicate clink of the spoon. 'I wish we had more time together,' she says.

I sit up straighter. 'How do you mean?'

She lifts her veil so I can see her full face, her rouged cheeks and pink lips, and cocks an eyebrow in reprimand. As though to say: *We both know how this will end. Why pretend otherwise?*

The waiter comes with our bill. Marianne gathers her things. 'But wait,' I say, panicking. 'I wanted to ask you . . .'

She stops, half up from her chair, and says Charlotte's exact words: 'Go live your life.'

My eyes widen.

Marianne is opening her makeup compact now, checking her look before going down into the street. She opens the café door; the little bell jingles. She turns back toward me, looking over her shoulder, but when her voice comes, it is directly in my ear, as though she's standing next to me. 'Don't suffer for me,' she says. 'For us.' I know that by 'us' she means Oskar and her; Vera's children, little Jan in his bathing suit, Eva with her halo of curls. Marianne holds my eye and says, for emphasis, 'There are better ways to honour us.'

TWENTY-ONE

I'VE BEEN GRANTED MY WISH to not have to face a circumcision. We have a simple baby-naming, instead. On a snowy morning in February, when Ayla is six months old, we clean and tidy, tucking tiny spit-up bibs and washcloths no larger than my palm out of sight. When the kitchen is spotless, I bring out a lace tablecloth that belonged to Vera, who died peacefully in 2001. I spread its elaborate pattern out on the table. I hang my framed photos of her lost children in the living room for everyone to see.

At eleven o'clock the doorbell starts ringing. Our family and friends arrive slowly and assemble in the living room, gathering around Rachel and Shayna, who will officiate together. Shayna begins to hum, softly and hypnotically; the crowd falls silent. I look out at their faces: Dad, my sister, Aaron and Sylvie, Debra. The faces of the many people who have been with me on this journey.

Ayla has been cloistered away with my mother, who has been given the honour of carrying her into the room. When they enter, a gasp of pleasure rises from the assembly. She is a beautiful baby. All parents think that of their child, but I am certain it is true. Pale-skinned and blue-eyed like her father, her fat limbs announcing the space she takes up in the world. Shayna's humming blooms into full song, and when she lets loose the first high clear notes, Ayla's body freezes and turns toward my friend, every bit of my daughter aimed at the beauty. A string of clear drool hangs from her plush pink lips; she blinks. Her first experience of being fully transported by art.

Ayla wears a white smock dress that was mine as a baby. Maybe it was the dress I wore to my christening.

Rachel explains that Ayla has entered the room to the same melody she will enter to on her wedding day. I can no more imagine Ayla getting married than I can imagine her speaking or walking, but there is something about Rachel's certainty – her *faith* – that makes me trust it is true.

Rachel leads us through the parents' dedication, but I am so overcome I cannot hear her words. I have to stop partway through the blessing because my throat is thick with feeling. I look into Rachel's eyes and hang on. *She* has been the one to shepherd us from a place of absence into presence. When she recites the prayer welcoming Ayla, Rachel, too, has tears in her eyes.

The centrepiece of any baby-naming ceremony is the parents talking about the names they have chosen. Degan starts, telling our friends about the first time he heard the name Ayla, and how he immediately fell in love with it. It was a Scottish name, but later, after I got pregnant, he began to harbour the idea that it was an old name, a name with other roots. Hebrew roots.

It was. It did. Ayla can be short for the Hebrew *ayala*, meaning 'deer'. Lithe and delicate, with light in the eyes.

Degan then speaks about the name Emily, passed down from both my sister and his paternal grandmother.

Then it is my turn to speak.

Ayla's third name is Ruzenka, I say, after Dad's paternal grandmother. She loved my father fiercely. She suffered the worst thing anyone can suffer – the deaths of two of her children in concentration camps. She grieved, and adapted with grace to what life dealt her. She believed, and taught Dad, that the most important thing was to have faith – of any kind – in God, the world and humanity.

But Ruzenka also believed in the particularity of religion. While the rest of her family pretended to be Christian, she held her Judaism close her entire life. She fasted on Yom Kippur. She lit candles on Shabbat. It is the light from Ruzenka's candles, I tell our family and friends, that we want Ayla to grow up in. A light that, despite great adversity, has shone down the generations.

I look out again into the faces of everyone gathered. Dad and I lock eyes. I smile. He smiles. It is done.

Somewhere rain falls into the open sea. Genocide continues. There are no easy answers. Snow falls on a tombstone, furring it over with memory. My great-grandmother is buried in an unmarked grave in the sky.

My Christian mother holds my Jewish child in her arms. The rabbi, full of love, blesses the baby in Hebrew: *bruchah haba'ah*.

We repeat the blessing in English.

Blessed is she who comes.

ACKNOWLEDGEMENTS

Acknowledgements play a particular role in a memoir. I'm grateful to have the chance to thank some of the many people who helped me with the writing and also who lived through various parts of this with me, who supported me in ways to numerous to list, and who offered conversation and company along the way:

Nicola Holmes. Aviva Chernick. Adam Sol. Rabbi Karen Thomashow. Rabbi Elyse Goldstein. Aaron Talbot and Miki Stricker Talbot. Hartley Weinberg and Sarah Margles. Rabbi Esther Lederman. Helen Bramer. The Traub-Werner family. Bernice Eisenstein. Allan Kaplan and Cheryl Reicin. Debra Bennett. Jordan and Ilana Stanger-Ross. John and Nora Freund. George Feldman and Deborah Orr. Sasha and the Mamas. Christine Pountney. Sonya Teece. Alexi Zentner. Matt Neff.

In many ways this book was a collaboration with my father, Thomas Pick, and I am particularly indebted to him, to Margot and Emily Pick, to Rabbi Yael Splansky who went above and beyond, to my longtime and beloved editor, Lynn Henry, and to Degan Davis for his incredible fortitude and compassion.

I could not have written this book without financial support from the Canada Council for the Arts, the Ontario Arts Council, the Toronto Arts Council and the Hadassah-Brandeis Institute. I was grateful for a fellowship from the Corporation of Yaddo during the final stages. Thanks to my agents Anne McDermid and Martha Magor Webb in Toronto, and to Zoe

Waldie and Stephen Edwards in London. And thanks also to Kristin Cochrane, Zoe Maslow and Sharon Klein at Doubleday Canada, to Claire Wachtel at HarperCollins in the US, and to Mary-Anne Harrington at Headline in the UK.

Between Gods is an emotional record, a spiritual and psychological snapshot of a particular time in my life. In order to highlight the essence of the events, I have taken artistic liberty with chronology. I have changed some names and distinguishing details, and I have also amalgamated some of the characters – rabbis, guides, friends who welcomed me to their tables. That I had to do so is a testament to the amount of support I received; I hope the work is taken in this spirit.

My final thanks goes to you, my reader.

You are invited to join us behind the scenes at Tinder Press

TINDER
PRESS

To meet our authors, browse our books
and discover exclusive content on our
blog visit us at

www.tinderpress.co.uk

For the latest news and views from the team
Follow us on Twitter

@TinderPress